# Understanding Nonverbal Communication

**ALSO AVAILABLE FROM BLOOMSBURY**

*An Introduction to Conversation Analysis,* Anthony J. Liddicoat
*Discourse Analysis,* Brian Paltridge
*Introduction to Multimodal Analysis*, David Machin and Per Ledin
*The Semiotics of Emoji*, Marcel Danesi
*Understanding Media Semiotics*, Marcel Danesi

# Understanding Nonverbal Communication
## *A Semiotic Guide*

**Marcel Danesi**

BLOOMSBURY ACADEMIC
LONDON • NEW YORK • OXFORD • NEW DELHI • SYDNEY

BLOOMSBURY ACADEMIC
Bloomsbury Publishing Plc
50 Bedford Square, London, WC1B 3DP, UK
1385 Broadway, New York, NY 10018, USA
29 Earlsfort Terrace, Dublin 2, Ireland

BLOOMSBURY, BLOOMSBURY ACADEMIC and the Diana logo are trademarks of
Bloomsbury Publishing Plc

First published in Great Britain 2022

Copyright © Marcel Danesi, 2022

Marcel Danesi has asserted his right under the Copyright, Designs and Patents Act, 1988, to be identified as Author of this work.

Cover design by Rebecca Heselton
Cover images: Sign-language © Jayesh/ iStock, Eyes © kowalska-art/ iStock, Handshake © natala krechetova/ iStock, Touching Hands © MarioGuti/ iStock. Other illustrations by Rebecca Heselton.

All rights reserved. No part of this publication may be reproduced or transmitted in any form or by any means, electronic or mechanical, including photocopying, recording, or any information storage or retrieval system, without prior permission in writing from the publishers.

Bloomsbury Publishing Plc does not have any control over, or responsibility for, any third-party websites referred to or in this book. All internet addresses given in this book were correct at the time of going to press. The author and publisher regret any inconvenience caused if addresses have changed or sites have ceased to exist, but can accept no responsibility for any such changes.

A catalogue record for this book is available from the British Library.

Library of Congress Cataloging-in-Publication Data
Names: Danesi, Marcel, 1946– author.
Title: Understanding nonverbal communication : a semiotic guide / Marcel Danesi.
Description: New York, NY : Bloomsbury Academic, 2021. |
Includes bibliographical references and index. |
Identifiers: LCCN 2021011481 (print) | LCCN 2021011482 (ebook) |
ISBN 9781350152649 (hardback) | ISBN 9781350152632 (paperback) |
ISBN 9781350152663 (ePDF) | ISBN 9781350152656 (eBook)
Subjects: LCSH: Body language. | Nonverbal communication.
Classification: LCC BF637.N66 D36 2021  (print) | LCC BF637.N66  (ebook) |
DDC 153.6/9—dc23
LC record available at https://lccn.loc.gov/2021011481
LC ebook record available at https://lccn.loc.gov/2021011482

| ISBN: | HB: | 978-1-3501-5264-9 |
|---|---|---|
| | PB: | 978-1-3501-5263-2 |
| | ePDF: | 978-1-3501-5266-3 |
| | eBook: | 978-1-3501-5265-6 |

Typeset by RefineCatch Limited, Bungay, Suffolk

To find out more about our authors and books, visit www.bloomsbury.com and sign up for our newsletters.

# Contents

*List of Figures* vi
*List of Tables* viii
*Preface* ix

1 **Nonverbal Communication** 1

2 **Kinesics** 27

3 **The Eyes** 49

4 **The Face** 75

5 **The Hands** 97

6 **Gesture** 121

7 **Proxemics** 147

8 **Extended Nonverbal Communication** 163

9 **Human–Machine Communication** 187

*Glossary* 203
*References* 211
*Index* 235

# List of Figures

| | | |
|---|---|---|
| 1.1 | Shannon's model of communication | 5 |
| 1.2 | Saussure's model of the sign | 17 |
| 1.3 | The Peircean model of the sign | 18 |
| 2.1 | Kinegraphs | 31 |
| 2.2 | Caspar Netscher, *Young Girl Holding a Letter*, c. 1665 | 40 |
| 3.1 | Müller-Lyer illusion | 51 |
| 3.2 | The Eye of Providence | 61 |
| 3.3 | Japanese dogū figurine | 63 |
| 3.4 | The Eye of Horus | 63 |
| 3.5 | Leonardo da Vinci, *Mona Lisa* (1503–06) | 65 |
| 3.6 | John William Waterhouse, *Hylas and the Nymphs* (1869) | 66 |
| 3.7 | Johannes Vermeer, *Girl with a Pearl Earring* (c. 1665) | 67 |
| 3.8 | Gustav Klimt, *The Kiss* (1908) | 70 |
| 3.9 | William Blake, *Kiss of Adam and Eve* (1808) | 72 |
| 4.1 | Facial expressions, from Guillaume Duchenne | 78 |
| 4.2 | Sketches of four facial expressions | 79 |
| 4.3 | The Buddha | 84 |
| 4.4 | Pacioli's illustration of the perfect human face | 89 |
| 4.5 | Giuseppe Arcimboldo, *Summer* | 94 |
| 5.1 | Human braincase | 100 |
| 5.2 | Sketch of the V-Sign | 101 |
| 5.3 | Vulcan salute | 102 |
| 5.4 | OK sign | 103 |
| 5.5 | Thumbs-up sign | 104 |
| 5.6 | Like and dislike | 105 |
| 5.7 | Hera and Athena shaking hands | 107 |
| 5.8 | Indian Namaste greeting | 108 |
| 5.9 | Michelangelo Buonarroti, *The Creation of Adam* (c. 1508–12) | 113 |
| 5.10 | Cuevas de las Manos (c. 9000 years ago) | 115 |
| 5.11 | Maurits C. Escher, *Drawing Hands* (1948) | 116 |
| 5.12 | Leonardo da Vinci, *Study of Hands* (c. 1474) | 117 |
| 5.13 | Albrecht Dürer, *Hands of the Apostle Praying* (1471–1528) | 118 |

| | | |
|---|---|---|
| 6.1 | The alphabet in sign language | 125 |
| 6.2 | Common hand gestures, John Bulwer (1644) | 127 |
| 6.3 | The sign of the horns | 128 |
| 6.4 | Edgar Degas, *The Dance Class* (1874) | 143 |
| 7.1 | Interpersonal zones | 152 |
| 7.2 | Actors in the four zones | 153 |
| 8.1 | Extension theory | 165 |
| 8.2 | Smiley and face with tears of joy emojis | 175 |
| 8.3 | Emoji gesture forms | 178 |
| 8.4 | Internet tetrad | 181 |
| 8.5 | Education tetrad | 182 |
| 8.6 | Writing tetrad | 184 |
| 9.1 | Feedback | 190 |
| 9.2 | Kismet | 197 |
| 9.3 | Connection between the body, mind, and culture | 201 |

# List of Tables

| | | |
|---|---|---:|
| 3.1 | A few illustrative eye-contact patterns | 52 |
| 3.2 | Examples of eye kinemes in basic emotions | 53 |
| 8.1 | Extensions | 167 |
| 8.2 | Emoji facial expressions | 176 |

# Preface

> Nonverbal communication is an elaborate secret code that is written nowhere, known by none, and understood by all.
>
> *Edward Sapir* (1884–1939)

Besides verbal language, humans transmit and exchange messages through postures, hand gestures, eye gazes, facial expressions, and other bodily activities. Charles Darwin saw such nonverbal communication (NVC) as an evolutionary link between humans and other animal species, designed to ensure survival (Darwin 1872: 352). But in human life NVC is not limited to serving a survival function. It is a crucial aspect in cultural rituals and performances, from theatrical acting to dancing; it complements oral speech systematically during routine interactions; it is a subject matter of artists, as the many paintings and sculptures focusing on the body indicate; and the list could go on and on. In effect, NVC is intrinsic not only to communication *per se*, but to meaning-making in all its dimensions.

As an instructor of anthropological linguistics and semiotics for five decades at the University of Toronto, I have always seen NVC as integral for understanding the origins and functions of signs. I have used various texts in this area over the years to supplement my teaching, but I found very few that focused on the interconnections between NVC and other sign systems. So, I decided to prepare one myself. The present book is thus intended as an introduction to nonverbal communication from a semiotic perspective, aiming to delineate its relation to verbal language, culture, mind, and representation generally. It is written in a synthetic way—that is, I have collated relevant research findings and theories on NVC, connecting them to the broader study of signs and representational activities. It is intended for a non-specialist readership, from students taking courses in linguistics, anthropology, psychology, semiotics, and other related fields, to the general public. For this reason, I have written it in a non-technical style, but without diluting the content excessively.

Nonverbal communication goes on "silently" all the time, as the anthropologist Edward T. Hall (1959) characterized it, ensuring that human interactions are regular and fluid. As a case in point, consider the following hypothetical, but hardly trivial, vignette that illustrates how this silent language unfolds in a specific way:

1. An individual in the United States is about to step into an elevator on the ground floor of a skyscraper in a major urban center. Inside, the person sees three other people.
2. The individual realizes instantly that they must be strangers to each other, because they are not conversing, standing near to, or leaning against, separate corners of the elevator, and avoiding eye contact.
3. Upon entering the elevator, the individual knows instinctively to go near the remaining corner and assume a similar posture as the others, maintaining silence.

If the individual decides to act or behave in some other way, the others might become uneasy, interpreting the behavior as rude, conflictual, or disturbed. To cope with the transgressor's breach of the rules of the silent language, they might ignore the behavior completely, as if it had not occurred; or else they might employ some strategy to counteract the emotional disruption that it likely brought about, such as initiating a brief conversation: "Is everything OK?" "Life is getting to all of us, isn't it?" and so on. In sum, the vignette makes it obvious that NVC is not random; it is coded culturally and applied to specific situations in a predictable way. In a similar elevator scenario in another country, the person entering the elevator would likely act differently, perhaps greeting the others politely and maybe initiating a brief conversation. This can happen in the US as well, but it is rarer. Like verbal language, nonverbal communication changes and adapts itself to new situations all the time.

The scientific study of NVC is carried out traditionally on the basis of face-to-face interactions (F2F); but today it has been extended to encompass computer-mediated communication (CMC) and communication between humans and their own machines. This textbook will deal with these different aspects of NVC to varying degrees. It will make use of findings and insights from various disciplinary sources—psychology, neuroscience, semiotics, linguistics, anthropology, culture studies, AI, among others. To keep its proportions within practical limits, I have streamlined the different topics in order to bring out general aspects. Nevertheless, I have tried to cast as broad a descriptive net as possible. The first two chapters provide an overview of the study of nonverbal communication. Chapters 3 to 7 cover the primary areas of NVC—eye contact, facial expression, tactile communication, gesture, and proxemic behavior (the zones people maintain between each other while speaking). Chapter 8 deals with how the study of NVC extends to clothing and architecture, and how it unfolds in cyberspace. Chapter 9 deals with cybernetic communication—communication between humans, computers, and robots. A glossary of the main technical terms is included at the end.

I should mention that this book was completed during the COVID-19 pandemic crisis, which altered some of the ways in which people communicated nonverbally, such as making elbow contact or fist-bumping in place of handshaking as part of greeting rituals. Some of these alterations will be discussed in various chapters.

I wish to thank Victoria College of the University of Toronto for having allowed me the privilege of teaching in, and coordinating, its Program in Semiotics and Communication Theory since the mid-1980s. I am indebted to the late Thomas A. Sebeok, a founder of the scientific study of nonverbal communication, and with whom I had the privilege of working for several decades, for constantly encouraging me to develop materials that would make semiotics and nonverbal communication understandable to a broad audience. Another debt of gratitude goes to the many students I have taught. Their insights and enthusiasm have made my job simply wonderful. They are the impetus for this book. I am also grateful to my grandchildren, Alex De Sousa and Sarah De Sousa, for all the insights they have provided me over the years. Any infelicities that this book may contain are my sole responsibility.

# 1

# Nonverbal Communication

## Chapter Outline

| | |
|---|---:|
| 1.0 Prologue | 1 |
| 1.1 Communication Models | 2 |
| 1.2 Modes and Media | 7 |
| 1.3 Mass Communications | 9 |
| 1.4 Computer-Mediated Communication | 11 |
| 1.5 Nonverbal Communication | 12 |
| 1.6 Useful Semiotic Notions | 16 |
| 1.7 Bimodality | 20 |
| 1.8 Epilogue | 24 |

## 1.0 Prologue

Communication exists in all species, serving survival in specialized ways. For example, birds have developed distinctive coos that are designed to signal mating, warnings, and distress; dolphins have evolved whistles, burst-pulsed sounds, and clicks to communicate similar types of messages over long distances underwater; gorillas and chimpanzees have developed facial expressions, postures, and hand gestures that are akin to those utilized by humans to convey a vast array of meanings, from predator warnings to complex emotional states. Communication in humans serves similar needs; but it transcends them in unique ways, serving cultural meanings that have little to do with mere survival. This blend of *nature* and *culture* is a key characteristic of human communication.

This chapter deals with several pivotal notions of communication theory in general and nonverbal communication in particular. A useful distinction between human and animal communication systems is the one between *signals* and *signs*. Although reductive, for the present purposes, a signal in animal systems can be defined as a message sent out instinctively in response to some need or environmental situation. Signaling is also typical of human communication, but in this case, it can be both instinctive *and* intentional, as will be discussed in due course. Signs are structures devised purposefully to stand for something in some way—words, symbols, images, etc. Although some species appear to possess the capacity for sign-based behavior, such as various primate species, by and large, signing is a unique human faculty. The study of nonverbal communication (NVC) in humans involves examining the origins, meanings, and functions of the elements in this dual system of signals and signs. Traditionally, it is carried out by observing people interacting physically in their social ambiances; but today it has been extended to study interactions in cyberspace, as well as how it relates to verbal language and other representational systems.

There is a common perception among people that nonverbal behaviors are natural, reflecting universal instinctual patterns. But this is not the case. Consider the behaviors that characterize courtship practices. Humans, like other animals, sense and respond instinctively to mating urges. Across the animal realm, such responses are communicated by specialized signals, according to species. From an evolutionary perspective, humans have also developed similar signals; but there is a difference—the signals are modified and regulated by cultural traditions, which transform them into signs and cultural codes (systems of signs) which guide, for example, how partners touch each other, how long they make eye contact, what postures are appropriate or not in romantic contexts, etc. In effect, in human NVC, nature is in a deep partnership with culture—a partnership that is meant to bring about a "mutual optimization," whereby the two—the natural and the cultural—function optimally in a symbiotic way.

## 1.1 Communication Models

Communication can be defined narrowly as the transmission and exchange of messages (in the form of either signals or signs, or both). The features of a communication system are specific to a species—that is, messages can be sent and received successfully (recognized as messages) by an organism if the sender and receiver belong to the same species. According to the early twentieth-century biologist Jakob von Uexküll (1909), system specialization relates to the anatomical structure of a species, as well as neural structure in the case of the higher primates, which shapes and delimits the kinds of information a species can receive and use.

Inter-species communication is possible to limited degrees, in some specific modes. Tactility and vocalization seem to be the primary modes that allow for interactions between humans and some animal species, such as cats and dogs. Caressing a dog companion to convey affection will typically motivate responses such as tail-wagging and friendly barking that indicate an understanding of the meaning of the caress in kind. Sharing the same living space, and being codependent on each other for affective exchanges, the two different species—human and canine—do indeed appear to transmit feeling-states to each other through nonverbal signals. However, even within the confines of the tactile communicative mode, there is no way for humans to be sure that dogs understand the intent and meaning of the caress in the same way that they do. Humans can only infer it.

The transmission of signals and signs in real space has a very limited span—a vocal utterance can only reach someone within a certain auditory range, a hand gesture within a specific visual range, and so on. However, even early hominid cultures had developed tools, artifacts, and various other means to extend the transmission range, including drums (extending the auditory range), fire and smoke signals (extending the visual range), etc. Messages were also attached to the legs of carrier pigeons trained to navigate their way to a destination and back home. In later societies, semaphore systems, such as flashing lights or flag-waving codes, were employed to send messages over difficult-to-cross distances, such as from hilltop to hilltop, or from one ship to another at sea. The late Canadian communications scholar Marshall McLuhan (1964) claimed that the type of technology developed to amplify the ability to transmit messages determined how societies evolved—that is, a major change in communications technologies would bring about a concomitant paradigm shift in social systems and even in human evolution.

The term *information* comes up in any discussion of communication, and thus requires some commentary. For the present purposes, it can be defined simply as the specific type of sensory input (vocal, visual, tactile, etc.) that is experienced as relevant or significant to a situation, producing differentiated reactions or interpretations. For instance, screaming is perceived as meaning something different from laughing; a ringing alarm evokes a different reaction than a silent alarm; and so on. The type of input provides the relevant information required to react accordingly, varying from biologically-based to culturally-based responses. Knowing that a ringing alarm indicates danger is something that is learned in cultural context, whereas screaming and laughing are natural modes of vocalization, although they too are constrained in their specific meanings by culture. One of the first modern-day theories of communication, by the American telecommunications engineer, Claude E. Shannon (1948; Shannon and Weaver 1949), was based on measuring the probability of some signal. He showed that the information in a signal was inversely proportional to its probability of occurrence—the more probable, the less information it carried; the less probable, the more information it bore. Shannon also elaborated a model of communication (Figure 1.1) that has remained a basic one in communication studies to this day. Its main components are as follows:

1. *Sender*: the source of a signal or message transmission.
2. *Message*: the information that the sender intends to transmit to a receiver in some way.
3. *Transmitter*: the organ or device that converts the message into a physical signal, in some medium. A verbal message, for instance, can involve a natural (biological) medium, if it is transmitted with the vocal organs. It can alternatively be transmitted through the medium of writing, or converted into electromagnetic signals for mechanical transmission.
4. *Noise*: some interfering element (physical or psychological) in the signal's transmitting channel that distorts or partially effaces the message. In radio and television transmissions, *noise* is equivalent to electronic static; in vocal speech, it can vary from any interfering exterior sound (physical noise) to the speaker's lapses of memory (psychological noise).
5. *Redundancy*: noise is why communication systems have redundant features built into them. These allow for a message to be decoded even if noise is present. For instance, in verbal communication the high predictability of certain words in many utterances or the predictability of specific sounds (phonemes) in common words greatly increase the likelihood that a verbal message will get decoded successfully.
6. *Receiver*: the organ or device that has the capacity to receive the signal and understand (or simply process) the information present in it; in verbal communication it is a human being; in telecommunications it could be a radio set.
7. *Destination*: the end-state or intended reach of a transmitted signal.

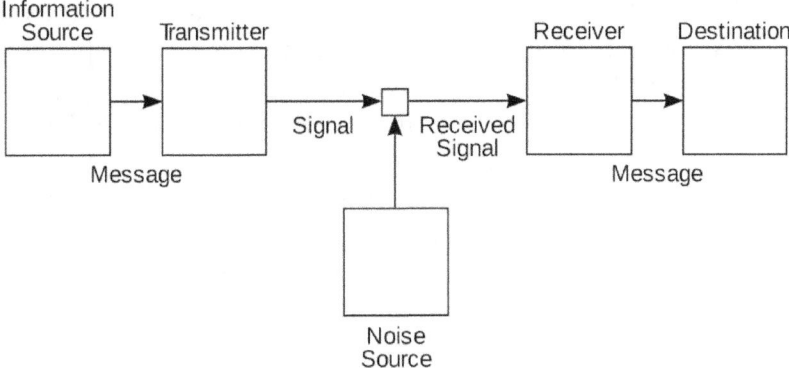

**Figure 1.1** Shannon's model of communication (Wikimedia Commons).

Shannon's model is called colloquially the *bull's-eye model*, because a sender (information source) is portrayed as someone or something aiming a message at a receiver—the bull's-eye—in a target range. The model thus depicts information transfer as a unidirectional process dependent on probability factors, that is, on the degree to which a message is to be expected or not in a given situation. Wilbur Schramm (1963) later expanded on this model, adding bidirectional dimensions to it, referring to senders as encoders and receivers as decoders, thus implying agency within the communicative system. He also refined several other notions, adding the cybernetic notion of *feedback* to the communication loop, defined as the modification of a message by the sender in response to a receiver's reactions. Feedback regulates the flow of communication, allowing for the adjustment or correction of errors that are introduced into it.

A model that has been applied to verbal communication in particular, but which can easily be extended to NVC, is the one put forward by the late semiotician and linguist, Roman Jakobson (1960). Taking his cue from the Danish philologist Otto Jespersen (1922), Jakobson saw speech acts as unfolding in terms of specific *constituents* and *functions*. He posited the following six constituents that must be present for any communicative act to become realizable in the first place:

1 *Addresser*: the person who initiates a communicative interaction, corresponding to the sender in the Shannon model; but the term *addresser* involves the dimension of *intentionality* to the communicative act, whereas a *sender* in Shannon's model does not—it can be any source that sends out messages automatically (if the source is mechanical) or instinctively (if it is biological).

2 *Message*: the information that the addresser shapes into verbal forms (utterances, speeches, conversations, repartees, etc.) in order to convey something meaningful to someone else.
3 *Addressee*: the receiver of the message, who responds to it with intent and interpretive modalities, not just automatically.
4 *Context*: the situation (psychological, physical, social, etc.) that provides the relevant input variables for interpreting the message correctly (to some degree). For example, the exhortation "Help me!" takes on a different meaning depending on whether it is uttered by someone lying motionless on the ground or by someone in a classroom who is working on a difficult math problem.
5 *Contact*: the actual interactional loop or medium (face-to-face, social media, etc.) by which the message is delivered between addressers and addressees.
6 *Code*: the sign-signal system or systems (language, gesture, etc.) providing the forms and the combinatory rules for creating and interpreting messages.

Jakobson then identified six functions which define the semiotic relations between messages and interlocutors:

1 *Emotive*: the intent of the addresser in creating a message and transmitting it. This reveals the reason or reasons why the addresser entered into a speech act in the first place.
2 *Conative*: the effect (physical, psychological, social, etc.) that the message has, or is intended to have, on its receiver.
3 *Referential*: any message constructed to convey information unambiguously; it is also the term Jakobson used to imply awareness that a message is perceived as referring to something other than itself ("Main Street is two blocks north of here").
4 *Poetic*: any message constructed to deliver meanings effectively from a rhetorical standpoint, like poetry ("I like it, I like it").
5 *Phatic*: any message designed to establish, acknowledge, or reinforce social relations ("Hi, how's it going?"), or else to be part of some ritualistic or performative speech situation.
6 *Metalingual*: any message that refers to the code used ("The word *noun* is a noun").

Jakobson's model suggests that human communication transcends a simple information-transfer loop; it involves intentionality and agency, and is shaped by the context, the reactions of the participants, and the personal goals of each one. While this model was developed initially to describe verbal communication, it can easily be applied to NVC. For example, a waving hand will likely have a phatic function; a facial expression conveys emotivity; gesture involves the use of a specific tactile code; etc.

## 1.2 Modes and Media

Consider the truly remarkable scenario that unfolds around a beehive. Worker honey bees returning to the hive from foraging trips have the extraordinary capacity to inform the other bees in the hive about the direction, distance, and quality of the food cache they located with amazing accuracy through movement sequences which biologists call a "dance," in obvious analogy to human dancing as a sequence of preset, repeatable bodily movements. The noteworthy thing about bee dancing is that it appears to share with human communication the feature of displacement; in other words, of conveying information in the absence of a stimulus, that is, the food cache itself—in the "round" dance, the bee moves in circles alternately to the left and to the right to indicate that the cache of food is nearby; in the "wagging" dance, the bee moves in a straight line while wagging its abdomen from side to side and then returning to its starting point, when the food source is further away.

Now, as sophisticated as this seems, it is ultimately an instinctual form of communication that cannot be learned by other bees (such as the queen bee). Human communications systems, on the other hand, can be learned by any member of the human species, and they can be modified and adapted according to new conditions, as they evolve historically. Moreover, the bee system is based on one mode of delivery of the message (bodily movement) and one medium (the space around the beehive). Human communication, on the other hand, is *multimodal* and *multimedial*. Multimodal forms include the following (Danesi 2019):

1 *Audition-vocalism*: communication via audio-oral channels, including vocal speech generally, spontaneous vocalizations (coughing and snoring), prosody (raising the tone of a vocal message to convey emotions of some kind), voice modulation (to communicate identity and feeling-states), etc.
2 *Visuality*: communication via some visual channel, such as writing, the sign languages of the hearing-impaired, visual representation (drawing, sculpting, etc.), website designs, emojis, etc.

3 *Tactility*: communication via touch. In humans, it also involves haptic forms of social interaction, such as handshaking or elbow touching.
4 *Corporeality*: communication via bodily forms, such as posture, gesture, pose, etc.
5 *Olfaction*: communication by means of smell; it includes pheromone communication and artificially-produced (chemical) smells in human systems.
6 *Gustation*: communication by means of taste; in human systems this includes the fabrication of food tastes via chemical processes.
7 *Spatiality*: communication via spatially-bound structures and behaviors; in humans this includes proxemic patterns (distances people maintain while interacting with each other) and habitation structures (such as towns and cities).

There are, clearly, overlaps between animal and human systems; but in the former the modes are specialized for acquired evolutionary purposes, such as mating and territorial assurance. In humans, multimodality involves a broad and sophisticated system of coordinated communication—the auditory-vocal mode is used in speech, the visual one in writing, the tactile one in social interactions, and so on. Communication between humans and animals will thus probably occur in some modes, but not in all (as discussed). If the communicative mode or modes of the species are vastly different, then virtually no message exchange is possible. It is unlikely that humans and ants will ever enter into a communicative exchange loop such as the one that has evolved between humans and cats or dogs.

The three main kinds of media that characterize human communication are:

1 *natural media*, such as the voice (speech), the face (expressions), and the body (gesture, posture, etc.);
2 *artifactual media*, such as books, paintings, sculptures, letters, etc.;
3 *mechanical media*, such as telephones, radios, television sets, computers, etc.

A verbal message, for instance, can be delivered through natural transmission, if it is articulated with the vocal organs; or else it can be transmitted by means of markings on a piece of paper through the artifactual medium of writing; and it can be converted into electromagnetic signals for mechanical transmission. In sum, human communication is a complex and sophisticated multimodal and multimedial system, standing apart from the communication systems of all other species.

## 1.3 Mass Communications

Because of technological inventions, human communication can be designed to reach mass audiences. Mass communication also occurs in other species, but, again, in a specialized instinctual way. One example is herd behavior, whereby an animal will move along with a fleeing herd to reduce the danger to itself. The signal to do so comes from the common movement, not from a particular source (Hamilton 1971). Another example is swarming, which is triggered by alarm pheromones to ward off predators, leading to potential mass attacks on the latter. Such mass instinctive behaviors might exist as well in humans; but the spreading of messages to convey non-instinctual meanings to masses of people via technology is unique to the human species.

The systematic study of mass communications media started in the 1920s, when electronic media such as radio, cinema, and sound recordings became widespread and popular. In his 1922 book, *Public Opinion*, the American journalist Walter Lippmann argued that the growth of such media had a powerful direct effect on people's minds and behavior. Although he did not use any empirical evidence to back up his argument, Lippmann's claim is the earliest version of what came to be called Hypodermic Needle Theory (HNT) a little later in psychology—namely, the view that the mass media can directly influence behavior in the same way that a hypodermic needle can directly affect the body (McQuail 2000). The American political scientist Harold Lasswell adopted Lippmann's basic argument a few years later in *Propaganda Technique in World War I* (1927), suggesting that mass-mediated propaganda affected people's politics, family relations, and general outlooks. In the same era, the Frankfurt School social theorists became prominent by critiquing the ever-expanding mass media culture as subserving a rampant "culture industry" spread by the institutions of consumer capitalism—a term coined to characterize the process by which mass forms of culture were created in analogy with the industrial manufacturing of commercial products, and spread by the mass media (Bottomore 1984).

This critical attitude towards mass communications shifted somewhat in 1955, when sociologists Paul Lazarsfeld and Elihu Katz conducted research which showed that the effects of mass media content were not as negatively impactful on people as the previous critics believed, because people interpreted the content in accordance to the values of the social class or group to which they belonged—that is, people reacted to it as members of interpretive communities, such as families, neighborhoods, churches, and so forth. In such communities, opinion leaders (for example, union leaders, church ministers) tend to influence or guide how the members will construe media content. So, in contrast to previous theories, which portrayed mass media content as a one-step flow reaching a homogeneous audience directly, the model put forth by Lazarsfeld and Katz saw it instead as a two-step flow, in which the first step is through the opinion leaders who filter the content which, in a second step, is passed on to group members, influencing their perceptions. A few decades later, George Gerbner and Larry Gross (1976) argued that the mass media actually had a conservative social function, rather than a negative psychological one, as Lippmann had claimed, because media content reflected what people wanted, reinforcing what they already valued and knew culturally. In this view, people are not passive consumers of media representations, but actively seek them out selectively for their own uses and gratifications (Katz 2002). British cultural theorist Stuart Hall (1973) also argued that people do not absorb media content univocally, but rather *read* it (interpret it) in one of three ways: (a) the *preferred* reading, which is the one that the makers of the content want audiences to accept; (b) the *negotiated* reading, which is the one that results when audiences agree only in part with the makers' intent; and (c) an *oppositional* reading, which occurs when audiences either reject the content outright, or critique it severely. An example is a speech by a politician, which might be received favorably by an audience of followers (preferred reading), in a partially critical way by, say, some journalist or media commentator (negotiated reading), or else in a hostile way by people who are opposed to the politician's opinions or policies (oppositional reading).

    Marshall McLuhan (1964) took yet another different approach, claiming that changes in mass communications technologies set off corresponding social changes. Each major period in history thus takes its character from the medium of mass communications used most widely at the time. McLuhan called the period from 1700 to the mid-1900s the age of print, because in that era print was the chief means by which people gained and shared knowledge massively. He called the twentieth century the electronic age, because of the emergence and spread of electronic communications technologies; in this age, people share knowledge through screens or other electronic devices. Each age is thus shaped cognitively and socially by the dominant mass communications technology used in the era—in the print age, people developed a sense of individualism based on reading the printed word; in the electronic age, people retrieved a more communal sense of identity, becoming immersed in the lives of people everywhere, in what

McLuhan called the "electronic global village." McLuhan's overall claim was, in effect, that mass communications media, knowledge, culture, society, cognition, and human behavior are intrinsically intertwined.

# 1.4 Computer-Mediated Communication

Computer-mediated communication (CMC), as an extension of face-to-face (F2F) communication, will be discussed in Chapter 8. Suffice it to say here that communicating through computer screens has not eliminated the nonverbal modes of F2F communication—it has projected them into a simulacrum. Although this notion has a broader definition in cultural studies, for the present purposes it is constrained to mean an artificial simulation of F2F communication via digital systems and artifacts. For example, the set of facial emojis used commonly in CMC are simulacra of facial expressions—that is, we understand that they represent these expressions in simulated form, retaining their meanings and functions in virtual environments. The word *simulacrum* was used for the first time in the late sixteenth century to describe a painting or statue that was created to resemble something in a verisimilar way—an idea that can be traced back to Plato, who, in the *Sophist*, spoke of two kinds of reproduction of art works—(a) faithful, which attempts to copy the original in a realistic way, and (b) distorted, which attempts to correct the image to viewers for some purpose.

This concept was taken up at length by the late French philosopher Jean Baudrillard (1983), who argued that a simulacrum is not just a copy of reality, but reshapes it so that it appears to be more real than real, or *hyperreal*, thus expanding upon Plato's second category. Baudrillard's analysis was meant as a critique of modern-day media and their effects on cognition; but in this book the term *simulacrum* is used to describe how F2F nonverbal communication is simulated in the CMC medium, as well as in communicative interfaces between humans and machines. Simulacrum theory can also be used to assess the implications of the digital creations of human figures who speak and act in ways that are practically indistinguishable from real human beings (Chapter 9).

CMC involves two different modes of communication: *synchronous* and *asynchronous*. Synchronous CMC occurs when the interlocutors are aware of the communication as an ongoing one—as, for instance, in Skype or Zoom interactions, or in a back-and-forth text-messaging loop. Asynchronous CMC occurs, instead, when interlocutors are not necessarily aware that a message has been created and sent—as, for example, in emails and blogs. A further distinction is to be made between screen-based visual communication, as in Zoom interactions, and written communications, as in text messages, social media posts, and emails. In some virtual spaces, a feeling of communal belonging emerges that is also based on a simulacrum effect. Some Twitter networks, for example, produce a hyperreal sense of community, which can be either "dense" or "weak." People in dense networks have frequent (daily) contact with each other, and are thus likely to be linked by more than one type of bond than are those with infrequent contact within weak networks. Dense networks put pressure on members to conform because their values can be more readily shared.

## 1.5 Nonverbal Communication

Nonverbal communication involves a broad range of modes, including eye contact, gazing, facial expressions, gestures, posture, touch, proxemics (the distances maintained between individuals while speaking), etc. It was Charles Darwin (1872) who first emphasized the evolutionary importance of such communication, given that humans share various modes with other species, such as baring the teeth when angry. Darwin traced this facial action to species that attacked their prey by biting it. Over time, this same facial action evolved into an expressive mode, separate from its original biting function. A similar process took place in humans, leaving its evolutionary residues in facial expressions of anger. These are thus residues of ancient *animal mechanisms*—a term coined by E. J. Marey in 1879. While this term is used rarely in biology today, it is a useful one nonetheless for discussing the origins of various nonverbal modes of communication, such as the facial expression of anger—although a caveat must be issued here. There is no way to directly trace some nonverbal action to a previous evolutionary stage; it can only be inferred, remaining largely conjectural. So too is it conjecture to connect aspects of verbal communication to animal mechanisms that undergird more primitive nonverbal systems. In some theories of the origin of language, in fact, NCV not only precedes verbal communication, but also constitutes its evolutionary source, as will be discussed in due course (Ruesch and Kees 1956).

Adam Kendon (2010: 45) defines NVC comprehensively as follows:

The term *nonverbal communication* is generally understood to refer to all of the ways in which communication is effected between persons in each other's presence by means other than words. It refers to the communicational functioning of bodily activity, gestures, facial expression and orientation, posture and spacing; of touch and smell; and of those aspects of utterance that can be considered apart from the referential content of what is said. Studies of "nonverbal communication" are usually concerned with the part these aspects of behavior play in establishing and maintaining interactions and interpersonal relationships.

NVC unfolds via bodily actions and expressions that may be conscious (voluntary, witting), unconscious (unvoluntary, unwitting), or a blend of the two (partially involuntary and voluntary). The unwitting mode emerges spontaneously in childhood, even in the absence of a rearing context, as has been documented in averbal feral children, who develop the same kind of instinctive gestures (such as the pointing index finger) and facial expressions (such as baring the teeth) of children reared in a normal upbringing (Classen 1991; Candland 1993). Now, while involuntary nonverbal behaviors may be based in biology, the voluntary ones are shaped instead by cultural upbringing. Moreover, in a version of evolutionary theory, called *autopoiesis* theory, humans may be able to reshape the animal mechanisms which they have inherited from their past. The term was introduced by Humberto Maturana and Francisco Varela in their famous 1973 book, *Autopoiesis and Cognition*, where they claim that an organism participates in its own evolution, since it has the ability to produce, or at least shape, its various biochemical agents and structures, in order to ensure their efficient and economical operation. Moreover, humans also evolve through their technologies, as McLuhan argued, which amplify physical and mental capacities.

Human NVC is, overall, a mixed system of signals and signs, partly instinctive and partly based on culture. Identifying which of the two systems is involved in some communicative act is often problematic. For example, in most parts of the world, nodding the head means agreement, and shaking it means disagreement, but this is not true everywhere (Morris et al. 1979). So, the head gesture might appear to be natural (in large part), but turns out to be conventional (in some cultures). Another main aspect of human NVC is that it can occur independently of vocal speech (as in sign languages) or in tandem with it, as in the use of gestures during speech, known as *co-speech* forms. Also, NVC can be dyadic—between two people—group-based, or massive, as discussed.

The technical term used commonly for the study of NVC is *kinesics*, introduced by anthropologist Ray Birdwhistell in 1952, who saw NVC as systematic as verbal communication and based on similar structures—as we shall see in the next chapter. This led in the mid-1950s to its systematic study in other fields, including psychology, semiotics, anthropology, and various other cognate disciplines. In 1954, the Center for Advanced Study in Behavioral Sciences at Stanford was founded to study NVC scientifically. Its original members included not only Birdwhistell, but also Gregory Bateson, Albert Scheflen, and Adam Kendon, among others. The first project at the Center was based on a film made by Bateson, which showed humans greeting each other, acting corporeally in certain ways at social gatherings, which were analyzed in great detail according to the common patterns they exhibited and the meanings and functions that they seemed to have. The results were never published, but were made available on microfilm in 1971 (see Scheflen 1973; Kendon, Harris, and Key 1975; and Kendon 1977). In the 1960s, researchers started focusing on specific aspects of NVC, such as eye-contact patterns in specific contexts, and on the zones people maintained during conversations. By the 1970s, the connection between nonverbal and verbal communication was also becoming a major topic of interest within various disciplines. Michael Argyle (1975; Argyle and Cook 1976), for example, was one of the first to examine the role of eye contact and gazing during conversations, concluding that there were five main functions of these nonverbal actions in co-speech situations: (1) self-presentation; (2) greeting; (3) expressing attitudes; (4) conveying emotions; and (5) supplementing speech. From the 1980s to today, the study of NVC has been expanded considerably, including how it unfolds in CMC contexts, in interactions between humans and machines (Riggio and Riggio 2012; Schrier and Shaenfeld 2016), and generally how it is adapting to new situations that involve multicultural interactions.

Among the main research approaches that have been used to study NVC since the 1950s, the following three remain primary ones to this day (Kendon 2010):

1 *Psychological:* this type of approach focuses on the relation between NVC and psychological states. Several experimental techniques have become standard within this research domain. One is called *method of judgment*. It involves presenting displays of nonverbal behavior to subjects, via video, who are then asked to make judgments on the

nonverbal aspects of specific interactions. Another method is called *interaction outcome assessment,* whereby subjects are asked to take part in some structured interaction, which is taped at the same time, and then asked to assess the encounter afterwards. Aspects of the interaction might be manipulated by the experimenter for a specific reason. For example, one of the interlocutors may be asked to smile or to gaze at the others in order to see what reactions this evokes. A third technique is called *method of behavior variable measurement*; it involves measuring some aspect of the behavior of subjects in an interaction, so as to correlate it to variables such as personality or social class.

2 *Structural:* the goal is to examine the extent to which an interaction is organized by verbal and nonverbal structures. The two main approaches are called *kinesics* (Chapter 2) and *proxemics* (Chapter 7). The former investigates bodily states, actions, or movements, such as gestures and postures as comparable or similar to verbal ones, and the latter measures and analyzes the zones that people maintain between each other while speaking. In both, the focus is on the meanings of the nonverbal structures and their relation to larger frames of cultural meaning. The main method of investigation is observational—that is, the interactions are recorded as they take place spontaneously and subsequently analyzed.

3 *Ethnographic*: this is a research technique practiced mainly by anthropologists and linguists whereby the researcher lives among groups of people, interacting with them and interviewing them in a systematic way, so as to observe and assess how they use verbal and nonverbal modes of communication.

A general method used in researching NVC involves detecting cues during interactions and then relating them to the intent or goals of a communicative act. Below are some examples:

1 *Conflicting Cues:* when people lie, specific nonverbal cues become noticeable, such as avoidance of eye contact or fidgeting, eye-pupil dilation, etc.
2 *Complementary Cues:* gestures and facial expressions reinforce verbally-transmitted information or content during interactions. As mentioned, this is called co-speech interactive behavior.
3 *Substitutive Cues:* when only NVC is possible in an interaction, such as one between speakers of different languages who know nothing of each

other's languages, then gesturing in particular becomes a substitutive system, based on cues that are felt to cross language barriers.
4 *Revelatory Cues:* Rolling the eyes, frowning, smirks, facial contortions, and the like during some interactions reveal what an interlocutor is thinking or feeling—disagreement, disbelief, doubt, etc. Similarly, smiling, head-nodding, moderate vocal tones, etc. indicate the opposite types of feelings and thought—agreement, belief, etc.

In the case of online or digital interactivity, the cues are created through simulation. In the emoji code, for instance, facial expressions are represented in outline form, including eye rolling, frowning, and smiling. They are constructed with the essential features of each expression, including eye configuration, mouth formation, and so on.

## 1.6 Useful Semiotic Notions

As mentioned, the study of NVC involves an interdisciplinary approach. One of the disciplines that is of particular relevance and utility is semiotics—the science of signs, meanings, and codes. The semiotic distinction between *signs* and *signals* is of special utility since it allows for a basic differentiation between voluntary (intentional, cultural), involuntary (instinctive), and mixed (partly instinctive, partly cultural) forms of nonverbal communication. The term *sign* in semiotics is defined as any structure (a word, a facial expression, etc.) that stands for something other than itself in some way. For example, the V-sign (Chapter 5) made by raising the index and third fingers does not constitute a meaningless shape in western culture, but rather a sign standing for several specific concepts (victory, peace, greeting, etc.). The term *structure* in this definition implies that a sign must have a distinctive, recognizable, and recurring physical form, consistent with the signs in the code or system in which it is forged (language, gestures, etc.). The Swiss philologist Ferdinand de Saussure (1916), one of the modern-day founders of semiotics (which he called *semiology*), called this component of the sign, the *signifier*, defined simply as the physical form of the sign. He termed the referent (concept) for which a physical signifier stands, the *signified*. The connection between the two, once established, is bidirectional—that is, one implies the other. For example, the word *tree* is a sign in English because it has a recognizable word structure that stands for a particular mental concept (an arboreal plant) (Figure 1.2).

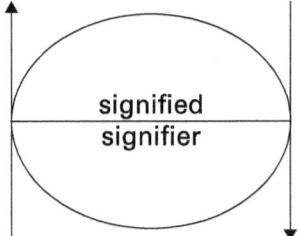 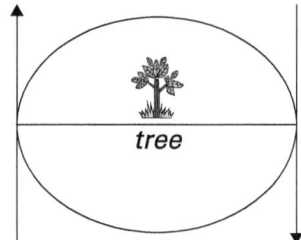

**Figure 1.2** Saussure's model of the sign (author's drawing, adapted from 1916).

When the word *tree* is uttered or written, the image of an arboreal plant comes spontaneously to mind; vice versa, when an arboreal plant comes into view, the word *tree* comes just as automatically to mind. Saussure argued further that the connection established between the two—the signifier and the signified—is an arbitrary one, forged by convention. In other words, there is no evident motivating reason for using, say, *tree* or *arbre* (French) to designate "an arboreal plant," other than to name it as such. Any other signifier could have been created for it, and then institutionalized by convention and usage. In contrast to Saussure, American philosopher Charles S. Peirce (1931), another modern-day founder of semiotics, saw an originating motivation between a sign and its referent, based on some physical sensory reaction or some ontological-associative linkage of sense. The word *tree*, from Old English *trēow*, is actually a variant of an Indo-European root shared by Greek *doru* "wood"—hence it constitutes a metaphorical linkage between *tree* and *wood*. It is unlikely that the word originated in a purely abstract, arbitrary way; it is more probable that it was created via this type of sense-based metaphorical association.

Peirce called the sign a *representamen*, in order to bring out the fact that a sign is something that "represents" something else, called the *object*, in order to suggest it "re-presents" it (as a mind object) in some way. Finally, Peirce added the *interpretant* to his model of the sign, which is the process of deciding or determining what a sign means in some context (cultural, historical, etc.)—a process that he called *semiosis* (Figure 1.3).

Without going into a detailed discussion here of the technical differences between these two models, suffice it to say that when they are used in tandem they can be applied to the study of NVC in a fruitful way. Now, a main difference between signs and signals is that the latter are, by and large, instinctive, conveying specific biological needs, alerting other members of

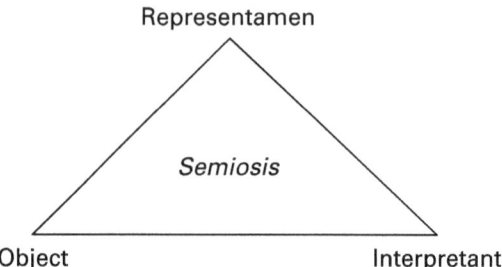

**Figure 1.3** The Peircean model of the sign (author's drawing).

the species to some need, event, danger, etc. This does not mean, however, that animal signaling is not subject to environmental conditioning. Vervet monkeys have the ability to use a specific set of signals to express their particular types of needs, but they also have developed another set of situation-based predator calls to alert other monkeys to the presence of specific predators—one alerting the monkeys to eagles, another to leopards, another still to snakes, and finally another to other primates. These calls are not instinctive; they are learned by an infant monkey by observing older monkeys and by trial and error. The infant vervet may at first deliver an aerial alarm to signal a vulture, a stork, or even a falling leaf, but eventually comes to ignore everything airborne except the eagle, using the appropriate alerting call.

The distinction between signs and signals in human communication is not clear-cut, because signals can also be voluntary or intentional, like signs. Blinking, throat clearing, and facial flushing are innate (involuntary) signaling forms, as are (to varying degrees) facial expressions of happiness, surprise, anger, disgust, and other basic emotions. However, laughing, weeping, and shrugging the shoulders are only partially instinctive—they are also shaped in meaning by cultural upbringing. While weeping is an instinctive reaction to something sad or else something happy, in some cultures it is a ritualistic sign. Among the Andaman Islanders in the east Bay of Bengal, the anthropologist Alfred Radcliffe-Brown (1922) found that weeping was not primarily an expression of joy or sorrow, but rather a ritualistic response to social events such as peace-making, marriage, and the reunion of long-separated intimates. In weeping together, the people renewed their ties of solidarity. Clearly, the line between signs and signals is a blurry one indeed, given that human communication systems are partially instinctive and partially guided in use and meaning by culture.

Another useful semiotic distinction is the one between *denotation* and *connotation*. Consider the word *cat*. As a sign it elicits an image of a "creature with four legs, whiskers, retractile claws." This is its *denotative* meaning, called more technically, the *denotatum*, defined as the image (object) itself, apart from any feelings, accrued notions, etc. it may evoke. Denotation has a primary classificatory differentiating function, allowing us to distinguish a *cat* from some other animal. Similarly, the denotatum of the word *square* implies an image of a geometrical figure consisting of "four equal straight lines meeting at right angles." Again, this allows us to differentiate a square from, say, a triangle or a circle. All other meanings that the words *cat* and *square* elicit are *connotative* ones, called technically *connotata*. Many of these are cultural extensions of denotative meanings. For example, in expressions such as *That person is so square* ("old fashioned"), *He has a square disposition* ("forthright," "honorable"), *Put it squarely on the table* ("evenly," "precisely"), the connotata associated with the word *square* are clearly extensions of the denotatum. Since the geometrical concept of square is an ancient one, the connotatum of "old-fashioned" fits in with this perception; it is also a figure in which every one of its parts is equal, hence the connotatum of "forthright;" and it is an even-sided figure, hence the connotatum of "evenly."

Connotation encompasses additional or expanded semiosis. It produces an archive of culture-specific meanings that signs have accrued over time. It is not a cognitive or semantic option, as some theories of meaning sustain; it is something we can easily extract from a sign if we have access to its cultural codes.

As this last comment implies, one other useful semiotic notion for the present purposes is that of *code*, which can be defined generally as a system of signs, which allows for the assignment of meaning to them. There are many uses of the term code within and outside of semiotics. But in all cases, the notion of collection of information elements or structures that assign meaning or function to signs is implicit. The genetic code, for example, consists of DNA and RNA molecules that carry genetic information in living cells; a computer code is a set of instructions forming a computer program which, like the Morse Code, can be translated into other codes, such as language. Language, dress, music, and gesture are examples of conventional social codes—that is, of systems of signs that are organized and used in specific ways, allowing for the creation of specific texts—conversations, clothing styles, etc. In the creation of these texts, the relevant codes specify what items to select (paradigmatic process), how to combine them (syntagmatic process), and what kinds of messages they convey.

Codes can vary in "size." A dress code has a limited range of applications, depending on era of usage. A language, on the other hand, has an infinite range of applications. Words are signs. But words in isolation are virtually meaningless outside of pure referential denotative function (naming things as in a dictionary), unless they can be combined to form texts. But to produce meaning-bearing texts, they cannot be stringed together haphazardly. This is also the case for forms and functions of language, from its sounds (phonemes) to its uses (conversations) which are structures that allow people to form and deliver meaning-bearing messages. Similarly, single musical notes are practically meaningless in themselves (although they might evoke some immediate response); they become part of some musically based text or message when they are combined according to specific codes, such as the harmonic code, the rhythm code, etc. Note that each code (or subcode) is an organizing grid of specific types of forms or signifiers—sounds, words, etc.

## 1.7 Bimodality

NVC and verbal language may be linked by evolutionary processes (discussed in Chapter 6). The connection between the two has left its traces in such interactional patterns as the use of gesticulation during vocal speech, revealing an integrated system of communication, with gestures reinforcing the speech forms (and vice versa). This integration of the two modes—verbal and nonverbal—can be called the principle of *bimodality*, defined simply, for the present purposes, as the instinctual integration of verbal and nonverbal communication modes during interactions. As research in neuroscience has shown, bimodality might be a consequence of the dual structure of the brain, with its right and left hemispheres, which control nonverbal and verbal modes respectively (broadly speaking). These can be labeled R-Mode and L-Mode for the sake of convenience. Communication is a bimodal process, with the R-Mode and L-Mode cooperating during message exchanges. The relevant neuroscientific findings that support the bimodality principle are as follows:

1 Nonverbal cues are processed by modules in the right side of the neocortex.
2 Feelings and sensory reactions are processed by the superior fiber linkages in the right hemisphere, expressed through nonverbal cues and actions. The superior neuronal volume of the left hemisphere makes it a better processor of the analytic forms associated with verbal communication.

3 The right hemisphere is involved in the processing of intonation and melody patterns during speech, while the left hemisphere processes phonetic and syntactic modules.
4 Assisting in the production and comprehension of nonverbal cues are the fiber links of white matter in the right hemisphere. Preadapted white-matter fibers link modules in the left hemisphere, forming the basis of various structures used in verbal speech.
5 Actions such as gesture, facial expression, and eye gazing, have been found to originate in specific areas of the right hemisphere.

Bimodality is consistent with work in the psychology of mental development. From his classic research studies, Swiss psychologist Jean Piaget (1969), for instance, concluded that childhood development undergoes sequential stages which flow from sensory-motor and concrete phases, associated with the right hemisphere, to abstract and formal-logical thinking phases connected with the left hemisphere. While this is a reductive assessment of Piaget's research, the point is that it can be mapped against the bimodality principle, suggesting a flow in cognitive growth that goes from the R-Mode to the L-Mode, ending in an integrated use of the two modes around the age of puberty. Piaget's theory has been called "genetic"—a term that he himself used to describe his approach (Piaget 1971)—because it posits intuitively that human development is guided by its genetic predispositions.

The work of Russian psychologist Lev S. Vygotsky (1962) is also relevant in shedding light on the bimodality principle. Vygotsky proposed developmental stages that go from external (physical and social) actions toward internal cognitive constructions and interior speech, via the mind's ability to construct images of external reality. His definition of speech as a "microcosm of consciousness" is particularly reflective of this. This is why the child first employs nonverbal semiosis (gesture, play, drawing, etc.), which has its source in the R-Mode, and then engages with imaginative constructions (narratives, fables, dramatizations, etc.), which extend the R-Mode towards the L-Mode, and finally full verbal language, which becomes the source of abstract thought.

As philosopher Karl Popper (1976; Popper and Eccles 1977) cogently argued, there are three main states of human consciousness, which he called "Worlds." "World 1" is the state whereby the human organism reacts instinctively to information and input; it is controlled by neuronal synapses transmitting messages along nerve paths that cause muscles to contract or limbs to move. This is the level at which instinctive communicative actions, such as facial expressions, occur. "World 2" is the level of conscious subjective experiences, allowing humans to differentiate themselves from the messages they make and their information content. This is the level at which verbal language emerges in tandem with various forms of nonverbal communication (including gesture) to shape human awareness and understanding. "World 3" is the level of cultural knowledge, allowing the mind to understand things and communicate in both concrete and abstract ways, as conditioned by upbringing, situation, period of time, and so on. Bimodality becomes dominant at this level. Animals also have a form of consciousness and specialized communication signal systems (Kowalski 1991; Griffin 1992), but they lack the bimodality dimension of human communication, which is unique among species.

The origin of NVC can be traced to the epoch of *homo habilis*, a genus of *homo* which possessed many traits that linked it to the earlier australopithecines and to later members of the genus—homo habilis made tools and had the ability to communicate through gesture (Cartmill, Pilbeam, and Isaac 1986). The fact that it was a tool-making species also strongly indicates that it had a form of consciousness that transcended the World 1 level in Popper's model, leading it to lay the basis of the formation of the first true human cultures based on the creation of sign systems and bimodal communication. The most likely estimate for this event is around 100,000 years ago—a period from which the plaster casts of skulls reveal that both Neanderthal and Cro-Magnon hominids had brains of similar size to modern humans (Lieberman 1972, 1975, 1984, 1991). The Cro-Magnons were representatives of the species *homo sapiens sapiens*. They lived during the last glacial age. The name "Cro-Magnon" is derived from a rock shelter of that name in the Dordogne department in southwestern France, where human remains were discovered in 1868. The physical characteristics that distinguished the Cro-Magnons from the Neanderthals were a high forehead and a well-defined chin. Artifacts attributed to the earliest period of Cro-Magnon culture demonstrate that they had mastered the art of fashioning many useful tools from stone, bone, and ivory. They also made fitted clothes and decorated their bodies with ornaments of shell and bone. A number of colored paintings left on the walls of caves near their habitats provide clear evidence that their form of social life was based on meaningful group interactions. About 10,000 years ago, they started to domesticate plants and animals, initiating an agricultural revolution that set the stage for the events in human history that eventually led to the founding of the first civilizations (Montagu 1983; Noble and Davidson 1996: 22–56).

One of the earliest of the major hominid characteristics to have evolved, distinguishing the species *homo* from its nearest primate relatives, was bipedalism, an adaptation to a completely erect posture and a two-footed striding walk. Almost all other mammals walk and run on four limbs. Those that stand on two have quite different postures and gaits from humans—kangaroos hop on their two feet; some monkeys walk bipedally, especially when carrying food; chimpanzees are capable of brief bipedal walks, but their usual means of locomotion is knuckle-walking, standing on their hind legs but stooping forward, resting their hands on the knuckles rather than on the palms or fingers. So, even though forms of bipedalism are observable in other animals, they are unlike the human type—all other forms of bipedal walking involve partially bowed spines, bent knees, grasping (prehensile) feet, and some use of the hands to bear part of the body weight during locomotion. The uniquely S-shaped spinal column of humans places the center of gravity of the body directly over the area of support provided by the feet, thus giving stability and balance in the upright position.

Complete bipedalism freed the human hand, allowing it to become a supremely sensitive limb for precise manipulation and grasping. The most important structural detail in this refinement was the human thumb, which can rotate freely and, thus, be fully opposable to the other fingers. No doubt, this development made it possible to use the hands and fingers for communicative purposes, leading, in all likelihood, to the emergence of gesture as a basic mode of interaction. Eventually, the erect posture gave rise to the evolution of the physiological apparatus for speech, since it brought about the lowering and positioning of the larynx for controlled breathing (by force of gravity). In a phrase, bipedalism, gesture, and verbal language were probably intertwined in their origins (as will be discussed subsequently), leading to the bimodal structure of human communication.

Shortly after becoming bipedal, the evidence suggests that the human species underwent rapid brain expansion. In the course of human evolution, the size of the brain has more than tripled. Modern humans have a braincase volume of between 1,300 and 1,500 cc. The human brain has also developed three major structural components that undergird the unique mental capacities of the species—the large dome-shaped cerebrum, the smaller somewhat spherical cerebellum, and the brainstem. The size of the brain does not determine the degree of intelligence of the individual; this appears to be governed instead by the number and type of functioning neurons and how they are structurally connected with one another. And since neuronal connections are conditioned by environmental input, the most likely hypothesis is that any form of conscious intelligence, however it is defined, is most likely a consequence of upbringing (in the main). Unlike the early hominid adult skulls, with their sloping foreheads and prominent jaws, the modern human skull—with biologically insignificant variations—retains a proportionately large size, in relation to the rest of the body.

The great increase in brain size was achieved by the process of *neoteny*, that is, by the prolongation of the juvenile stage of brain and skull development in neonates. As a result, human infants must go through an extended period of dependency on, and stimulation by, adults. In the absence of this close bond with adults in the early years of life, the development of the infant's bimodal communication would remain incomplete, even though some aspects of instinctive NVC will emerge no matter what the rearing environment is.

## 1.8 Epilogue

The study NVC today consists of a sophisticated interdisciplinary approach to understanding the role and meaning of such communicative patterns of interaction as eye contact, facial expressions, gestures, posture, and the distance that individuals keep between each other as they talk. The first work that approached NVC broadly and systematically is Darwin's *The Expression of the Emotions in Man and Animals* (1872), mentioned above. In the book, Darwin demonstrated that both humans and animals showed emotion through similar facial expressions, thus laying the foundation for understanding NVC as a principle of all life. The study of NVC was not formalized, however, until the middle part of the twentieth century, with the work of several psychologists, linguists, and communication theorists (as mentioned above) at the Center for Advanced Study in Behavioral Sciences at Stanford through a project which came to be called the *Natural History of an Interview*, based on a film made by Gregory Bateson (as discussed), using an analytic method which today would be called context analysis—the analysis of how context shapes the functions and constituents of a communicative act. Research on NVC started proliferating in the 1960s and has developed substantively in scope ever since to include the use of technologies that allow for the measurement of facial actions, gestural forms, etc. during interactions. With the advent of computers and AI, NVC can now be studied ever more precisely.

The research has largely focused on bimodality—that is, on the relationship between verbal and nonverbal forms of communication, including: the role of eye contact and facial expressions during conversations; patterns of gazing as people speak and listen; the type of zones people maintain between each other according to the social register of speech; and the like. Today, the domain of NVC study has been amplified considerably, and includes understanding the transference of nonverbal meanings to material artifacts such as clothing and architecture, as well as to the evolution of NVC in cyberspace and its simulation in artificial systems. The remainder of the book will deal with the various domains of research that constitute the science of nonverbal communication today.

# 2

# Kinesics

## Chapter Outline

| | | |
|---|---|---|
| 2.0 | Prologue | 27 |
| 2.1 | Kinesic Analysis | 29 |
| 2.2 | Kinesic Codes | 33 |
| 2.3 | Posture and Pose | 35 |
| 2.4 | Therapeutic Applications | 41 |
| 2.5 | Forensic Applications | 44 |
| 2.6 | Epilogue | 46 |

## 2.0 Prologue

"Body language" is a colloquial term used commonly to refer to NVC in general—that is, it is used characteristically in reference to gestures, postures, eye contact, facial expressions, etc., as well as to body modifications and decorations such as hairstyle, clothing, tattooing, piercing, etc. The term "body language" is meant to literally convey how people communicate "silent" information about their identity, thoughts, moods, motivations, and attitudes, as well as identifying the nature of interpersonal relationships during conversations. The scientific study of body language is called *kinesics*, a term coined by the American anthropologist Ray L. Birdwhistell, as mentioned in Chapter 1, who used films of conversations to document and analyze speakers' nonverbal behaviors. He adopted terms and techniques from linguistics to characterize the basic movements, actions, and schemas that made up meaningful body language. He reported the main results of his findings and the methods he used to conduct the relevant research in two major books, *Introduction to Kinesics* (1952) and *Kinesics and Context* (1970). The goal of this chapter is to present and discuss the general findings and research methods that make up kinesic analysis. The specific areas—eye contact, gesture, posture, etc.—will be covered in subsequent chapters.

Some kinesic actions, such as blinking the eyes, clearing the throat, and facial flushing, are innate (inborn, involuntary) signals, as are, in large part, some facial expressions such as those conveying happiness, surprise, anger, sadness and disgust. Other forms may originate as innate signals, but their meanings are shaped by culture—a spontaneous action such as head nodding could mean approval or disapproval according to culture (Morris et al. 1979). Others still are veritable signs based on cultural connotative codes. For instance, hand gestures, such as the thumbs up or a military salute, are learned (culture-based) signs; so too is the V-sign made with the index and third fingers meaning "peace," "victory" or even the number "two." Some kinesic forms reveal states of mind. For example, pressing the lips together may indicate disagreement or doubt, even if the person's verbal statements seem contrastively to convey agreement. When verbal language and body language are in conflict, an asymmetry of meaning emerges. For this reason, kinesic insights are used both in psychiatric assessments and in criminal interrogations—a topic that will be discussed at the end of this chapter.

Kinesic signs cohere into *kinesic codes* that regulate how people behave and interact in certain social situations. The sounds made by the body (sneezing, coughing, burping, etc.), and the fluids that issue forth from it, are interpreted in terms of such codes, ranging from denotative meanings (sneezing is interpreted normally as a sign of a cold virus) to connotative ones (lip-kissing is perceived in most contexts as a sign of romance). The concept of kinesic code has been extended in semiotics to enfold the symbolic meanings that the body or body parts have in cultural settings. For example, as the late French philosopher Michel Foucault (1976) argued, perceptions of which body parts are erotic or not are hardly universal. English Puritans saw any exposure of the body from the neck down as sinful, unless it occurred in a marriage, whereby it was accepted as a kind of "necessary sin." On the other hand, many ancient rituals exalted and glorified the nude body as part of the human condition. Obviously, what is acceptable to some, is unacceptable to others; and the acceptability pattern is imprinted in specific kinesic codes.

## 2.1 Kinesic Analysis

Kinesics can be defined as the study of the bodily actions, schemas, and movements that typify communicative interactions or situations. These include hand gestures, facial expressions, eye contact patterns, posture, and other corporeal schemas that convey some psychologically or socially-relevant meaning. The founder of the discipline, as already mentioned, was Ray L. Birdwhistell, who, as a member of the Center for Advanced Study in Behavioral Sciences, was inspired by anthropologists Margaret Mead and Gregory Bateson (Chapter 1), and by the previous research on gesture by David Efron (1941), to conduct a systematic study of NVC. Although aspects of Birdwhistell's methods and theories have been critiqued somewhat (Jolly 2000), his overall approach remains a plausible and highly useful one. One of its premises is what has been called the bimodality principle here (Chapter 1), which specifies that the verbal and nonverbal modes of communication form an integrated system and that the codes of both modes mirror each other in form and function, even when they are used autonomously.

Birdwhistell started analyzing the ways in which people interacted kinesically by filming conversational interactions already in the late 1940s. As noted above, his first book, *Introduction to Kinesics*, was published in 1952. In a series of subsequent works (for example, 1955, 1960, 1961, 1963, 1970, 1974, 1979), he institutionalized kinesics as a branch of anthropology and several other disciplines, including semiotics, linguistics, and psychology, in which it is still utilized to varying degrees to carry out research on NVC. His main assumption was that: "developing a notational system for body language is to assume that all movements of the body have meaning. None are accidental" (Birdwhistell 1970: 157). In analogy with the concept of *phoneme*, or minimal sound unit that differentiates meaning in language, he named meaning-bearing body cues *kinemes*, which "can be construed as having a definite organization or structure, just as language" (Duncan and Fiske 1977: xi).

Birdwhistell divided the study of kinesic phenomena into four main phases:

1 *Prekinesics*: this is the initial phase during which the relevant movements, called *kines*, observed on film, are simply described. Kines constitute the raw data of kinesic research—they include movements of the head, face, trunk, shoulder, hands, fingers, legs, feet, neck, etc.

2 *Microkinesics*: this is the stage of determination of which kines can be classified as *kinemes* (meaningful units) and which can be assigned to variant status, called *allokines* (in analogy with *allophones*, which are phonetic variants of phonemes). For example, a slanting of the head to the side may constitute a kineme, indicating (perhaps) consternation, or it may be analyzed as a variant of the consent nod, depending on situation and type of interaction.
3 *Social kinesics*: this is the phase of analysis of the social meanings of the kinemes as utilized in a specific interactional scenario. For instance, gesticulating in certain ways during conversations may imply friendliness or the opposite, again depending on context.
4 *Parakinesics*: this phase completes the analysis. It involves examining the role of qualifiers such as intensity, range, velocity of movement in the kinesic system or code employed.

As a simple example of this four-phase analytical process, consider the use of the index finger in conversations. During the prekinesic stage, the analyst would just single it out as a kine, without ascribing any meaning to it at that point. If it is observed to accompany an utterance such as "Look over there," then it can be assigned a specific kinemic status, since it functions as an indexical sign (a sign indicating the location of something); now, the direction of the pointing, which does not alter the underlying kinemic meaning, allows the analyst to describe it as a particular allokine. As part of social kinesics, the pointing would then be connected to the various potential meanings that it might entail in the interactional scenario—for instance, pointing out something concretely ("Look over here"), or indicating reprobation, if the finger is shaken up and down or side to side ("You shouldn't say that"). At the parakinesic stage, the ways in which the pointing finger is modulated (pointed, shaken, etc.) are connected bimodally to the verbal parts of the interaction, allowing the analyst to complete the analysis of this gestural sign.

As mentioned, Birdwhistell used films to record interactions—a research method introduced by Bateson and Mead (1942) and Mead and MacGreggor (1951). The kinesic analysis of the scenarios on the film was called *context analysis* a little later (Scheflen 1966; Kendon 1979). Overall, kinesics has shown rather conclusively that everyday communication is based on bimodality (verbal and nonverbal) and the multimodality of potential sensory channels. Birdwhistell (1970: 70) put it as follows:

> We cannot investigate communication by isolating and measuring one channel, the acoustic. Communication, upon investigation, appears to be a system

which makes use of the channels of all of the sensory modalities. By this model, communication is a continuous process utilizing the various channels and the combinations of them as appropriate to the particular situation. If we think of Channel 1 as being the audio-acoustic (vocal) channel, Channel 2 as the kinesthetic-visual channel, Channel 3 would be the odor-producing-olfactory channel, Channel 4 would be the tactile and so on. Thus, while no single channel is in constant use, one or more channels are always in operation. Communication is the term which I apply to this continuous process.

To annotate the kines that can be observed in an interactional scenario, Birdwhistell developed a system of notation that he called *kinegraphs*, which are symbols standing for specific kinesic schemas. Figure 2.1 shows examples of kinegraphs for annotating eye and facial kines.

Kinesics remains an overarching method for studying and analyzing NVC in all its facets. Its main research and theoretical aspects were adopted by American psychologist Paul Ekman, whose work will be discussed in the next few chapters. For the present purposes, it is sufficient to point out that Ekman and his team of researchers (for example, Ekman and Friesen 1969a) have identified five basic types of kinemes, which have remained standard ones within nonverbal communication science:

1 *Emblems*: kinemes that can be translated directly into words. For example, the OK-sign made with the raised thumb on a fist matches the word "OK" in English-speaking culture. In other cultures, however, it might have an obscene meaning. Other examples include the beckoning ("come here") sign, waving, obscene gestures, and the like.

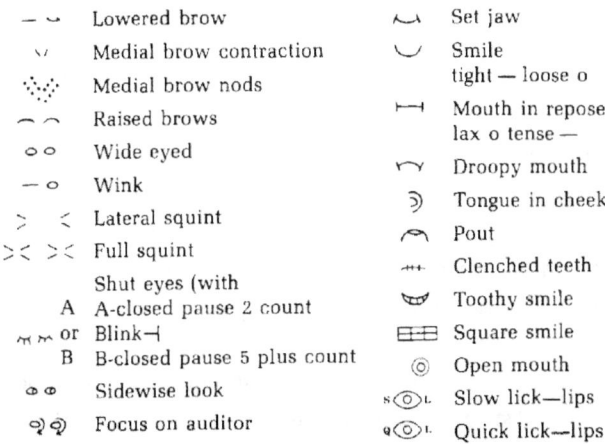

**Figure 2.1** Kinegraphs (from Birdwhistell 1952; 1970).

One of the first researchers to identify this type of kineme was David Efron (1941), who carried out extensive fieldwork in southern Italy and Eastern Europe.

2 *Illustrators*: kinemes that complement verbal communication by reinforcing the message through gesture, facial expressions, or head movements. Examples include indicating the increasing size of something being described orally by drawing the hands outward ("This is getting to be larger and larger"), putting the open hands forward as if giving something to someone ("Let me give you some advice"), shaking the head left and right to indicate disapprobation or displeasure ("This makes no sense whatsoever"), and so on.

3 *Affect displays*: bodily or facial kinemes that communicate an emotional or affective state, as for instance smiling to convey pleasure or frowning to communicate displeasure instead. In other words, these communicate emotional meaning (emotivity)— happiness, surprise, fear, anger, sadness, contempt, disgust, etc.—and can be both co-speech forms or independent modes of communication.

4 *Regulators*: kinemes that accompany speech to control or regulate what is being said, including such actions as head nodding to indicate agreement, or raising a finger to indicate the desire to intervene in a conversation. Other examples include the hand movements that accompany utterances such as "Keep going," "Slow down," "What else happened?"

5 *Adaptors*: kinemic actions such as scratching one's head, tugging one's ear, swinging one's legs, etc., which constitute cues as to how someone is feeling.

Today, computers are used to record and analyze kinesic phenomena, with computer laboratories in various universities throughout the world that are making it possible to analyze eye contact, gesture, posture, and other bodily schemas with a precision that has never before been possible. To give just one example, the Human Media Lab, which was founded in 2012 at Queen's University in Ontario, Canada, allows for many uses of computers to study communicative interactions and to precisely analyze kinesic schemas. Such laboratories also make it possible to investigate human-computer interactions (Chapter 9).

Overall, kinesics has shown that F2F communication occurs both through the body and vocal speech in tandem. This implies, as Charles Peirce (1931–58, volume V: 551) argued, that bimodal communication emanates from the organic world: "Not only is thought in the organic world, but it develops there."

## 2.2 Kinesic Codes

Recall the elevator vignette described in the preface. This time, let us suppose that the stomach of one of the passengers emits one of those uncontrollable growls that result from hunger or digestion. More than likely, the person will feel embarrassed or uneasy. This is because of an unconscious social rule of what behavior or type of noise is appropriate in the "elevator scene," including bodily sounds, such as a rumbling stomach, that break the measured silence in the cubicle. The same social knowledge provides strategies of socially redeeming repair—the individual might make some excuse, a facetious remark about the sound, or ignore it completely as if it had not occurred. Such behaviors are governed by an unconscious kinesic code, which is based on the enactment of silence as an appropriate social rule in this particular context. It is based, in effect, on the social meanings of silence.

On the other hand, in many other kinds of daily interactions, silence is felt to be uncomfortable, as for example when friends meet each other, whereby long stretches of silence between utterances is felt to be awkward. So, people feel that they must say something, no matter how trivial, fearing that the silence might otherwise be misinterpreted as a sign of inattentiveness or indifference. Silence is also intrinsic to the successful enactment of certain communicative situations—for example, a teacher expects students to remain silent during specific instructional phrases, as does a preacher during a religious service, especially to commemorate someone or something—it is, in other words, perceived as a sign of respect or deference in many communicative interactions. In various Native American cultures, silence conveys contemplation, and speaking for the sake of speaking is seen as a "waste of breath," as some have called it (Epes-Brown 1992). As such examples show, the silence code varies in meaning from situation to situation, enfolding a vast array of connotative meanings (Schroeter and Taylor 2018).

Te reiterate, a kinesic code constitutes a semiotic grid of social meaning that guides the enactment and interpretation of nonverbal behaviors according to situation (Lévi-Strauss 1951; Krampen 2010). The reason why the elevator scene makes sense is because those involved in the situation have internalized the relevant code, which, in this case, regulates the sound environment, the allowable glances, postures, etc. that are seen as appropriate. In other words, kinesic codes provide unconscious social scripts for determining what kind of nonverbal behaviors are appropriate in a specific situation. The code may have a natural (biological) origin, but its implementations in human interactions are shaped by culture. So, the elevator code may be a reflex of some evolutionary mechanism that cautions people latently to be wary of unknown people or situations—a mechanism that characterizes many species. However, when it is contextualized in some social scene, such as in an elevator, its manifestations are shaped by a specific kinesic code, which ascribes silence situationally. The underlying function of the code is to make contact and interaction fluid and non-threatening. Joseph Jordania (2009) has argued that in social animals, silence can be a sign of danger. Darwin (1871: 123) also wrote about this type of silent behavior in relation to horses and cattle.

The silence code is a paralinguistic code, involving the deployment of a specific vocal strategy—in this case, absence of voice—for some communicative purpose. All codes subserve specific communicative functions. The following are of particular relevance to the study of NVC. These are listed here for the sake of illustration. Detailed discussions will follow subsequently:

1 *Posture codes:* these regulate the orientation and tension (tautness) of the body—for example, a loose body pose and a leaning forward orientation might indicate a sense of relaxation and comfort with a familiar interlocutor, while an upright and more taut body posture generally characterizes formal social interactions.
2 *Eye-contact codes:* these regulate the frequency and pattern of looking into an interlocutor's eyes during an interaction. In some cultures, men and women do not make eye contact outside of marriage; in contemporary urbanized courtship displays, on the other hand, gazing is seen as part of romantic behavior between potential partners.
3 *Haptic and tactile codes*: these regulate the type, mode, and frequency of touching between interlocutors during an interaction—each of which communicates relevant social meanings. In many courtship-based situations, touching and hugging are perceived as key aspects of romance, but these would violate behavioral norms in most other contact rituals, such as those involving strangers or superiors.
4 *Gesture codes*: these involve the use of the hands and the arms to communicate something, either independently of language or integrated with it during speech. The gestures that accompany speech are known more specifically as gesticulants (to be discussed subsequently).
5 *Proxemic codes:* these regulate the zones people maintain between each other during F2F conversational interactions, varying according to context and type of relation that exists between the interlocutors. The elevator scene above included not only a silence code, but an

overlapping proxemic code, which implied that the people in the cubicle must keep a formal distance between each other; any violation of that distance, such as one person standing right in front of another, would be felt as aberrant or conflictual.

6 *Paralinguistic codes*: these regulate the tone, pitch, volume, rhythm, and rapidity of speech, supporting the emotive function of communication—for example a high pitched voice may indicate happiness, a low one sadness; a loud voice may indicate anger, a low one, indifference; etc.
7 *Buccal-nasal codes*: these relate to the meanings of actions and behaviors involving the mouth or nose, including spitting, coughing, sniffling, snorting, puffing etc. These assume specific connotations according to context—for example, spitting might be construed as a gesture of anger or contempt, while snorting might be seen as an act of displeasure or derision.
8 *Chronemic codes*: these regulate how people manage time and how events are perceived as structured in some sequential way. For example, appointments in many cultures are established at specific times; not respecting the particular time frame might engender negative interpretations of the violation.
9 *Personal presentation and appearance codes*: these regulate the ways in which people present themselves to others, including clothing, hairstyle, and other aspects of appearance that are designed to convey to others certain personal or social meanings.

The bimodality principle applies to all these codes—that is, the verbal and nonverbal forms involved are reflexive of each other in specific ways during a communicative event; or else, when they are not part of such an event, the structural properties of verbal language and kinesic codes are isomorphic, as Birdwhistell showed by relating kinemes to phonemes. Another principle that applies is that of multimodality (Chapter 1). This implies that different modes of communication occur in tandem systematically in communicative situations, whereby such behaviors related to eye contact, posture, language etc., will match the semantic content of speech.

## 2.3 Posture and Pose

After Birdwhistell's 1952 book, it became obvious that NVC could be studied as systematically as verbal language—kinesics was to body language what linguistics was to verbal language. The study of posture and posing, for instance, could be carried out in the same manner that linguists conducted fieldwork, using kinegraphic annotations rather than phonemic or grammatical symbols. Birdwhistell based his overall approach on the previous work of Allport and Vernon (1933) and Laban (1950), which showed how the choreography of dance movements and postures reflected cultural meanings. An early survey of postural codes, published after Birdwhistell's book, was the one by Gordon Hewes (1955). So, by the mid-1950s it was becoming evermore obvious that the ways in which someone comports their body when standing or sitting, or the particular poses adopted by people during conversations, were hardly random or idiosyncratic. Rather, they formed a system that was comparable to the structures and combinatory rules of linguistic grammar.

Research has since shown that posture codes direct enactments of social rank, with relaxed postures generally indicative of a lower rank and more upright (rigid) ones of a higher rank, within varying ranges of social meaning (Mehrabian 1968). They may change, of course, from one phase of the encounter to the next, but these would generally fall under the allokinetic category (above), rather than constitute differential kinemic structures. Scheflen (1964) found that postural changes occur in relation to changes in the intent or function of an interaction; so, the posture assumed to question someone shows a different bodily composure than the one assumed as people listen to someone else talk. The differential postures signal attitude or role in an interaction, while falling under the same kind of functional (kinemic) category. Among the postural and posing forms that characterize interactions in contemporary urban settings, the following have been identified by the relevant research conducted mainly in western urban locales:

1 *Inclination*: this refers to the ways in which someone might lean toward a person during an interaction. A forward inclination is generally an unconscious expression of sympathy or acceptance, while inclining away from the interlocutor might signal disapproval. Inclinations of the head bear the same pattern of meanings.
2 *Unconscious mimesis*: during a conversation, people have a tendency to imitate each other, especially when the interaction is fluid and positive. This can be seen in gestures and postures that are mimetic (of each other), suggesting an empathic bond between the interlocutors. Lack of such mimetic behavior may induce the subconscious sense that the interaction is artificial or conflictual (Olson and Hergenhahn 2009).

3  *Orientation*: how people orient their bodies toward each other reveals various emotive states. For example, a close F2F orientation might be indicative of a confrontational situation, while looking at each other at an angle might indicate that the interaction is positive and smooth.
4  *Hands and arms*: these play significant roles in assigning meanings to certain postures and poses. For example, the arms crossed over the chest or the hands clasped in front of the body might convey an impression of disinterest or even hostility, while open hands and arms convey opposite meanings (Rossberg-Gemton and Poole 1993).
5  *Clenching the hands*: in a central, raised, or lowered position (depending on whether the person is standing or sitting) is a sign of confidence. But it can also be a frustration sign if the clenching is robust to the point of turning the knuckles white.
6  *Steepling*: the term used by Birdwhistell (1970) to indicate the gesture of touching the fingers together to form a steeple. It invariably communicates confidence and authority. It is a kind of "know-it-all" positional kineme. The raised steeple is used when the steepler is doing the talking and the lowered one when the same person is listening.
7  *Gripping*: the hands, arms, and wrists behind the body conveys superiority or confidence. The palm-in-palm gesture (behind the back) is the most common manifestation of this positional gesture.
8  *Thumb displays*: with the other fingers in a pocket or under a jacket lapel, as the thumbs protrude out, convey confidence or a sense of superiority. These manifest themselves saliently when the person gives a contradictory verbal message. For instance, when an attorney turns to a jury and says "In my humble opinion," displaying the thumbs, tilting back the head, the effect on the jury is likely to be a negative or counteractive one, making the jury feel that the lawyer might be insincere or pompous. If the lawyer approaches the jury with an open palm display and a slight sloop, the jury will be more inclined to believe the lawyer's words.
9  *Folding the arms*: generally indicates that the person has negative thoughts about the other speaker, indicating a lack of attention to what the interlocutor is saying. Folding both arms together might imply an attempt to hide from an unfavorable situation or else to indicate disagreement. A variant of this sign is the partial arm gesture, with one hand holding the other near or at the elbow. This seems to imply lack of self-confidence or humility.

While *posture* refers to the position, tension, inclination, or orientation of the body in certain situations, *pose* implies a specific implementation of posture for various reasons—aesthetic, athletic, ritualistic, romantic, etc.—and *positioning* to how the body is disposed with respect to a speaker. There is, however, much overlap between the three. For example, kneeling is a posture if deployed as a resting position (rather than sitting), such as after running for a while in order to regain breath, but it can also constitute a religious pose indicating reverence or veneration—a bodily schema that applies as well in situations of regal communication (between, say, kings and subjects), in which case it is more precisely a positioning of the body in a specific way. Similarly, lying down in a supine position can be a simple resting posture, but it may also be a pose of sexual enticement in some situations. The same kind of kinemic modulation among posture, pose, and positioning can be applied to such actions as squatting, sitting, crouching, bending, bowing, jumping, etc. In all cases, the context and kinesic code constrain the meaning of each bodily schema: for instance, in Japan, bowing—*ojigi*—is a greeting posture, but it can also mean apologizing or showing respect in other contexts. However, sitting cross-legged is seen as a disrespectful pose in that country, especially in the presence of an elder or someone of superior social rank (Caradec and Cousin 2018).

Positioning is divided broadly into two schemas—*open* and *closed*. The former bespeaks of openness toward interlocutors, with the torso leaning toward them and the arms typically at the sides. This communicates agreement and emotional consonance with the speaker. In contrast, a closed posture, such as leaning back, while crossing the arms on the chest, communicates that the person is less receptive to the intelocutor. In many East Asian cultures, the open positional schema also communicates modesty and humility. Overall, the open-versus-closed code corresponds to positive-versus-negative emotivity, as can be seen in the following nonverbal actions that typify many urbanized (western) communicative events (Scheflen 1964; Argyle 1975):

*Positive:*
- tilting the head to a side indicates that a person is (likely) listening attentively and thus interested in what is being said;
- rubbing the hands briskly suggests an eagerness to receive certain information;
- the palms facing upward is a sign of openness and of honesty; it can also convey sincerity or innocence; but in a religious context it is a sign of spiritual submission or imploration;
- standing straight with the shoulders back conveys self-confidence and openness to what is being said;

- stroking the chin indicates interest or thoughtfulness;
- leaning towards interlocutors indicates that they are perceived as trustworthy or as saying something of interest;
- direct eye contact conveys confidence and trust in an interlocutor; however, unwavering direct eye contact can produce a feeling of conflict;
- head nodding communicates agreement with what is being said (in most situations and cultures, but not all).

*Negative:*
- crossing the arms over the chest conveys defensiveness or disagreement with what is being said;
- nail-biting might reveal stress or insecurity;
- placing a hand on a cheek might indicate that someone is thinking negatively about what is being said;
- a furrowed brow might suggest that the person is no longer listening, or is in disagreement with what is being said;
- finger-tapping implies (generally) that someone is growing impatient or bored with something;
- touching or rubbing the nose might indicate disbelief or outright rejection of what is being said;
- placing the head in the hands may indicate boredom or being upset;
- pulling an earlobe might suggest indecision;
- fidgeting with something might convey nervousness or insecurity.

Given the obvious importance of bodily schemas in everyday communication, it is not surprising to find that artists have depicted them throughout history, focusing on their meanings from an aesthetic perspective (Morris 2019). As an example, consider the painting by seventeenth-century Dutch painter Caspar Netscher, titled *Young Girl Holding a Letter* (Figure 2.2).

The girl's pose, with her head resting on her arm in support of seemingly desperate inner thoughts, while her left hand holds a letter in a positioning that seems to indicate disappointment, is a portrait of what can be called a "pose of hopelessness." This message is relayed visually by the kinemic schemas themselves, which, although open to various other interpretations, are arguably suggestive of the young woman's state of mind (Mehrabian 1973). The artist seems to have understood that the girl's postural schemas were indexes of emotional states and even existential ones.

**Figure 2.2** Caspar Netscher, *Young Girl Holding a Letter*, c. 1665 (Wikimedia Commons).

A relevant research study of classic Mayan art, conducted by Maitland Gardner (2017), confirms the symbolic-cultural power of postural and gestural forms in that culture and its overall worldview:

> This research situates (and re-negotiates) the meanings of postures and gestures within the Maya worldview (and our understanding of it), but also stresses the importance of cross-cultural perspectives on bodily communication, particularly by considering the relationship between the physical forms of postures and gestures and the meanings that they communicate. It is argued

that broad practices beyond elites in Maya society formed the repertoire from which gestures were drawn to function in particular iconographic contexts during the Classic Period. The postures and gestures represented in Maya art may not be part of an exclusively courtly etiquette but rather originate in a common body language that communicates meaning.

Already in the 1920s, anthropologist Bronislaw Malinowski (1922, 1923) saw the modes of communication that characterize ritualistic encounters, verbal and nonverbal, as critical in maintaining social relations fluent and smooth. In the 1950s, anthropologist Edward T. Hall showed that the positioning of bodies between people while they interacted was imbued with powerful emotional meanings (Chapter 7). Since then, it has become increasingly obvious that the schemas of posture, pose, and positioning are hardly superficial matters—they form a silent code, as Hall called it, that regulates common interactions and the meanings assigned to them.

## 2.4 Therapeutic Applications

The early study of body language was seen almost immediately to have specific implications for psychotherapy, starting with the work of Albert Scheflen (1964) and Gregory Bateson (1972). Research has shown, in fact, that posture conveys more therapeutically relevant information to counselors than does verbal dialogue (Haase and Tepper 1972). The reason for this is that states of the body, such as posture, represent mental-emotional states in a fairly stable patterned way—a view called *embodied emotion theory* (Hadjikhani and De Gelder 2003; Briñol, Petty, and Wagner 2009; McHugh et al. 2009). Changing postures has been found to correspond to shifting emotions in an interaction, starting with Scheflen (1964, 1973).

The first to apply research on body language directly to psychotherapy, even before the advent of kinesics as a distinct discipline, was Gregory Bateson who, in his 1936 book *Naven* stressed the importance of ritualistic bodily communication to wellbeing and cultural stability in general—a conclusion he reached from his fieldwork among the Iatmul, an indigenous society of New Guinea. The word *naven* refers to a ceremony in which sex and gender categories in Iatmul interactions transcend typical, formulaic phatic communication. Such ceremonies revealed to him what he called *metacommunication* (Bateson 1951), defined as the exchange of codified cues that unconsciously suggest relationships between interlocutors. Metacommunication may or may not be congruent to verbal communication, but it can always be deciphered via the nonverbal cues that accompany speech.

His observations of how Balinese children were reared (Bateson 1942), led Bateson to formulate the hypothesis that many mental illnesses result from a difficulty in processing unstated metacommunicative structures, such as those that manifest themselves at different levels of actual communication—including the use of mixed messaging—a theory that he called *double bind* (Bateson 1956). This refers to the type of paradoxical messages consisting of a primary negative injunction ("Do not this") followed by a secondary negative follow-up meant to assuage the previous one emotively ("Do not see this as a punishment"). The problem arises when someone is unable to discriminate the discursive-cognitive relation between such messages. This inability has therapeutic implications, since, as Bateson claimed, a schizophrenic patient, for example, will have difficulties differentiating them and relating them metacommuncatively (that is, as part of an interactional strategy). So, he suggested that the environment of a schizophrenic patient must be created and maintained as a holistically positive discursive system, with no contrasting signals of meaning. Schizophrenic patients might also be incapable of commenting on the message themselves, which, therefore, prevents them from escaping from the emotional double bind. To put it more concretely, a double bind is a dilemma that arises during communicative events whereby an individual receives seemingly conflicting messages, with one negating the other for socially strategic purposes, which are meant to complement each other. These might induce a state of mental conflict, whereby the interaction will fall into the double bind with no resolution. Double-bind theory has been influential in drawing psychiatrists into the study of nonverbal communication as a key to unraveling mental health problems.

Another domain of therapeutic application of kinesic research is in so-called *body psychotherapy*, which is a branch of clinical psychology. It is based on the view that there is an intrinsic link between the mind and the body, a link which, as Foley and Gentile (2010: 38) point out, allows for a more comprehensive diagnosis than using verbal dialogue alone:

> The mental status examination is the objective portion of any comprehensive psychiatric assessment and has key diagnostic and treatment implications. This includes elements such as a patient's baseline general appearance and behavior, affect, eye contact, and psychomotor functioning. Changes in these parameters from session to session allow the psychiatrist to gather important

information about the patient. In psychiatry, much emphasis is placed on not only listening to what patients communicate verbally but also observing their interactions with the environment and the psychiatrist. In a complementary fashion, psychiatrists must be aware of their own nonverbal behaviors and communication, as these can serve to either facilitate or hinder the patient–physician interaction . . . Being aware of these unspoken subtleties can offer a psychiatrist valuable information that a patient may be unwilling or unable to put into words.

As early as the late 1930s, anthropologist Eliot Chapple (1939, 1940) was drawing attention to the role of turn-taking cues in conversations, observing that interlocutors display specific interaction rhythms that guided turn-taking. His findings had immediate implications for communication theory and for clinical practices. Adam Kendon (1967), for example, showed that gazing patterns were directive of conversational turn-taking—a co-speech phenomenon that became a salient one in early conversation studies (Beattie 1978). It is now a documented fact that gaze directions are often relied upon by interlocutors as cues to emotional states—a fact that has obvious clinical implications as well. Kendon (2010: 51) characterizes the general importance of such research aptly as follows:

> Close analyses of human interaction using films has led to the realization that when people interact they do not respond merely to each other as if each provides a succession of discrete acts which can be responded to as if they are discrete signals cueing the other to a succession of separate acts. People in interaction, it appears, often enter into a sustained coordination of action with one another, each continually adjusting his/her behavior to the other, as partners do in a waltz. This suggests that people in interaction may often be so highly familiar with the structure and timing of each other's actions that they are able to anticipate the course of development of each other's actions and so achieve extremely close temporal coordination of action.

It is remarkable to note that the Greek physician Hippocrates—the western founder of both medicine and semiotics—was aware of the importance of the body–mind nexus in any treatment: "It's far more important to know what person the disease has than what disease the person has" (cited in Chadwick and Mann 1950). Hippocrates realized that disease was in both the body and the mind (so to speak). A mental illness, such as schizophrenia, as Bateson certainly suggested, is simultaneously a biological phenomenon and one that is subject to cultural systems—with one affecting the other mutually.

## 2.5 Forensic Applications

A major finding of kinesic science is that body language can reveal feelings that a person may wish to hide, as that person speaks deceptively. For this reason, kinesic methods have been taught to investigators to carry out effective interrogations of suspects in various police forces across the world (Danesi 2013a). Lying involves an asymmetry between verbal and nonverbal features of communication, producing sign traces that indicate that mendacity is occurring—a fact called "emotional leakage" (Ekman and Friesen 1969b; Porter, Brinke, and Wallace 2012). Leakage occurs, in other words, when someone says one thing, but their body language (facial movements and hand-to-face gestures) indicates something else. The reason may be, as Darwin had hypothesized, that humans cannot consciously control their emotions and therefore cannot inhibit the body schemas associated with them.

In criminal interrogations, it is expected that criminals will lie to protect themselves. Observing the criminal's postures, facial expressions, eye contact patterns, etc., has become a standard practice among investigators, because of the phenomenon of emotional leakage, which is a form of asymmetrical semiosis. As Umberto Eco (1976: 58) has put it: "Every time there is possibility of lying there is a sign function; which is to signify (and then to communicate) something to which no real state of things corresponds. The possibility of lying is the proprium of semiosis." In effect, lying sets off a series of nonverbal actions that leak the deceptive strategies to the interlocutor (DePaulo et al. 1996; Cohen, Beattie and Shovelton 2010). For example, open palms normally accompany honest speech (as discussed). When someone hides the palms (usually behind the back), the person is likely trying to hide something or is not being open about something—a gesture that might be accompanied by fidgeting and sweating. People find it difficult, if not impossible, to lie with their palms exposed.

Because kinemic behaviors are partly involuntary and partly learned in context, criminal interrogations will have to take into account variables such as subjective uses of nonverbal actions and the cultural shaping of gestures. Nonetheless, as psychologist Meier-Faust (2002) argues, kinesic information can be used to assess the intensity of emotion involved during verbal communication and, thus, to examine if the two—body language and verbalization—are complementary (consonant) or not (dissonant). Dissonance produces bodily signs that usually imply deceit; consonance does not. Needless to say, there are some people, such as actors and skilled orators, as well as inveterate criminals, who can control their body language, impeding its leakage, to give the impression that they are telling the truth. Knowing how to use smiles, nods, and winks to cover up lies takes skill, but it is possible to do. However, even in such cases, facial muscular twitching, expansion and contraction of the pupils, an increased rate of eye blinking, and a general lack of composure in posture are kinemic actions that can rarely be contained, no matter how skilled a liar may be. These are monitored by the brain's "lie detector" apparatus, so to speak. To lie successfully, the body must be hidden from sight. It is easier to lie in writing or on the phone than it is in a face-to-face encounter.

However, even paralinguistic or writing features might reveal that deception is involved. In forensics, voiceprinting analysis is used as an investigatory tool for detecting if someone might be lying based on the stress patterns (and other paralinguistic features) in the voice. A common method is called the *Psychological Stress Evaluator* (PSE). Relevant research has found that the voice will tend to be at higher pitch when someone is lying, emitting inaudible vibrations called *micro-tremors* that can be recorded (Tanner and Tanner 2004). Stress causes the vocal muscles to tighten and the micro-tremors to decrease, producing flattened lines on the screen of a computerized speech synthesizer. A version of this method, called the *Computer Voice Stress Analyzer* (CVSA), has proven to be more reliable than the PSE. The CVSA checks for voice shifts during interrogations, complementing the findings produced by other truth-telling devices.

Voiceprinting has helped solve a number of famous cases (Danesi 2013a), such as that of Gloria Carpenter, whose body was found in her bathroom in Modesto, California, in 1973 with a mark around her neck indicating that she had been strangled. Investigators located her partner, John Wayne Glenn, at a pub, who admitted to taking her home while vowing that he did not enter her apartment. Detectives persuaded Glenn to take the PSE test. The results showed significant stress in his voice, suggesting that Glenn was likely involved. So, the detectives returned to the apartment; and after meticulous forensic research turned up a palm print that belonged to him. Glenn confessed, even though the PSE evidence could not be used in court.

The forensic use of voice analysis did not start until the late 1960s following its utilization by the Michigan State Police. It is now part of a larger approach, based on the fact that voiceprints are unique, shaped by the sizes of the oral and nasal cavities of individuals, as well as the quality of the vocal cords located in the larynx. The cavities are resonators, reinforcing some of the overtones produced by the vocal cords. Also, the articulators (the lips, teeth, tongue, soft palate and jaw muscles) are controlled in unique ways by individual speakers, producing the kinds of sounds and prosodic patterns that we can easily recognize as belonging to them. The FBI has examined thousands of voiceprint cases and found the reliability to be high. For this reason, many police forces now conserve voiceprints as a permanent record alongside fingerprints, DNA, and other kinds of evidence.

In 1984, Frederik Link and Glenn Foster devised an interview system, which they called the *Kinesic Interview Technique* (KIT), that incorporates many of the kinesic concepts discussed above. Link taught the technique at military police schools, to agents of the FBI, and at other federal government agencies; Foster used the technique in connection with the polygraph and other lie-detection devices, finding that it produced highly synchronous results with these devices. Another interview technique based on kinesic notions that has been adopted by police forces is the *Reid Technique* system, named after John Reid (1991). The interrogation session in this case is based on interpreting facial expressions, poses, hand movements, etc., to assess if there is any emotional leakage. But there is a caveat here. Because of cultural kinesic codes, one must always be wary of applying such techniques broadly. Looking people in the eyes when spoken to, especially by authority figures, is considered bad manners by some people, not a sign of evasion or guilt.

## 2.6 Epilogue

All aspects of one's body, from the eye and face to postures and poses, are sources for transmitting messages, wittingly or unwittingly. As Ekman and Friesen (1975: 7) observe, body language is a dominant mode of communication, especially in the conveyance of emotional states:

> Emotions are shown primarily in the face, not in the body. The body instead shows how people are coping with emotion. There is no specific body movement pattern that always signals anger or fear, but there are facial patterns specific to each emotion. If someone is angry, his body may show how he is coping with the anger. He may be tense and constrained (tight muscular tension in arms and legs, stiff posture). He may be withdrawing (a particular retreated position). There may be verbal attack (certain types of hand movements with his words), or the likelihood of physical attack (posture, orientation, hand movements). However, any of these movements can occur just as well when a person is afraid as when he is angry. Body

movement reveals, of course, not just how someone copes with emotion, but also what a person's attitudes, interpersonal orientations, etc. might be.

Kinesics has become an important branch of various disciplines, from anthropology and semiotics to psychology and linguistics, showing the power of nonverbal signs in regulating how people behave in certain social situations and in manifesting inner states of feeling and thinking. Kinesic semiosis is a product of both our biological ancestry and specific cultural histories. The eye patterns that manifest themselves when speaking, the kinds of touching routines humans utilize during discourse, the kinds of gestures and gesticulations that accompany speech, and the like, are based both in biology and in rearing practices; that is, they are the outcome of nature and culture cooperating in an exclusive form of partnership.

To conclude this chapter, it is relevant to note that there is now a sub-field of Artificial Intelligence aiming to study and develop software and devices that can recognize and simulate human emotions. Called Affective Computing (AC) software, it has been designed to detect emotional states in people on the basis of the algorithmic analysis of facial expressions, muscle tension, postures, gestures, speech tones, pupil dilation, etc. (Picard 1997). The relevant technology includes sensors, cameras, big data, and deep learning software. The aim of this branch of AI is to construct algorithms that can decode emotional states or influence them. This line of research has led to the building of so-called Empathy Machines, which are companion robots that display the ability to respond to human emotional states by simulation. To actually achieve empathy, however, a robot would have to be able to experience emotion and comprehend it bimodally; to do so it would need a biological body.

There is also another problem (for now). When someone makes a facial expression, such as furrowing the brow, the AC software might identify it as confusion as opposed to happiness, which may or may not correspond to how someone is actually feeling. To reinforce the interpretation, there are now gesture recognition algorithms used in conjunction with facial expression ones. The topic of human-computer communication will be taken up subsequently. For the present purposes, it is relevant to note that the insights used in AC computing are derived from kinesics, a development that has also been of great benefit, in turn, to kinesics itself, since it can now make use of computer technology to expand its traditional methods of research.

# 3
# The Eyes

## Chapter Outline

| | |
|---|---|
| 3.0 Prologue | 49 |
| 3.1 Eye Contact | 51 |
| 3.2 Gazing | 55 |
| 3.3 Eye Metaphors | 58 |
| 3.4 Eye Symbolism | 60 |
| 3.5 The Eye in Art | 64 |
| 3.6 Epilogue | 72 |

## 3.0 Prologue

The second century CE Greek physician, Galen of Pergamon, was one of the first to describe the anatomy and physiology of the eye with scientific precision (De Lacy 2010). He identified ocular structures such as the retina, the cornea, the iris, the uvea, tear ducts, and eyelids, as well as two fluids he called the vitreous and aqueous humors. The eye became a subject of great scientific interest in subsequent medieval and Renaissance medicine. However, the interest in the eyes as a source of nonverbal communication did not surface in any significant way until after Darwin's book *Expression of the Emotions in Man and Animals* (1872), in which he emphasized how eye movements revealed intentions, emotions, and inner thought processes.

At a biological level, the eyes permit vision, which is a survival function, allowing a species to scour the environment to detect prey, danger, a mating partner, etc. At a psychological level, the eye, as Darwin pointed out, provides access to inner states, emotional and cognitive. At a communicative level, the eye allows for the transmission of signs and signals that have specific meanings—a function that often comes out in interactional patterns such as making eye contact (gazing, looking, staring, etc.) to communicate an emotional state, a need, a social relationship, etc. Some of these functions, especially the biological one, are found in other species. A dog will form a direct stare as a threat or challenge to another dog, only breaking eye contact as a sign of surrender to a more dominant (powerful) dog. In contacts with people, a dog will similarly use a menacing stare if the person is unknown, and seemingly interpret a human stare as a threat, leading to an attack on the looker. Staring in such ways appears to be instinctive and not limited to human NVC. However, in humans eye-based communication transcends biology, constituting culturally-coded behavior that enfolds a vast array of meaning exchanges, complementing vocal speech, reinforcing its content and intent in various ways. Given its importance in human life, the eye has also been incorporated into symbolic practices and treated by visual artists across eras and cultures.

This chapter will deal with the eye as: (a) a source of NVC; (b) as connected bimodally to verbal interaction; and (c) as a symbolic structure in culture and art. As in other chapters, a selection of the vast array of possible topics connected with the eye has been made, based on the main ideas and findings that are relevant to the chapter themes. Although not part of the subject matter of this chapter, it is nonetheless useful to stress here, as a side-note, that seeing and visual perception, although intertwined, are not one and the same. Evidence that the two are autonomous yet mutually influential comes from the domain of optical illusions, which caution us to be careful about what our eyes tell us. One of the best known is the so-called Müller-Lyer Illusion, named after the German psychologist Franz Carl Müller-Lyer, who invented it in 1889, a version of which is shown in Figure 3.1.

Most people in western culture see the bottom line as longer than the top one, even though the two are equal in length. The source of the illusion is the different orientation of the two arrowheads. One plausible explanation why this dupes the eye into seeing the figure incorrectly is that we tend to interpret arrowheads that jut out as lengthening something, and vice versa, those pointing inwards as shortening something. Another possibility is that the illusion affects those who live in built environments, such as urban centers where rectilinear architecture is common. Whatever the explanation, research has shown that perception of the illusion varies from culture to

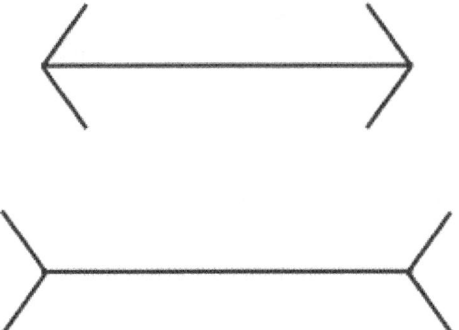

**Figure 3.1** Müller-Lyer illusion (Wikimedia Commons).

culture, exposing visual perception as unreliable, because it is influenced by contextual and cultural factors.

## 3.1 Eye Contact

The term *eye contact* came into broad use around the same time as Birdwhistell's work on kinesics (Chapter 2). More technically, its study comes under the rubric of *oculesics,* defined simply as the study of communication with the eyes. Research in this area has shown that the ways in which people look at each other, and the ways in which they use eye configurations (gazing, staring, etc.) are hardly random; they are guided by both natural instincts (shared with other species) and cultural practices, conveying personal and social meanings (Knapp and Hall 2010).

As the work of Paul Ekman (2003) has shown, eye contact, also called *mutual gazing,* is a major mode of nonverbal communication, accompanying oral speech or used independently of verbal interaction. Eye-contact patterns vary broadly. But whatever their specific function or modality, as Erhardt Güttgemanns (2010: 95) suggests, of all the nonverbal communicative modes, these seem to have primacy across the world:

> While the tactile channel (e.g., dance, clothing, circumcision), the gustatory channel (food, drink), the olfactory channel (smells), and the thermic channel (hot vs. cold) are much more reduced, the optic channel is the most important. It is correlated to the "door" of the eyes, which represses the ears. Even liturgic speaking is not so much acoustic and "verbal" as optic, since a pragmatically perlocutionary speech aims at "evidence".

Semiotically, eye contact codes constitute mixed sign systems—natural (instinctive, involuntary), conventionally-based (cultural, voluntary), or a combination of the two. Table 3.1 shows a few examples (Ellsberg 2010).

The eyes are a focal point on the face, and because the pupils work independently of other neural and cognitive systems, a person who is being dishonest or is holding back information will avoid eye contact around one-third of the time more than others (Marsh 1991). When there is prolonged eye contact between two people, the pupils tend to dilate if romantic interest is involved or else they will constrict if there is hostility. If the rapport with another person is amicable or neutral, the pupils remain normal. Mutual gazing produces similar ocular patterns and is typically constrained by cultural traditions (Binetti et al. 2016). Some southern Europeans, for

**Table 3.1** A few illustrative eye-contact patterns.

| Instinctive | Cultural |
| --- | --- |
| • Depending on situation, staring is interpreted as a challenge across various mammalian species (including humans).<br>• Like other species, humans perceive a direct stare as a threat or challenge and, like dogs and primates, will break eye contact as a signal of surrender. | • "Making eyes" (prolonged erotic-romantic eye contact) is interpreted as an acceptable flirtation signal in some cultures or social contexts, but disallowed in others.<br>• The length of time involved in eye contact conveys what kinds of relationships people have with each other in contextualized ways. This varies from culture to culture and, even within one culture, from situation to situation. |
| • Across human cultures, when the pupils contract during excited states, they convey certain common meanings and elicit specific response and interpretive mechanisms (usually unconscious), such as romantic interest or deceit. | • Making eye contact early or late during a verbal exchange indicates the kind of relationship one has, or wishes to have, with the interlocutor.<br>• The frequency, intensity, and duration of eye contact varies along cultural (and subjective) lines. |
| • Narrow eyelids imply pensiveness across cultures. | • People in some cultures tend to look more into each other's eyes during conversations than in others. |
| • Making the eyebrows come nearer together implies thoughtfulness across most cultures.<br>• When they are made to rise, they convey surprise. | • In some cultures, males are not expected to look into women's eyes, and vice versa, unless they are married to each other or else are members of the same family. |

example, are habituated to deploying frequent mutual gazing in all kinds of interactions, whereas in some Asian cultures, the tendency is to avoid it, pointing the eyes at the neck while conversing or else lowering them to indicate respect.

In a phrase, mutual gazing conveys a complex set of social connotations. Among early studies of this code are those of Paul Ekman (1982, 1999) and Robert Plutchik (1991), who initially identified aspects of eye contact that are universal, found across cultures, and thus likely based in biology. The examples in Table 3.2 appear to signal basic emotions.

As this shows, the eyes convey feelings and thoughts in anatomically structured ways. These unwittingly regulate conversations, establishing an unconscious connection with others, positive or negative.

In various disciplines, four theoretical approaches to eye contact patterns can be discerned: (1) the basic emotion approach; (2) the appraisal approach; (3) the constructivist approach; and (4) the eye-contact-effect approach. Approach (1) began with Darwin (1872), who maintained that mammals express inner mental-affective states in similar ways, through facial expressions and gazing patterns. In this framework, eye kinemes are seen as residues of humanity's evolutionary past, connecting humans with other animals. As people interact, it is believed that they will experience the same sensations, regardless of situation or culture, as manifested in isomorphic eye contact patterns across the world, with predictable variation. Adam Kendon (2010: 52) gives the example of the "eyebrow flash," as a case-in-point:

> Eibl-Eibesfeldt has undertaken an extensive program of filming social behavior in a number of widely separated cultures and has shown that there are certain facial gestures that may be observed worldwide, most notably a

**Table 3.2** Examples of eye kinemes in basic emotions.

| Emotion | Kineme |
| --- | --- |
| anger | glaring, staring |
| desire | dilation of the pupils, enlarging of gaze |
| disgust | turning away both eyes |
| fear | widening of the eyes, looking away or downward |
| happiness | eyes wide open, wrinkling at the sides |
| pity | soft form of gazing, eye moisture |
| sadness | looking downward, tearing |
| shame | looking downward, with head bent |
| surprise | eyes wide open |

certain gesture of greeting in which the eyebrows are rapidly raised and lowered—the so-called "eyebrow flash." This study is especially seminal in providing a model in terms of which a basic expressive action can be taken up and employed in diverse ways in different cultural settings and contexts.

Approach (2) can be traced first to American psychologist David Irons in 1894, elaborated much later by Magda Arnold in *Emotion and Personality* (1960). According to this approach, emotional eye configurations and contact patterns (such as those discerned in mutual gazing) result from a person's interpretation, or appraisal, of an event or situation—hence the different subjective interpretations of gazing patterns. In this framework, an event is seen as provoking a series of appraisals in the person's mind, resulting in an emotional experience that is unique to that person and situation. Thus, different appraisals produce different degrees of anger, sadness, fear, and other emotions. Approach (3) started with psychologist William James in 1884, who maintained that the emotions are meaningful reactions to events. It was expanded by Stanley Schachter and Jerome Singer (1962), who proposed that specific emotions are produced (or constructed) by two factors: (a) physical changes in the body; and (b) the reason someone gives for those changes. So, pleasant and unpleasant events can trigger an increase in heartbeat, but memories and experience help the brain determine which specific emotion is involved. Approach (4) is based in contemporary neuroscience, aiming to study what areas of the brain are involved in processing eye contact patterns and how these impact, in turn, the perception of the meanings of those patterns (Senju and Johnson 2009). Three main regions and ensuing effects have been documented within this research paradigm:

1 *Affective arousal*: specific brain arousal modules are activated by eye-contact situations, which then influence social interaction patterns.
2 *Communicative intention detector*: brain region which processes the intent and social significance of eye contact during interactions.
3 *First-track modulator*: neural pathways involved in face recognition that overlap with eye contact patterns, fusing the two into one modality (this is why we associate a certain facial expression with a specific gaze).

A major approach within linguistics and semiotics is one based on the bimodality principle (Chapter 1)—namely, the study of eye-contact patterns mapped against specific functions and forms of verbal communication. For example, emotivity levels during speech (Jakobson 1960), which involve states of mind (opinion, judgment, attitude, outlook, sentiments, etc.), and which can be identified via interjections, intonation, and other prosodic strategies, are reflected in an integrated fashion by simultaneous eye kinemic patterns. For example, the raised eyebrow typically accompanies a raised tone of voice; the downward eye movement co-occurs with a lowered tone of voice (Hietanen 2018). In phatic communicative acts, such as greeting rituals (Jakobson 1960), mutual eye contact may be direct, indirect, or completely avoided, according to cultural rules of greeting. When cultural codes are in conflict, as in immigrant situations, then misunderstanding might ensue. Uono and Hietanen (2015) studied how these emerge in the children of Korean immigrants who live in the United States. When scolding students, American teachers might require Korean children to look at them directly to keep their attentiveness, while at home making eye contact during parental reprimands would make the situation worse, since the children are supposed to look down as a sign of deference and respect. So, eye avoidance, rather than eye contact, is perceived as the relevant sign of respect with regard to teachers, which stands in contrast to teacher expectations. The same pattern of eye avoidance to show respect applies to the traditional cultures of East Asia and Nigeria (Galanti 2004: 34)—a pattern that might be interpreted contrastively as being shifty in some western cultures.

## 3.2 Gazing

Gazing is a form of looking that involves staring steadily and intently at someone or something, indicating admiration, curiosity. Kobayashi and Kohshima (2002) have posited that gazing among primates, including humans, was the event that produced the visual-perceptive functions of the eye—a theory they call the *cooperative eye hypothesis*, which suggests that the eye's visual-perceptive mechanisms evolved to make it easier for humans (and other primates) to understand the intent of another's gaze while collaborating on tasks. This hypothesis has been corroborated to some extent by research on childhood development. Tomasello et al. (2007) investigated the effects of changing gaze direction in human infants and great apes, finding that the apes were most likely to follow the gaze of the experimenter when the person's head moved somewhat, while infants followed the gaze more often in itself, paying no attention to head movement. The experiment suggested, in effect, that humans depend more instinctively on the gaze than other nonverbal cues when trying to interpret the actions and expressions of others, inferring cooperative or conflictual intentions from the gaze itself. Similar research has shown that children become aware of the functions and meanings of the gaze early on and infer intent from it to varying degrees according to situation (Samuels 1985; Hains and Muir 1996; Brooks and Meltzoff 2002; Farroni, Johnson, and Csibra 2004; Reid and Striano 2005).

Gazing patterns during courtship and romance situations across the world lend further credence to the cooperative eye hypothesis (Peck 1987; Simon 2005). The length of time involved in gazing, for example, conveys what kinds of romantic relationships people have, or wish to have, in contextualized ways; people in some cultures will tend to look more into each other's eyes during romance, while in others, the paramours tend to avoid eye contact entirely for reasons of deference and respect; in other cultures still, the partners are not expected to look into each other's eyes unless they are married. Accompanying the gaze during courtship rituals is head movement. It has been found, for example, that the "head tilt" position is assumed to convey interest in the partner, whereas the "head down" position signals a negative or judgmental attitude, across virtually every culture (Duncan and Fiske 1977).

The cooperative eye hypothesis might also explain why gazing is perceived as emotionally and socially powerful, depending on who the gazer and the gaze recipient are. Laura Mulvey (1975) coined the term the *male gaze* as a culturally based form of looking by males that traditionally meant "control" over women (emotionally and psychologically), in contrast to the *female gaze*, which has traditionally implied subservience. Now, while this pattern of gendered gazing has changed in many contemporary cultures since Mulvey put forth her analysis, it is still a mode of indicating gender roles to this day, albeit in altered fashion. Like Mulvey, French philosophers Michel Foucault (1975) and Jacques Derrida (Derrida and Wills 2002) saw the gaze as a social control mechanism—the gender or social class that was allowed to control the gaze was the one that had dominance or priority in a society. In such situations the cooperative eye hypothesis manifests itself as a control mechanism, whereby the gazer is perceived as being superior to the recipient of the gaze (Sturken and Cartwright 2009). Foucault (1963) coined the term "medical gaze" to illustrate what this meant, referring to the unequal power dynamics between medical practitioners and patients, indicating an unconscious intellectual authority assigned to doctors by society.

Mutual gazing during speech interactions involves the bimodality principle—that is, it accompanies speech in specific ways, as research in the area of discourse and conversation analysis has shown (Bavelas, Coates, and

Johnson 2002; Lance and Marsella 2007; Rossano 2012; Mondada 2018). Among the first to argue for the importance of researching mutual gazing patterns as co-speech features was Adam Kendon, who summarized its importance as follows (Kendon 2010: 53):

> Direction of gaze is an aspect of behavior that has also received a very great deal of attention although studies pertaining to it only began to appear in the mid 1960s. Where a person is looking provides an indication of where he/she is directing his/her attention, and for one person to look at another has always been recognized as an act of great significance. Simmel (1921) pointed out the special nature of the eye-to-eye look, for here each person simultaneously sees the other and sees that he/she is being seen by the other. Initial studies on gaze direction in interaction were conducted by Nielsen (1964), Exline (1972), Argyle and Dean (1965), and Kendon (1967) ... The possible role of gaze direction in the regulation of turn-taking or talk in conversation and other aspects of action in interaction have already been mentioned. Studies of gaze direction, however, have dealt with numerous other aspects, although the patterning of gaze directions and the whole issue of how gaze may be modified expressively have received far less attention, although these aspects have been widely noted.

The relevant studies have shown, generally, that co-speech gazing has regulating functions. One of these is turn-taking, signaling unconsciously that the speaker has finished talking, handing over the platform to continue the interaction to another speaker. Another pattern documented by the research is that speakers tend to gaze away at the beginning of turn-taking in conversations, looking toward the other interlocutors when they are approaching completion (Kendon 1967). Bavelas, Coates and Johnson (2002) also found that the gaze guided the responses that emerged between interlocutors—so, for example, the listener typically looks more at the speaker than vice versa, but at key points the speaker seeks a response by looking directly at the listener. Other co-speech gazing patterns are the following:

1 The *eye shuttle* involves shuttling the eyes back and forth, signaling unease, a desire to get out of a conversation, or imploring an interlocutor to speed up the delivery of the utterance.
2 The *sideways glance* can convey different messages depending on context: for example, turning the head away and furrowing the eyebrows as someone is speaking might communicate hostility or suspicion, or in other contexts interest in what the person is saying.

3   The *looking-up gaze* is generally perceived as a flirtation strategy in many contemporary cultures, whereby the eyelids are lowered and the eyebrows raised as interlocutors exchange messages (usually of a romantic type)

4   *Winking* might signal a variety of meanings during interactions, including a special kind of secret understanding between interlocutors or a sign of empathy, depending on context.

The meanings of the gaze are modified by the length of time that it is maintained, to whom or to where it is placed, the positions and actions of the other parts of the face, such as the head, the configuration of the eyebrows, and the size of the pupils. Whatever the evolutionary source of gazing, it is clear that it plays a host of roles in human life, constituting a common kinesic form of interaction between people involving an array of connotative meaning patterns.

## 3.3  Eye Metaphors

One way to assess the cultural significance assigned to the body or any of its parts is to deconstruct the metaphorical language that incorporates them into everyday speech. A useful technique for this purpose is so-called *conceptual metaphor theory*, which was elaborated by George Lakoff and Mark Johnson in their 1980 book, *Metaphors We Live By*, but which derives from previous work on figurative language (for example, Richards 1936; Black 1962; Pollio et al. 1977; Ortony 1979; Honeck and Hoffman 1980). The following utterances, for example, indicate that we perceive gazing and eye contact as a form of vicarious tactile contact and the eye as an object itself that can be easily manipulated (Lakoff 2012: 166):

1   I felt his *eyes on me.*
2   He *ran his eyes* over my whole face.
3   Please *take your eyes off* me.
4   My *glance* fell on that picture.
5   Our *eyes met*.

In conceptual metaphor theory, the above expressions are called *linguistic metaphors*, while the concept they reveal is called a *conceptual metaphor*. The linguistic metaphors above are, in other words, instantiations of an unconscious concept that can be formulated as follows: *eye (contact) is touching (manipulating)*. Utterance (1) implies that gazing is perceived as a tactile form of conversing (touching with the eyes in a figurative way); (2) implies that the eyes are perceived as substitutes for the hands, used for "touching" or "manipulating" the other person's face; (3) also connects gazing with touching, which is placed on someone and must be taken off, like a hand; (4) indicates that the eyes are physical objects that can fall onto something; and (5) implies that eye contact is, again, equivalent to physical tactile contact.

The last utterance likely derives from the common experience of gazing as a way to make social or physical contact with others. Now, when this concept becomes established culturally, it is extended connotatively in various ways, as can be seen in the following typical utterances, whose meanings mirror the actual communicative-semiotic functions of gazing:

1. When their eyes met, he knew it was time to get moving (*Function:* conveying relevant information about an event or situation).
2. After our eyes met, we started smiling (*Function:* flirtation, mutual interest or understanding of a situation).
3. Their eyes met, allowing them to complete the transaction (*Function:* mutual agreement).
4. Their eyes met one day, and they became romantic partners (*Function:* romance, courtship).
5. I was bored, until her eyes met mine (*Function:* conveyance of interest or flirtation)
6. Their eyes met, but they said nothing fearing the worst (*Function:* conveying that something is amiss).

Lakoff and Johnson trace the cognitive source of conceptual metaphors to what they call image schemas (Lakoff 1987; Johnson 1987; Lakoff and Johnson 1999). These are schematic mental images that convert concrete experiences into figurative structures for grasping abstractions. Whatever their neural substrate, they not only permit people to recognize patterns in the world, but also to anticipate new ones and to draw inferences from them. For example, the image schema of orientation—*looking up* vs. *down, back* vs. *forward*, etc.—renders the perception of the eyes as conveyors of emotional states as well as of perspective and outlook:

1. Life is starting to *look up*.
2. Do not *look down* on what I said.
3. It is time to stop *looking back* and start *looking forward*.
4. Stop *looking around*; it is time to do something concrete.
5. No matter which *way you look*, nothing will change.

In effect, these image schemas allow us to identify how we perceive the role of the eyes and vision in mental and cultural states. Philosopher Martin Heidegger (1962: 214) saw our linguistic abstractions as indexes of how "the world [is] encountered by us in perception." Lakoff and Johnson's theory may also explain why eye and seeing metaphors have been used throughout history as analogues of intelligence and wisdom. One of the first attestations of this is found in Book VII of Plato's *Republic* (1992: 514), where Socrates depicts human beings as being held in bondage in a cave, forced to watch the shadows cast on the wall before them by "a fire burning far above and behind them." The implication is that we cannot trust the truth behind what we see. As Maurice Merleau-Ponty (1993) put it, such allegories, metaphors, and analogies suggest that understanding and vision are intertwined in our evolution, and that metaphor is a semiotic reflex of evolutionary tendencies to grasp abstractions via sensory or practical experiences.

## 3.4 Eye Symbolism

The importance of the eyes in human life is corroborated not only by metaphorical language and allegorical traditions, but also by the fact that they have been part of symbolism and ritualistic practices since antiquity. In many ancient traditions, for example, the eye is the symbol of divine (all-seeing) knowledge. It is found commonly in versions of the so-called Eye of Providence, consisting of an eye inside a triangle from which rays of light emanate; it is an archetypal symbol found in various religious and philosophical traditions, representing the divine eye watching over humanity (Figure 3.2).

A use of the all-seeing eye symbol is on the Great Seal of the United States, and it appears on the American one-dollar bill in a pyramid (another archetypal symbol). The counterpart of the "divine eye" is the "evil eye," which is found across cultures as a symbolic curse designed to bring injury or misfortune to someone. Various spells, charms, amulets, and talismans have been created to ward off the evil eye, constituting part of many cultural traditions to this day. For instance, the use of horns, phallic shapes, and the devil's hand symbol in Italy likely emerged to distract the evil-eye spell casters, as symbols of evil themselves constituting a kind of "fight-fire-with-fire" strategy—that is, using the same kind of symbolic weapons or tactics of the casters against them.

The origins of evil eye symbolism are traced back to ancient Sumerian and Egyptian culture. In later Greek culture, it is referenced by many leading figures, from Hesiod and Plato to Plutarch (Walcot 1978). Plutarch traced

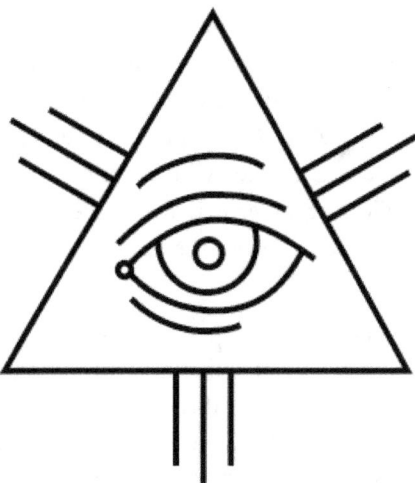

**Figure 3.2** The Eye of Providence (Wikimedia Commons).

the source of the evil eye to the power of the malignant stare, writing that the deadly rays that were supposed to emanate from this stare affected people negatively. In a similar vein, Pliny the Elder (1857, vol. VIII: 2) described enchanters as having the "power of fascination with the eyes and can even kill those on whom they fix their gaze." As anthropologist Alan Dundes (1992) found in his in-depth study of the evil eye, since ancient times it has been based on the notion that the eye has the power to shape events. It is seen, in other words, as a magical-telekinetic force, whereby the conveyor of the evil eye has the power to influence someone without physical interaction. It thus constitutes a form of sympathetic magic, or the belief that anyone can be affected by symbolic actions performed against them. Interestingly, a recent scientific study by Guterstam et al. (2020) looked at this type of belief, using fMRI scans of subjects to determine whether intense gazing has any effect on brain processes. The researchers found that the brain does in fact assign significance to the gaze of others, reacting to it as it would to dangerous situations of various kinds. This might suggest that the evil eye may be the result of emotion-detecting and emotion-producing systems hardwired into the brain, perhaps as cultural adaptations of some evolutionary function, such as the ability to perceive in another's gaze evil intent.

Interestingly, in some Aegean countries, people with light-colored eyes are thought to have particularly powerful gazes and thus regarded as naturally capable of casting the evil eye; so, amulets in areas of Greece and

Turkey are designed with blue orbs, likely connecting the rarity of such eye coloration in the region with the potential for evil—a concept that is archetypal in the Jungian sense (Jung 1956, 1959), appearing in myths, engravings, and paintings across time and across cultures.

Interestingly, Jung also used the evil eye concept as part of his therapy with patients. The following excerpt is from a letter he sent to Sigmund Freud in 1909 in which he describes the case of a particular patient (Jung 1973: 9–11):

> The case I told you about—evil eye, paranoiac impression—was cleared up as follows. She was abandoned by her last lover, who is altogether pathological; abandoned also by an earlier lover-this one even spent a year in an asylum. Now the infantile pattern: hardly knew her father and mother, loving instead her brother, 8 years older than she and at 22 a catatonic. Thus the psychological stereotype holds good ... I had the feeling that under it all there must be some quite special complex, a universal one having to do with the prospective tendencies in man. If there is a "psycho-analysis" there must also be a "psychosynthesis" which creates future events according to the same laws. The leap towards psychosynthesis proceeds via the person of my patient, whose unconscious is right now preparing, apparently with nothing to stop it, a new stereotype into which everything from outside, as it were, fits in conformity with the complex.

As this excerpt implies, Jung saw the perception of the evil eye as a psycho-synthetic teleological force, embedded in the unconscious mind, affecting states of mind, reflecting the symbolic history of the concept itself. Jung was also aware of the eye as an archetypal divine force illuminating aspects of reality. This dual symbolism of the eye is a common one, as Jung knew—as both a source of knowledge and wisdom and a source of evil. In some traditions, the symbolic power of the eyes is reflected in the great size used to depict them. An example is found in ancient Japanese clay figurines known as the *dogū*, from the Jōmon period (14,000–400 BCE) (Figure 3.3).

Archeologists are unsure as to what these figurines mean—some see them as effigies of people that are equivalent to the biblical scapegoats, whereby illnesses or curses could be transferred to the *dogū*, who is believed to destroy them (Insolla 2012). *Dogū* are typically female, with big eyes, small waists, large abdomens, and wide hips—hence the possibility that they represented mother goddesses. Big eyes also stand for beauty and knowledge—the opposite of beady eyes, which suggest deviousness. So, they might indeed be an antidote to the evil eye, implying that the *dogū* is a goddess who looks over humanity with her big eyes in order to protect people from evil or, at least metaphorically,

**Figure 3.3** Japanese *dogū* figurine (Wikimedia Commons).

**Figure 3.4** The Eye of Horus (Wikimedia Commons).

to impel them to open their own eyes wide to evil and embrace only goodness. This symbolism finds parallels in other mythic traditions, such as the ancient eyes of the Horus in Egyptian lore (Figure 3.4).

The Horus was a falcon-headed god, whose eyes had special meanings to the ancient Egyptians. The left eye represented femininity, the moon, and history, while the right eye symbolized masculinity, the sun, and the future. Together the two eyes represented the all-seeing power of Horus. In one version of the legend, Horus lost his left eye in a battle with the evil god Seth, who then cut the eye into six pieces, dispersing them into the River Nile.

Another god named Thoth recovered the eye and reconstructed it, turning it into a symbol of good winning against evil.

Eye symbols in myths and legends are manifestations of a common ancient belief that the eye has spiritual-teleological powers, able to change people's destiny (Haiman 2010). Another example comes from Hinduism, where the *Ajna chakra*, or "third eye," represents the eye as the source of inner spiritualism and a predictor of character. The symbol is traced to the myth of Shiva, one of the primary deities, who possessed a third eye, giving him the ability to see things that two eyes alone cannot. In humans, the *Ajna* is thought to be located in a region of the brain which can be exercised through meditation. Whereas our two eyes see the physical world, the third eye reveals insights about the future. It is the source of intuition and inner clairvoyance. It corresponds roughly with the notion of the *mind's eye* in other cultures.

Taoist and Zen traditions practice "third eye training," which involves getting someone to focus the mind on the point between the eyebrows with closed eyes, while the body is in various postures. The goal is to allow an individual to tap into the correct vibration of the cosmos and thus to understand reality through this meditative gesture. Interestingly, it has been found that reptiles and amphibians sense light via a third parietal eye, connected to the pineal gland, which regulates circadian rhythms. It has even been speculated, somewhat incredulously, that the inner eye might be capable of even seeing objects as small as quarks (Phillips 1980). According to another belief, humans are said to have actually had a third eye in the back of the head, which atrophied over time, sinking into the pineal gland. Whatever the truth, the gist of the foregoing discussion is that the eye is much more than a seeing organ; it is also perceived across time and cultural spaces as a thinking and divinatory organ, which comes out in specific forms of archetypal symbolism, traditions, and the like.

## 3.5 The Eye in Art

The *dogū* is an example of ancient symbolic art that portrays the eyes as signs with multiple levels of meaning, as a basis of understanding human character and destiny. Portraits based on the eyes and its connection to the smile, as art curator Angus Trumble (2004: 49) has written, bring out the "power of wordless communication."

Perhaps the painting that symbolizes the powerful messages that gazing and smiling entail, from intrigue, provocativeness, and mischievousness to romantic allure, is Leonardo da Vinci's masterwork, the *Mona Lisa* (*La gioconda* in Italian, meaning "the playful one")—said to have been the portrait of a woman named Lisa Gherardini (Figure 3.5).

Much has been read into the gaze of *la gioconda*. A computer analysis conducted at the University of Amsterdam in 2006, which mapped her expression to known facial expressions in psychology (Lin et al. 2006), found that she is 83 percent happy, 9 percent disgusted, 6 percent fearful, and 2 percent angry—a finding that brings out the inbuilt ambiguity of her gaze and her accompanying enigmatic smile. But artificial intelligence cannot explain the subtleties of meaning imprinted in the gaze, with its promise of sexual excitement or, in contrast, of anticipated rejection. The interpretation of *la gioconda*'s gaze as a signal of interest, romantic or otherwise, is likely embedded, again, in the evolutionary history of the eyes as a source of

**Figure 3.5** Leonardo da Vinci, *Mona Lisa (La gioconda)*, 1503–06 (Wikimedia Commons).

spiritual understanding, not just of vision. The gaze seems to trigger a primitive part of the human brain that processes both approach and retreat, since the eyes of another that are fixed on us cannot be ignored. They beckon us on to do something, persuading us to come forth or else to retreat apprehensively. Da Vinci seems to have captured these deeply-embedded meanings of the gaze to aesthetic perfection, leaving viewers only to figure out what *la gioconda's* gaze means to them in subjective terms.

*La gioconda's* small dark eyes appear soft and tender, gazing directly into the eyes of viewers, drawing them in. Upon close scrutiny, it can be seen that they are dilated, perhaps reflecting subtle flirtation, as she looks askance to her left (Zaremba Filipczak 1977). Research has shown that women with large pupils are perceived as attractive, a fact corroborated indirectly by the popularity of the cosmetic called *belladonna* ("beautiful woman" in Italian) in the 1920s and 1930s, which was a crystalline alkaloid eye-drop liquid that was claimed to make someone "more beautiful" (Sebeok 1990). This might explain why the playful-flirtatious gaze with large pupils has always been a subject in art. Da Vinci's masterwork is a powerful exemplar in a tradition of such "gaze portraits."

Another famous painting that represents the symbolic power of the gaze is John William Waterhouse's suggestive painting, *Hylas and the Nymphs* (1869) (Figure 3.6).

**Figure 3.6** John William Waterhouse, *Hylas and the Nymphs,* 1869 (Wikimedia Commons).

A possible interpretation is that the enticing gazes of the water nymphs, which are not as coy and flirtatious as those of *la gioconda*, are alluring nonetheless for the erotic awe (or is it fear?) that they seem to convey. The painting depicts the tragic legend of young Hylas of Greek and Roman mythology, who was abducted by the nymphs to fulfil their desires, while he sought water. The faraway and distracted gazes, with dilated eyes, suggest that the nymphs may be daydreaming or mesmerized by the power of love itself. Unlike *la gioconda*, they suggest the innocence of youthful infatuation and the lure of romance in itself.

Another painting that brings out the power of the gaze in youth, akin to da Vinci's portrayal, is Johannes Vermeer's *Girl with a Pearl Earring* (c. 1665) (Figure 3.7).

**Figure 3.7** Johannes Vermeer, *Girl with a Pearl Earring*, c. 1665 (Wikimedia Commons).

The young female in the portrait is thought to be Vermeer's maid. She is tilting her face, again to the left (as in da Vinci's *gioconda*), allowing her to project her gaze askance, suggesting distrust and even fear in the flirtatious pose, drawing attention to her assumed innocence. Like *la gioconda,* her gaze is ambiguous, making it emotionally powerful; combined with her slightly parted lips in an equally ambiguous combination suggesting flirtation, shyness, and fearfulness, at once, her gaze seems to indicate that something unusual has caught her eye, even though it is not possible to determine if it is something to which she is attracted or which she fears. The gaze is thus a question mark: Who or what is she looking at? This emphasizes that she is hardly just using her gaze to look, but rather to question reality. As existentialist philosopher Jean-Paul Sartre (1943) argued, the mere presence of another human in the line of sight causes one to look at oneself and thus to see the world as it appears to the other person. In effect, by gazing at others we come to realize that we are alive through the act itself.

The first theory of art of any scope was that of Plato (1992), who believed that it was an imitation of forms in reality. He also felt that art encouraged immorality, and that certain artworks caused laziness and immoderacy. He thus suggested banishing some types of artists from society. Paintings such as those above would have been condemned by Plato as immoral since they were evocative of chaotic urges within the human soul. Aristotle (1952) also saw art as imitation, but not in the same way that his teacher Plato did. The role of art, thought Aristotle, was to complete what nature did not finish, separating the form from its content, such as the form of the human body from its manifestations in people, and then transferring it onto some physical medium, such as marble. In an Aristotelian framework, the portraits of gazing such as those above would likely have been seen as imitative of the functions of the eye in understanding abstract principles of life. They complete nature in human terms: "And that time is a good discoverer or partner in such a work; to which facts the advances of the arts are due; for any one can add what is lacking" (Aristotle 1952 Book I: 23).

Artists in the Middle Ages were considered to be primarily servants of the Church, as is evidenced in no small part by the absence of portraits based on the human gaze, focusing instead on spiritual eye symbolism as can be seen in portraits of religious figures. It was during the Renaissance that art became focused on human qualities of the eyes, of which da Vinci's work is only one example. The Renaissance, moreover, saw little difference between the artist and the scientist. Indeed, many were both—da Vinci was a painter, writer, and scientist, Michelangelo a visual artist and writer, to mention but two well known figures. It was only after the Enlightenment and the Romantic period that an artificial split came about, separating art from science, a separation that persists to this day. The view of artists as unique geniuses impelled by inner creative energies to free themselves from the shackles of society is very much a product of Romanticism. In ancient times artists were workers paid by rulers for their services. Ancient Egyptian architects, for instance, were hired to build structures designed to glorify the pharaoh and his life after death. In medieval Europe, visual artists were hired by the Church to create art works designed to extol Christian themes, especially in churches. The choice to be an artist was a matter of social custom, not of some esoteric inclination at birth. Artists, like other people, customarily followed their fathers' profession. It was only after the eighteenth century that the choice to become an artist became an individualistic-subjective one.

It is noteworthy that in all periods the eyes, whether human or divine, have always been central to the art of portraiture. The examples above only scratch the surface of the ancientness and power of such art. Through such representations, we come to see vision as telling us something about the human condition. The American philosopher Susanne Langer (1948, 1957) claimed that we do not experience art as we do something spoken or written, but as a holistic emotional experience. It is only when we try to understand rationally why an artwork had such an effect on us that the aesthetic experience is transformed by reasoning into one in which its parts can be taken apart, discussed, critiqued, etc. But, no matter how many times people try to understand the experience logically, it somehow escapes understanding, remaining larger than the sum of its parts. One can analyze the gazes in the paintings above in terms of their outlines and their suggestive nuances, but in the end, we can never totally grasp what they truly tell us about ourselves.

Viewing *la gioconda* or Vermeer's maid involves making eye contact with each one. The women in the paintings do not blink; they hold a constant gaze that is difficult to resist, impelling us to stare back. It is we, the viewers, who will have to break the connection, as in any communicative interaction. But this is not always the case. In pop artist Roy Lichtenstein's *Crying Girl* (1963), we see a comic-book drawing of a young lady in tears—an image of sadness that is reinforced by her fearful look, which bespeaks of inner turmoil. Like Vermeer's maid, the subject is gazing at something which is making her upset, but unlike the maid or *la gioconda*, she is not looking at us, the viewer, making us wonder what is making her so distressed. Without the implied mutual gaze, we tend to see the sadness from a different perspective.

So, what happens when the eyes are distorted in some way? Take, as an example, the *Weeping Woman* (1937) by Pablo Picasso, a portrait of Picasso's lover, Dora Maar. Like the Lichtenstein drawing, there is the image of a woman crying, exuding pain and suffering through the distorted parts of facial anatomy put together via assemblages of the parts as triangular shapes. The distress on the woman's face is represented in fractured images, suggesting physical illness, expressed as well through the pain apparent in the eyes, which are noticeably distorted, small and dark, and wide open as if in shock and disbelief. One eyeball is jutting out trying to eject itself from the face, perhaps as a way to stop the crying and the pain.

In some paintings, the eyes are shut, implying a sense of rapture. An example is the famous 1908 painting by Austrian nouveau style artist Gustav Klimt, a painting that brings out the delicate romantic and passionate qualities of a kiss—implied by the woman's shut eyes (Figure 3.8).

**Figure 3.8** Gustav Klimt, *The Kiss*, 1908 (Wikimedia Commons).

The lovers are kissing on the edge of a flowery precipice, their bodies pressed together in a tender embrace. The man presses his lips against his lover's cheek, not her lips, which emphasizes the tenderness of the act, rather than its sexuality. Her head is tilted again to the left (as in the other paintings discussed above). He wears an all-enveloping gown made of black and white rectangles and squares, which forms a sharp contrast to the woman's gown full of colors and concentric circles. We can only see the back of his head while her face is visible, with her eyes closed, without eye contact, which would likely break the spell of the kiss. The two seem to be in a cocoon, with the kiss insulating them from the vagaries and tribulations of everyday life.

The third-century philosopher Plotinus claimed that art revealed how we see reality internally, rather than externally with physical eyes. This implies that art is our mythical "third eye." English artist and writer, John Berger (1972) has even suggested that this eye cannot be suppressed even in textual writing. To illustrate this, Berger wrote his book, *Ways of Seeing*, in a hybrid script—in some chapters he used a combination of words and images, and in others only images. Rudolph Arnheim's book, *Visual Thinking* (1969), also showed how art works reveal a propensity to see the world through the eyes of the artist, rather than through our own eyes, allowing us to have a perspective of the world that we might not have had otherwise. Extending Berger's and Arnheim's approaches, it can be argued that artworks such as those discussed here have brought to awareness our intuitive sense of what looking and gazing mean to us.

As a final example of the artistic treatment of the gaze as a means to ask existential questions about reality, consider the well-known painting by William Blake, *Kiss of Adam and Eve*, which he drew as an illustration to John Milton's book, *Paradise Lost* (1808). In it, we see Adam gazing directly into Eve's eyes in a state of terror or fright, implying a rhetorical question: What is this all about? Eve looks back in a state of wonderment, perhaps trying to grasp the implications of the same question. The hands that touch both personages are unidentified—they could be divine or satanic. The ambiguity and uncertainty of the scene are powerful—gazing into each other's eyes is a fundamental means for understanding the world, or at least for asking "silent" philosophical questions about it (Figure 3.9).

Throughout history, art has allowed us to see reality through a third eye—the eye of the artist. It is a form of silent communication that paradoxically seems to tell us as much about the human condition, if not more so, than words.

**Figure 3.9** William Blake, *Kiss of Adam and Eve*, 1808 (Wikimedia Commons).

## 3.6 Epilogue

Vision is a key survival function for various animals. Birds, for instance, cannot locate food if they cannot see it. In contrast, hearing is vital to bats. If a bat's ears are covered, it will crash into objects when it tries to fly. A keen sense of smell enables dogs and wolves to find food, follow trails, and recognize danger, although they also rely on vision to assist them. The eyes have similar vision functions in humans. As children grow, however, they learn that the they have other functions, beyond survival.

The archetypal symbolism of the third eye reveals an embedded perception that "seeing" the world involves more than vision, as does the conversion of visual phenomena into image schemas. Consider the image schema of an *obstacle*. An obstacle is something, such as a wall, a boulder, or another person that blocks our forward movement. Familiarity with seeing obstacles in everyday life produces the image schema of an inner eye designed to see abstract obstacles in the mind and then react to them as if they were concrete. This comes out in metaphorical phraseology such as going *around* some abstract obstacle, *over* it, *under* it, *through* it, and so on. On the other hand, the obstacle could successfully impede us, so that we would have to *stop* and *turn back*. All of these actions relate to the physical eye seeing the outside world, but are transferred to the inner eye imagining the inner world: "We *got through* that difficult time;" "Jim felt better after he *got over* his cold;" "You want to *steer clear of* financial debt;" "With the bulk of the work *out of the way*, he was able to call it a day;" "The rain *stopped* us from enjoying our picnic;" "You cannot *go* any *further* with that idea; you'll just have to *turn back*;" and so on and so forth. The "mind's eye" is, clearly, as crucial to human life as are the physical eyes. As Ralph Waldo Emerson (1903: 194) aptly put it: "Truth is always present; it only needs to lift the iron lids of the mind's eye to read its oracles."

# 4

# The Face

## Chapter Outline

| | |
|---|---|
| 4.0 Prologue | 75 |
| 4.1 Facial Expression | 76 |
| 4.2 The Head and Hair | 82 |
| 4.3 Facial Figurative Language | 85 |
| 4.4 Face Recognition | 86 |
| 4.5 The Face as *Persona* | 89 |
| 4.6 Epilogue | 92 |

## 4.0 Prologue

In 1963, Paul Ekman established the Human Interaction Laboratory in the Department of Psychiatry at the University of California at San Francisco for the purpose of researching and studying facial expressions cross-culturally—it was one of the first such labs designed to study NVC systematically. He was joined by Wallace V. Friesen in 1965 and Maureen O'Sullivan in 1974. Over the years, Ekman and his team have extensively researched, documented, and analyzed facial expressions, mapping them against other modes of NVC, showing overall that, like other nonverbal systems, they are partly instinctive, partly learned, and partly a mix of the two. The central method of analysis used by Ekman was to break down the different expressions into their characteristic components—eyebrow position, eye shape, mouth shape, nostril size, etc.—recalling the kinesic approach of Ray Birdwhistell (Chapter 2). In so doing, Ekman has shown that it is possible to write a "grammar" of the face that shows less cross-cultural variation than language grammars (Ekman 1976, 1980; Ekman and Friesen 1975).

This chapter will deal with several aspects of the face as a source of NVC: (a) as a co-speech system; (b) as a stand-alone communicative system; (c) as a code for assessing character; (d) as a source of symbolism; and (e) as the main feature in portraiture. Also discussed briefly is the advent of face recognition technologies and what they potentially tell us about facial expression itself. As in previous chapters, the discussion is a selective one, so as to keep the chapter within the limits of a textbook ..

Although there is some controversy about the origins of facial expressions in human communication, there is broad consensus that they serve many of the same functions of other nonverbal systems (Fridlund 1994; Russell and Fernandez-Dols 1997). In the evolution of mammals, the face reveals emotional states by its different configurations. This is true as well in humans, but in their case the face has also been perceived as a kind of "mask" that people wear for various social and psychological purposes. As anthropologist Helen Fisher (1992) has argued, this is the reason why facial decorations and alterations to the face go back to antiquity and even prehistory, indicating that the face has always been perceived as a sign of character, in addition to a conveyor of emotional states.

## 4.1 Facial Expression

As mentioned, Darwin (1872) claimed that human facial expressions in different cultures, infants, and other animal species, reveal common (instinctive) patterns. For example, he noted that when "a dog is on the point of springing on his antagonist, he utters a savage growl; the ears are pressed closely backwards, and the upper lip is retracted out of the way of his teeth, especially of his canines" (Darwin 1872: 115). He pointed out the same kind of expression pattern in humans, albeit with structural modifications. Darwin also noted that children's understanding of certain facial expressions, and their reactions to them, were instinctive and similar to those of other animals (Russell 1994). The more infants are exposed to different faces and expressions, the more they seem capable of recognizing emotions and imitating them. Paul Ekman has largely validated Darwin's observations, but he has gone far beyond them, separating the facial expressions that are connected to the basic emotions from other kinds that are instead culturally coded (Ekman 2006).

In effect, as Ekman has documented, facial expressions in humans constitute a hybrid system of signals and signs—some are unwitting (instinctive), resulting from reactions to emotional stimuli, some constructed for specific reasons, and others the result of a blending of the two. An example of the latter can be seen during deception (Glass 2013), which involves instinctive and learned behavior in tandem. Studies have shown that pupil dilation occurs frequently during lying, and is thus a reaction based in biology (Meyer 2010; Heussen, Binkofski, and Jolij 2011). However, the liar may also use intentional looking strategies that deflect attention from the deceptive intent, such as looking away or else employing reassuring signals such as smiling or looking into someone's eyes. This means that, by and large, lying generates instinctive reactions in the face and eyes, but the liar will also know how to modify these and use deflection strategies to conceal the deception. Those who are skilled at artifice can suppress facial expressions effectively. Nonetheless, it is nearly impossible to trick one's brain into camouflaging all the facial reactions that might give away one's true thoughts.

Darwin was influenced by the 1862 book by French neurologist Guillaume Duchenne, *Mécanisme de la physionomie humaine*, as can be discerned in the correspondence between Darwin and Duchenne. In that book, Duchenne included photographs of faces that he described in terms of muscles that were activated by electrical stimulation, producing different facial expressions—Darwin would later republish some of these, comparing them to the facial expressions of some animals (Figure 4.1).

Duchenne and Darwin thus laid the groundwork for a scientific study of facial expressions in the subsequent century, connecting specific facial expressions to specific muscle movements and facial configurations and features, which they saw as conveying specific emotions—for instance, smiling is a sign of happiness, tearing of sadness, jaw clenching of anger, grimacing of fear, eye-brow raising of surprise, nose wrinkling of disgust, and so on. These are universal because they occur independently of culture or rearing; on the other hand, emotions such as shame, pride, jealousy, envy, etc. will vary according to culture. Called the "universality hypothesis," it was the first theory of the role of facial expressions in human communication—a theory that has had both support (Izard 1971; Ekman, Friesen, and Ellsworth 1972) and criticism (Jack et al. 2012; Nelson and Russell 2013). The counter-hypothesis—namely that facial expressions vary according to culture, because the emotions themselves have differential social functions—was put forth in a detailed way by anthropologist Margaret Mead (1964), who studied the connection between facial expressions and emotional states

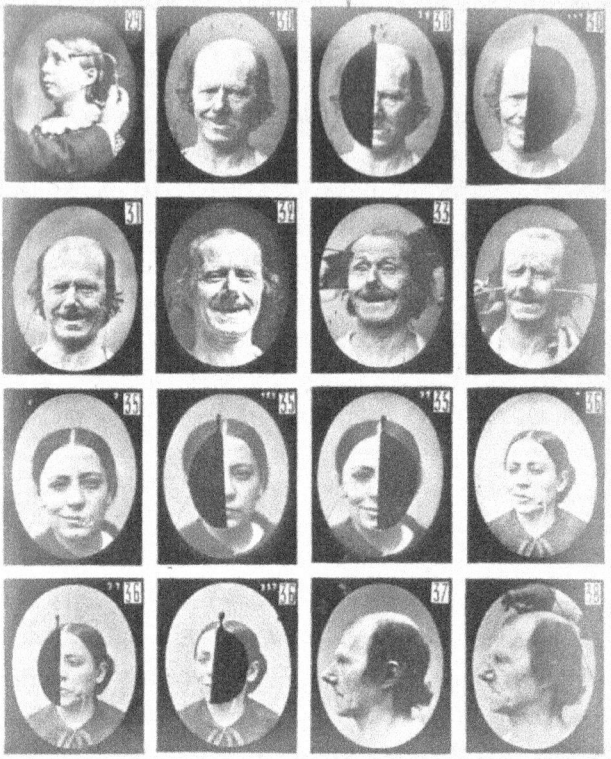

**Figure 4.1** Facial Expressions, from Guillaume Duchenne 1862: 277 (Wikimedia Commons).

in isolated communities, coming to the conclusion that they are largely culture-specific—a conclusion supported two decades later by the work of psychologist Gordon H. Bower (1980), who also concluded that facial expressions as shaped largely by contextual factors.

Darwin's universality hypothesis received empirical support by psychologist Silvan Tomkins, who conducted studies demonstrating that specific facial expressions were invariably associated with emotional states (Tomkins 1962; Tomkins and McCarter 1964; Tomkins and Izard 1965). Tomkins recruited Paul Ekman to conduct research on this hypothesis, becoming himself a major researcher in the field, documenting and analyzing differences between universal and culture-specific facial expressions. Ekman went to Papua New Guinea where the South Fore people, a pre-industrial culture, had little contact with westerners at the time. This allowed him to assay whether or not there was any demonstrable validity to the universality hypothesis (Ekman and Friesen 1971).

To collect relevant data, Ekman told brief stories about emotional situations involving the basic emotions of anger, happiness, disgust, sadness, surprise, and fear, and then asked the Fore people to match each emotion to a photographed facial expression from a set of three. The matches were 60 to 90 percent consistent with western interpretations of the same facial expressions, except for the one associated with fear, which the Fore people had difficulty distinguishing from the facial expression of surprise. Overall, however, Ekman concluded that his results strongly suggested that there is a set of facial expressions which convey the same emotional information universally, given that the Fore people had no previous contact with images of these expressions found in western culture.

Variability in facial expression does occur, but it does so in the domain of non-basic emotions. These are learned through imitation (or osmosis) in childhood, the period when facial recognition also plays a central role in shaping how expressive patterns develop. A study by Allen, Peterson, and Rhodes (2006) found that such recognition may be an evolutionary residue, related to "parent-infant attraction, a quick and low-effort means by which parents and infants form an internal representation of each other, reducing the likelihood that the parent will abandon his or her offspring because of recognition failure" (Allen, Peterson, and Rhodes 2006: 311) Interestingly, this pattern has been found located in the same area of the brain that evaluates attractiveness. As Chatterjee et al. (2009: 135) note: "Facial beauty evokes a widely distributed neural network involving perceptual, decision-making and reward circuits, even when subjects were not attending explicitly to facial beauty."

Ekman's work laid the foundations for a broad scientific approach to the study of facial expression as both an instinctive and cultural phenomenon. Ekman broke facial expressions into micro-units which, when combined, determine their meaning or function. Consider the sketches in Figure 4.2 representing four basic emotions in outline form.

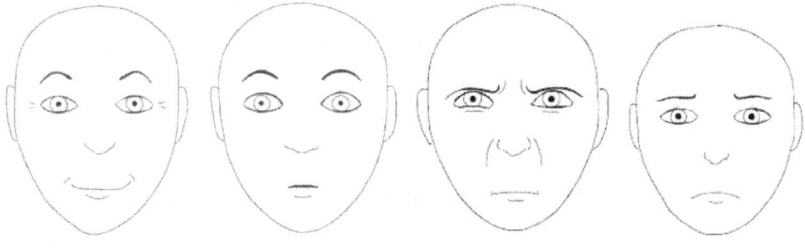

1. *Amusement*  2. *Surprise*  3. *Anger*  4. *Sadness*

**Figure 4.2** Sketches of four facial expressions (Wikimedia Commons).

We perceive each face as expressing specific emotions—amusement or surprise, anger, and sadness—because of the orientation and shape of the eyes, the eyebrows, the mouth, and wrinkles:

1 *Amusement*: the eyebrows are raised and slightly arched; the eyelids are also raised; and the mouth assumes the form of a smile;
2 *Surprise*: this includes lifting the eyebrows; opening the eyes; raising the eyelids; and keeping the mouth even;
3 *Anger*: for this emotion the eyebrows are furled and drawn together; the eyes assume a glaring form; and the lips are narrowed;
4 *Sadness*: for this emotion, the inner corners of the eyebrows are raised; the eyelids loosened; and the lip corners are pulled down.

It is the combination of the micro-units (raised eyebrows, narrow lips, etc.) that produces the relevant facial expression, akin to the syntactic combination of words in sentences (Peck 1987). Ekman (2003) has called them *microexpressions*, organizing them into a classification system that he has termed the *Facial Action Coding System* (FACS) (Ekman and Friesen 1978), adapted from the work of Swedish anatomist Carl-Herman Hjortsjö (1970). The features of microexpressions are called *action units* (AU). Today, researchers use computers to automatically identify the AUs and to simulate facial expressions. Interestingly, AUs similar to human ones have been documented in several non-human primates (Vick et al. 2007).

Overall, research on the basic emotions (disgust, fear, anger, contempt, sadness, surprise, happiness) has largely confirmed that they activate similar microexpressions across the world. These were researched extensively by Haggard and Isaacs in 1966, who called them "micro-momentary" expressions—the term *microexpression* was coined a few years later (Ekman and Friesen 1969). Haggard and Isaacs used films of psychotherapy sessions to identify repeating facial expressions between therapists and patients, which corresponded to those documented by Ekman and his team of researchers in different cultural settings (Ekman and Friesen 1971; Ekman 1989; Matsumoto 1992). In 1991, Ekman expanded the list of universal microexpressions to include the AUs connected with embarrassment, anxiety, guilt, pride, relief, contentment, pleasure, shame, and a few others, some of which crossed cultural lines, including chewing on the bottom lip as a reaction to worry, fear, or insecurity, covering the mouth as a sign of politeness, tightening the lips to indicate distaste or disapproval, and closing the mouth to hide an emotional response (Fernández-Dols and Russell 2017).

A particularly interesting expression is the smile, which may be an instinctive reaction to a feeling of happiness, but also constructed intentionally to express irony, false happiness, sarcasm, or cynicism. The particular AUs that might indicate each emotive state need not concern us here. Suffice it to say that the smile is an example of how human facial expressions are based in both biology and culture, forming a hybrid sign system, which produces overlapping and divergent interpretations across cultures, according to how the muscles at the sides of the mouth are flexed and what type of gaze is involved during the smile. Some of the functions of smiling that have been found to be similar across societies are the following (Messinger, Fogel, and Dickson 2001; Gladstone 2002; Haakana 2010; Tracy and Beall 2011):

1. a pre-laughter expression;
2. a response to humor or to someone else's laughter;
3. a sign of romantic interest, enhancing appeal;
4. a reinforcement of what someone is saying, showing consent or approval;
5. a deceptive sign employed for manipulative purposes—known as a *superficial smile*;
6. a forced or posed smile, known as a *Pan Am smile* (after Pan American World Airways which required its flight attendants to produce a perfunctory smile to all passengers.

Murphy, Lehrfeld, and Isaacowitz (2010) designed an interesting experiment to examine the forced smile. They asked a group of subjects, young and elderly, to judge individuals using forced and genuine smiles, finding that all subjects could equally tell the difference, even though the older group was slightly better at distinguishing between the two types. Actually, the distinction, between spontaneous and posed, can be extended to all kinds of facial expressions. The latter serve social functions such as the following:

1. *Simulation*: any facial expression can be simulated or mimicked for some purpose, ranging from deception to ironic humor.
2. *Neutralization*: any facial expression can be suppressed to show a neutral stance on something, decreasing the emotivity of the situation.
3. *Masking*: any emotion can be masked by a posed facial expression.
4. *Construction*: A facial expression can be constructed on purpose, rather than occurring spontaneously, to indicate some reaction to a situation.

Pathological liars have a greater ability to control posing strategies. However, anyone can intentionally construct a facial expression to convey the impression that they feel, even when this is not true. This implies an ability to shape the face according to situation, constituting a social mask. An interesting relevant study by Matsumoto and Willingham (2009) utilized thousands of photographs taken at the 2004 Olympic and Paralympic Games so as to compare the facial expressions of sighted and congenitally non-sighted judo athletes who posed for media or publicity photographs. The researchers discovered that both types of competitors displayed similar posed expressions, during victories and losses, suggesting that the posing of the face to fit the social setting is not learned, but is likely an inherent trait.

To summarize the foregoing discussion, facial expressions can be divided broadly into spontaneous and constructed. The interpretation of the former is consistent across cultures, as the review of relevant studies by Matsumoto (2001) has shown, with some variation. The latter are simulated for social purposes, showing an ability to construct the face as if it were a mask—a theme to be discussed below. So, while the primary emotions are imprinted in common facial expressions across the world, human ingenuity can modify them artfully and artificially to make messages on purpose.

## 4.2 The Head and Hair

AUs that involve the head contribute to the meanings of facial expressions. These too can be involuntary or voluntary, natural or conventional. As in other domains of NVC, there are also mixed-sign head movements. For instance, as discussed, an up-down head nod is typically a positive gesture indicating agreement, but in some cultures the opposite is true, as Morris et al. (1979) discovered in some Slavic cultures, where nodding means disapproval, while shaking the head from left to right means approval. In some Asian cultures nodding connotes respect, as it does in various other non-western cultures.

Common cross-cultural head gestures are the following (Burgoon, Guerrero, and Floyd 2016):

1. The "heads up" pose (with the head remaining taut) conveys a neutral attitude about what is being said.
2. The "head raising" movement might indicate interest, especially if accompanied by other microexpressions such as raised eyebrows; on the other hand, in certain situations, it may also signal boredom or disinterest.

3 The "head tilt" position is assumed by someone who is likely interested in what is being said or in who is speaking. It can also be a flirting signal or an indication of curiosity, depending on context. A tilted head pulled back might indicate suspicion or even submission.
4 The "head lowering" movement might signal a negative or judgmental attitude; it can also be a defensive pose in reaction to perceived threat; lowering the head also lowers the eyes and hence can be a sign of submission.
5 The "hands behind the head" pose conveys confidence and authority.

By and large, however, head movements are regulated by cultural rules. Alternately tilting the head to each side can imply uncertainty in western culture, but in Southern India it means affirmation. It might constitute a strategy to avoid direct eye contact, especially if it is socially disconcerting. Tapping the head with a finger can be a sign of regret or of foolishness in some cultures. In others, the head is considered a spiritual part of the person and, thus, tapping it might be considered sacrilegious.

The hair on the head is a semiotic code that communicates various presented meanings. Since prehistoric times, people have cut, braided, and dyed their hair and changed it in various ways as part of grooming and fashion (McCracken 1995). Hairstyle is a social code that is used to communicate personality, social status, ideology, etc. The oldest known images of hairstyling date back around 30,000 years. Some are imbued with symbolism. For example, the tight curls on the Buddha are connected to the Buddha narrative—the curls indicate that he had cut his long locks, leaving his former life behind, but retaining the curls on his head (Figure 4.3).

In Egypt, men and women alike often shaved their heads to combat the heat. As a result, baldness became a fashion style in its own right. A shaved head in other cultures can instead indicate sacrifice and submission of a spiritual nature—Buddhist monks shave their heads for this reason. In the late Middle Ages, married women had to cover their heads in public for modesty, and only husbands were allowed to see their wives' hair. In the Renaissance and for several centuries afterward, most noblemen had long, flowing curls—a hairstyle that became a symbol despised by the bourgeoisie and the lower classes. The chief opponents of King Charles I during the civil war in England were the Puritans, called Roundheads because they cut their hair short, frowning upon the long hairstyles and cosmetic fashions of the aristocracy, which they saw as signs of a degenerate lifestyle.

In the 1920s, hairstyle fashions became a form of rebellion against staid puritanical lifestyles and a declaration of moralistic independence. Young

**Figure 4.3** The Buddha (Wikimedia Commons).

women wore short hair as part of the so-called Flapper look; young men slicked down their hair with oil in the manner of movie stars. During the 1950s, some teenagers wore a crew cut, a very short hairstyle combed upward to resemble a brush. Others wore their hair long on the sides, and swept back, so that it looked like a duck's tail. During the 1960s young males wore long hair that covered the forehead as did the females, creating a so-called unisex style. The subsequent decades have seen hairstyles vary constantly according to group, ideology, or dominant fashion trends.

Facial hair has also borne culture-specific meanings throughout history. Some religions consider a full beard to be essential for all men, constituting a principle of dogma. Various cultures may view a beard as a sign of virility, others as indicative of wisdom or high social status. In ancient China, facial hair and the hair on the head were traditionally left uncut and untouched because of Confucianism.

In sum, hairstyle and facial hair constitute specific kinds of nonverbal codes. Along with the face, we tend to interpret personality and character in part through the type of hairstyle someone wears. If someone we knew well were to change hairstyle, our tendency would be to assess it as a change in self-image or even in personality, not just a change in style.

## 4.3 Facial Figurative Language

Like other nonverbal modes of communication, the face, as mentioned, is much more than a channel for expression; it is also a sign system. A way to access its meanings is to examine the type of figurative language that incorporates the face and the head into discourse (Chapter 3). For example, metonymic expressions provide useful cultural information on the meanings of the face, as a sign of character and of other referents:

1. *They argued face to face*: this indicates that the face is perceived to be of primary importance in discourse.
2. *Don't show your face around here anymore*: this implies that the face is equated with the actual person.
3. *She criticized the boss to her face*: this is another allusion to the face as representing the person.
4. *We must always put on a happy face*: this implies that the face is a social mask, constructed by posing the face in some intentional way.
5. *I always wear my feelings on my face*: this indicates that the face is a conveyor of emotions and that feelings are the "metaphorical clothes" that identify the emotions.
6. *He's just another pretty face*: this implies that we judge appearance and personality in terms of a person's face.

The underlying concept in these expressions is: *the face is the person*—a concept that is incorporated not only in figurative language, but also in portraiture art, which is a visual representation of a subject whose facial appearance, as depicted by the artist, is a sign of the Self—an image that we interpret as revealing the subject's character (as will be discussed below). It is relevant to note that an anonymous or unknown person is occasionally referred to as *faceless*.

The *head* is also a source for figurative language:

1. She is the *head* of the class = the leader (intellectually, socially).
2. There are a lot of good *heads* in this place = intelligent people.
3. My friend is *big-headed* = supercilious, conceited.

4  He always bites my *head* off = criticizes strongly.
5  She is *head* and shoulders above everyone else = better.
6  I keep banging my *head* against a brick wall = unsuccessful.
7  My brother also has his *head* in the clouds = distracted, absent-minded.

Other parts of the face, such as the lips and the mouth, are also imprinted in common discourse as figurative images:

1  You always pay *lip* service to some unusual cause = approval or support, indicating that the approval comes through the lips during speech.
2  He always keeps a stiff upper *lip* = containing one's emotion, based on the physical experience that the taut lips impede potentially conflictual speech.
3  My *lips* are sealed = promise not to reveal a secret, based on the physical fact that sealing the lips impedes the possibility of speaking.
4  After eating I had to smack my *lips* = pleasure, based on the AU of lip-smacking upon eating pleasurable food.
5  Keep your *mouth* shut = the mouth is the part of the face through which oral speech is emitted—therefore, shutting it means blocking speech, literally and metaphorically.
6  You took the words out of my *mouth* = anticipated agreement based on the fact that the mouth is required for vocal expression.

The number of expressions that involve the face, its parts, and the physiology of speech is a vast one. These indicate, overall, that the face is perceived as the expressive conveyor of the mind's various states. William Shakespeare said it best as follows: "There's no art to find the mind's construction in the face" (*Macbeth,* Act I, scene 4, line 11).

## 4.4  Face Recognition

In the nineteenth century, French neurologist Jean Martin Charcot (1886) discovered a type of "face blindness" in a patient who had difficulty recognizing a close friend by his face—a syndrome called *prosopagnosia*. One of the most widely known cases of this syndrome is reported by neurologist Oliver Sacks in his popular book, *The Man Who Mistook His Wife for a Hat* (1985). Sacks' patient was able to recognize his wife if she wore a hat or some other item which was familiar to him as associated with her, but he could not recognize her by facial information alone. The neurological reason for this selective blindness is traced to a cluster of cortical cells vital for facial recognition, which do not function when impaired or damaged in some way.

Neuroscience has identified specific regions of the brain where face perception and recognition are located, including an area within the fusiform gyrus (Gauthier et al. 1999, 2000). The amygdala has also been shown to play an important role in facial recognition—an area that processes emotions and hence the neural connection between facial expressions and emotivity (Rinn 1984; Adolphs 2010). There is also evidence of the existence of two separate neural systems for face recognition: one for familiar faces and another for new faces, linking face recognition with episodic memory (Leube et al. 2003). It was Endel Tulving (1972) who first divided memory into episodic and semantic systems. The former specifies and stores events as "episodes." It is useful for getting on with the practical matters of life—recognizing faces, friends, family members, telephone numbers, etc. The semantic memory system, on the other hand, is involved in providing concepts in the form of language and other symbol systems to serve recall of events and people.

It has also been found that gazing and facial expression influence how we interpret interactions and even how we remember unfamiliar faces (Li and Jain 2011). A relevant experiment by Nakashima, Langton, and Yoshikawa (2012) showed how gaze direction and facial expression cooperated in facial recollection. The researchers showed subjects a set of unfamiliar faces with either happy or angry faces and which were either gazing straight ahead or sideways. They found that memory for faces with angry expressions was poorer when accompanied by a sideways gaze, whereas recognition of happy faces was unaffected by gaze direction.

The recognition of facial features emerges early in life, as children learn that facial features and expressions carry psychological and social information. Neonates show an instinctive ability of mimicking the facial expressions of others, displaying a remarkable knowledge of the role of eye and mouth shape in the production of facial expressions, using them effectively, even though they may not be aware of the emotional content in the expressions. Around the age of seven to eight months, the child recognizes a facial expression as indicating fear, anger, or happiness. After that, the ability to interpret the face and its meaning states grows considerably, matching developments in language and other faculties.

Another general finding of neuroscientific research is that the anatomical structure of the face is processed as unique by the brain and thus can be compared to a fingerprint. The bones involved in shaping the face are the maxilla, mandible, nasal bone, and zygomatic bone. Other features are color tinge, size of lips, eye shape, eyebrow pattern, jaw and chin musculature, nose shape and size, its position with respect to other parts, and overall shape of the head. These are the "parts of speech" of a kinesic facial grammar. While the parts are the same in all humans, their variant shapes, sizes, and ways in which they are juxtaposed to each other produce the facial fingerprint. Some of these features are studied under the rubric of *biometrics*, which is the mathematical analysis of human features, from fingerprints to facial qualities, that can be used to determine identity.

In the last decade, work in AI has come forth to help understand how the brain creates facial recognition, producing software capable of recognizing a person's identity from a digital image or a video source. The software compares the image with biometric images of people within databases, including social media network databases, where profiles include photos. Programs such as DeepFace, developed by Facebook, can determine whether two faces belong to the same person, with a high accuracy rate. There is now also a subfield of AI, called Affective Computing (AC), aiming to develop computer systems that can recognize and simulate human emotions on the basis of the algorithmic scanning of facial expressions, muscle tension, postures, gestures, speech tones, pupil dilation, etc. The relevant technology includes sensors, cameras, big data, and deep learning software. Research in AC has led to the creation of systems that allow users to employ animated shapes to perform a set of gestures and so is now used in psychology as a tool for modeling or deconstructing human emotions into their microexpressions.

The face is also a primary factor in how we assign aesthetic qualities to a person, including how we interpret a face as "beautiful" or "ideal," which has not only been a target of neuroscience, but also of artists and philosophers. It was in the Renaissance that artists became especially fascinated by the face and its connection to perceptions and models of aesthetic beauty. In that era, the concept of symmetry and proportion of the face was developed artistically. Mathematician Luca Pacioli (1509), for example, showed how to draw the human face according to the divine proportion (also known as the sacred ratio), claiming that it made a face beautiful. Figure 4.4 shows his illustration.

Aesthetic models of the ideal face impel us to make certain interpretations of actual faces. In a relevant study, Apicella, Little, and Marlowe (2007) compared two cultural groups—British and Hazda, a hunter-gatherer society in Tanzania, which had not been exposed to western canons of beauty. Both groups were shown two facial images and asked to choose the more attractive one. The main finding was that the British subjects found both Hadza and

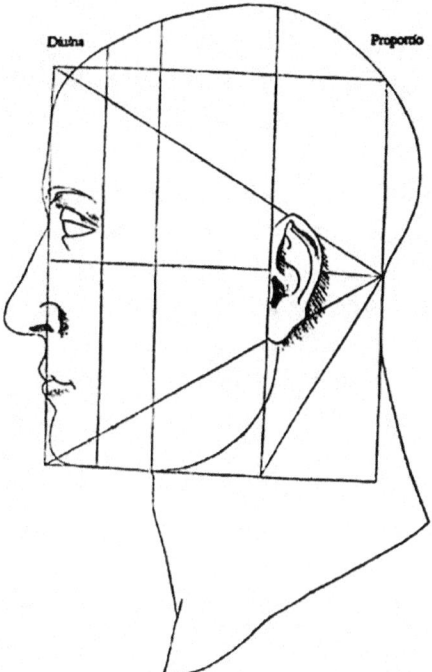

**Figure 4.4** Pacioli's illustration of the perfect human face (Wikimedia Commons).

British faces beautiful, whereas the Hadza preferred only Hadza faces. The reason, the study asserted, was that the Hazda had no familiarity with western faces, not recognizing what an average western face looks like. The findings suggested that culture clearly has an impact on the meanings of the face, and thus that beauty is, as the figurative expression so aptly puts it, "in the eye of the beholder."

## 4.5 The Face as *Persona*

Like the eyes, the face is perceived across the world as a sign system, with coded cultural meanings, especially as a sign of character. This is evident in the art of portraiture. In the early civilizations the subjects were typically rulers, people in authority, and mythic personages. However, there was also some interest in the faces of common people. In China, for instance, murals depicting commoners go back to the Han Dynasty (206 BCE–220 CE), conveying the subject's character through facial features, clothing, and pose. The stone heads made by the Maya peoples, the "laughing clay sculptures" of the Veracruz region in Mexico, the effigy vessels of the Mohican culture, and other examples of Native American portraiture also put on display the faces of common folks.

This type of art, which reaches back to the dawn of history, is a probe of the human face, and can be called the art of *persona*—a term that encapsulates how we equate the face with the person. In ancient Greece and Rome, the term meant the mask worn by an actor on stage, from the Etruscan word *phersu*. Subsequently, in the Roman era, it came to have the meaning of "the character of the mask-wearer." This meaning persists to this day in the Latin theater term *dramatis personae* "cast of characters" (literally "the masks of the drama"). Eventually, the word came to have its present meaning as identifying features of someone's character, starting in the later Roman era when it became apparent that individuals could play different roles in life, like actors on the stage. This meaning of the term—as the social mask people wear and present in public—has been adopted by psychoanalysis (Jung 1971) and, more recently, linguistics (Leary 1996, 2011). Jung warned against the constant presentation of different personas, fearing that the sense of true individuality would be lost. Moreover, if the presentation was not successful it could have negative consequences and psychological effects. In one relevant study, Danielle Jackson (2017), showed that the persona can affect health—the more acceptable socially the more health benefits experienced by the person, the less acceptable, the more likelihood of negative mental health consequences. This is especially noticeable when the person becomes unstable and incapable of acting outside their persona.

Sociologist Erving Goffman (1959), like Jung, saw a person's understanding of the Self as imprinted in the persona that people create, arguing that social life was very much like the theater, in which people perceived themselves as playing specific roles and adapting them to the situation. Goffman's work has spurred psychological-sociological investigations into the contrivance of social interactions based on the concept of persona. In all such interactions, the face plays a critical role—how it is made up, how it is controlled in conveying expressive states, what hairstyle is adopted, etc. This scripting of persona will fail, however, if not accompanied by acceptance, as just mentioned. Smiling, eye contact, nods of agreement, accompanied by appropriate verbal mannerisms coalesce to convey the intended persona.

Goffman originated the concept of *frame analysis*—the technique of dividing human interaction into separate frames of behavior that can then be analyzed in terms of constituent units of self-portrayal, recognizable by others intuitively as part of persona. Taking his cue from anthropologist Gregory Bateson (1972, 1979), he called the sequence of actions that identify a person's behavioral characteristics a "strip" (in reference to the comic strip as a structured sequence of actions). The method consists of: (1) describing the strip (the actual behavioral scene); (2) classifying the cues that indicate self-presentation; and (3) interpreting the cues in terms of their social meanings. In effect, with his work, Goffman drew attention to the fact that social interaction unfolds very much like a sequence in a theatrical script, wherein the social actors seek to skillfully stage their persona according to social context. As part of his analytical framework, Goffman introduced the notions of "situational effects," "role-playing," and "presentation of Self" into the human and communicative sciences.

The face is the key to self-presentation, since it is perceived the world over as a sign of Selfhood, character, social rank, etc. This is why we tend to evaluate a stranger's personality almost instinctively on the basis of facial appearance. This is also why facial decorations constitute Self-presentational props that reach back into the origins of culture. The cosmetic make-up that we use today has a long and unbroken connection to ancient self-presentation practices during various stages of courtship. As the anthropologist Helen Fisher (1992: 272–3) has aptly remarked, the archeological evidence suggests that the altered face is a phenomenon that goes right back to our Cro-Magnon ancestors, who spent hours decorating themselves, plaiting their hair, and donning garlands of flowers to show off for one another around the fire's glow. The contemporary cosmetic and jewelry industries are modern-day versions of these age-old traditions.

Interestingly, psychologists have found that specific individuals are responsive romantically to certain particular kinds of faces and not to others from puberty onwards. One explanation as to why such preferences surface at puberty is the presence of what the psychologist John Money (1986) calls "lovemaps" in the mind. He defines these as mental images acquired and embedded in the mind during childhood that determine the specific kinds of features of the face that will evoke love moods (such as infatuation) in a pubescent individual. Lovemaps unconsciously generate an image schema of what the ideal romantic partner should be like, as to details of the poterntial mate's facial physiognomy. While this concept now has a psychological name, it is an ancient one based on the metonymic principle that the *face-is-the-person* (above). Fertility rites practiced and performed along the Tigris and Euphrates Rivers, as Herodotus noted in his *Historia*

(440 BCE), celebrate the made-up face as the basis of romantic attraction. British anthropologist James Frazer was one of the first to study such rites systematically in his book, *The Golden Bough* (1890). Frazer differentiated between types of rites—including the making-up of the face to indicate a passage from childhood to maturity or its alteration to indicate a courtship pact. It is informative to note that these rituals may all have a common source—namely the view that people have both a male and a female persona, as evidence somewhat by the ancient myth of Hermaphrodite, the peculiar creature with two faces, two sets of limbs, and one large body. Hermaphrodite was resented by the gods, who ended up dividing the creature into two biologically separate sections—male and female, each with its own persona. This Hermaphroditic notion was developed psychologically by Carl Jung (1971) and his concepts of the *animus* and the *anima*—respectively, the unconscious masculine side of a woman and the unconscious feminine side of a man, present in the psyche to varying degrees.

Myths, legends, and artistic artifacts have dealt with archetypes of persona in different ways. The Greek version of the animus was *eros*, depicted as a winged youth, often with his eyes covered to symbolize the blindness of love. Eros is the source of new life. Sigmund Freud (1931: 48) described it as follows:

> Civilization is a process in the service of Eros, whose purpose is to combine single human individuals, and after that families, then races, peoples and nations, into one great unity, the unity of mankind. Why this has to happen, we do not know; the work of Eros is precisely this.

*Agape*, on the other hand, was the Greek version of the *anima*. Aphrodite was the mythical personification of agape. Artists and poets have traditionally portrayed Aphrodite as the goddess of love and beauty, even though her functions in ancient Greece were more varied and complex. In Christian belief, marriage was a union of these two spiritual forces, meant to fulfill the scriptural requirement that "the two shall become one flesh."

## 4.6 Epilogue

As Darwin noted, canines, felines, primates, and other mammals have a similar facial anatomy—two eyes, a nose, a forehead, a mouth, a chin, and a head that are in the same relative positions. Darwin emphasized that such physiognomy optimizes survival. The location of the eyes a little higher up than the nose provides a more panoramic and commanding view of surroundings; the nose turned down allows an animal to block rain from entering into its head; the mouth, which is below the nose and the eyes, is situated in this relative position so that the two organs can provide it simultaneously with relevant information about whether to ingest food or not. These features are based in biology, leading to the emergence of similar kinds of facial expressions in diverse animals.

However, in humans, as discussed in this chapter, facial expressions transcend this evolutionary paradigm. We use facial expressions to understand each other as much as we rely on language to comprehend intentions and states of mind. Being able to read someone's face is as fundamental as decoding the person's words so as to be able to understand actions and behaviors (Bänziger, Grandjean, and Scherer 2009). Overall, it would seem that anatomical structures shaped by evolution, known as *morphogenesis*, are not only contributors to instinctive communication, but are adapted for intentional communication. Facial expressions and head movements form a coordinated system of communication that can complement, supplement, or even substitute vocal language (Knapp 1978: 94–5). As Duncan and Fiske (1977: xi) observe, all morphogenetic structures work in unity, that is, with a "definite organization."

Gregory Bateson (1979) understood the importance of this communicative unity as affecting states of mind. As discussed (Chapter 2), his notion of the *double bind* was a source of disruption of this unity, deriving from conflicting messages in daily communication acts. The main implication is that communication must be balanced, equal, and based on mutual trust, not one in which there are contrasts of meaning. Bateson saw it as the source of mental illnesses such as schizophrenia (Bateson 1956: 251):

> Schizophrenia—its nature, etiology, and the kind of therapy to use for it—remains one of the most puzzling of the mental illnesses. The theory of schizophrenia presented here is based on communications analysis, and specifically on the Theory of Logical Types. From this theory and from observations of schizophrenic patients is derived a description, and the necessary conditions for, a situation called the "double bind"—a situation in which no matter what a person does, he "can't win." It is hypothesized that a person caught in the double bind may develop schizophrenic symptoms.

A key to understanding the double bind is facial expression—which Bateson came to realize while conducting fieldwork among the Balinese of Indonesia, noticing that Balinese mothers ignored their children's emotional outbursts, avoiding to utilize facial expressions of approval or disapproval, or at least attenuating them. In the West, Bateson pointed out, the outbursts would evoke a conflictual response in kind, accompanied by attendant facial expressions. In the Balinese world, the mother was inclined, by cultural conditioning, to see the child's behaviors as part of character development. The Balinese approach to rearing injected stability in the child, which Bateson called *stasis* in social behavior, diminishing the likelihood of emotional disturbances arising in adulthood. On the other hand, in societies where stasis is not part of rearing patterns, such as in the West, where a dominance-based relation is encouraged between mother and child, the risk of developing unstable emotional behaviors in adulthood increases considerably. He called this *schismogenesis*. Avoiding contradictory emotional messages, verbally and nonverbally, is the main practical therapeutic implication of double-bind

**Figure 4.5** Giuseppe Arcimboldo, *Summer*, sixteenth century (Wikimedia Commons).

theory. Like other organisms, humans instinctively seek homeostasis, or the ability to maintain a stable set of conditions inside the body and the mind vis-à-vis external information and states. The more homeostatic the cultural system, the less aberrant behaviors and emotional states. As Bateson understood, human communication is complex, consisting in an integrated system of words, tone of voice, and body language. Any breaking or leakage within this system causes breakdowns in understanding. Saying something like "I love you" can only be interpreted in a context, including who uttered it, the tone of voice used, and the facial expression that accompanies it. From this coordinated set of features, its meaning can then be assayed (to some degree)—as a declaration of romance, as an ironic joke, and so forth.

In the unified system of communication, known appropriately as face-to-face, clearly the face is a dominant factor. We are programmed to look for cues of meaning in faces, and this instinctual propensity even leads to a common optical illusion of seeing hidden faces in things. Called "chance faces," they include seeing faces in clouds, in geographical shapes, and so on. Some artists have intentionally created hidden faces for effect. A famous one is the sixteenth-century painter, Giuseppe Arcimboldo of Milan, who arranged images of things on his canvasses so that the arrangement formed a portrait. Above is his painting of various fruits, vegetables, and various plants or substances that are put together to show a face (Figure 4.5).

Arcimboldo's composite faces and heads were imitated by his contemporaries, but relatively forgotten until various subsequent artists, such as the Dadaists and Surrealists, rediscovered them, realizing that we are predisposed by our evolution to see faces everywhere, as Darwin so persuasively argued. Even though Darwin did not treat the communicative value of facial expressions explicitly, he was among the first to realize that they both unite and distinguish humans from other animals, suggesting a historical paradigm that predisposes humans to perceive faces as equivalent to personhood and even to see them hidden everywhere.

# 5
# The Hands

## Chapter Outline

| | |
|---|---|
| 5.0 Prologue | 97 |
| 5.1 Bipedalism | 98 |
| 5.2 Haptic Signing | 101 |
| 5.3 Tactile Communication | 106 |
| 5.4 Tactile Metaphors | 109 |
| 5.5 Handedness | 112 |
| 5.6 The Hands in Art | 115 |
| 5.7 Epilogue | 118 |

## 5.0 Prologue

At a certain point in its evolution, the species *homo* became bipedal, freeing the hands to play a critical role in its life, from tool-making and tool-use to the development of gestural and haptic (touching) modes of communication and the use of the fingers to create symbols, such as numerical ones. The communicative functions of the hands include greetings, such as handshaking, and hugging to indicate affection or consolation. The hands have also been of interest to artists and psychologists, perceived as playing vital roles in human life. As Joe Navarro (2010) has aptly put it:

> Among all species, our human hands are unique—not only in what they can accomplish, but also in how they communicate. Human hands can paint the Sistine Chapel, pluck a guitar, maneuver surgical instruments, chisel a David, forge steel, and write poetry. They can grasp, scratch, poke, punch, feel, sense,

evaluate, hold and mold the world around us. Our hands are extremely expressive; they can sign for the [hearing-impaired], help tell a story, or reveal our innermost thoughts.

This chapter will deal with the hands as part of a manual communicative kinesic code. The next chapter will deal with the use of the hands in gesturing and gesticulating. The study of hand-based communication falls specifically under the rubric of *haptics* (from Greek *haptikos* "grasping," "touching"). The term was first used by the German psychologist Max Dessoir in 1892, to give a name to the research he was conducting into the sense of touch (Gibson 1966).

Haptic signage in communication forms a mixed system—voluntary (intentional, cultural) and involuntary (instinctive, natural). Using the hands to shield oneself from an attack is an instinctive haptic action. So too is raising the hand to warn someone. But most other haptic signs are culture-specific, although they may still have some evolutionary function. These include patting someone on the arm, shoulder, or back to indicate agreement or praise, linking arms to designate companionship, putting an arm around the shoulder to communicate friendship or intimacy, holding hands to express intimacy, hugging to convey happiness, and so on. It is unclear why haptic communication varies so much across cultures. The reason may have a basis in cultural perceptions of the body's meanings. Some people perceive the skin to be a surface "sheath." Others regard the body as a "container" and thus think of themselves as "contained" in their skin. The zones of privacy that define Self-space in these cultures, therefore, include the clothes that cover the skin. Others feel instead that the Self is located down within the body shell, resulting in a totally different expression of haptic behaviors. People in such cultures are in general more tolerant of crowds, of noise levels, of the touching of hands, of eye contact, and of body odors than others.

The study of the hands for communicative purposes falls more directly under *tactile communication*, rather than *haptics*, although the boundary line between the two is a thin one—it is used here for clarity, rather than for any theoretical reason.

## 5.1 Bipedalism

The liberation of the hands for communicative, expressive, and representational purposes is, as mentioned above, the result of bipedalism, an adaptation to a completely erect posture and a two-footed striding walk. Many of the higher primates can manipulate even very small objects. In humans prehensile (grasping) hands have allowed for manipulation in a skillful manner.

Fossils discovered in Africa provide evidence that hominids walked erect, had a bipedal stride, and had prehensile hands even before the great increase in their brain size. The most important structural detail in this refinement was the elongated human thumb, which could rotate freely for the first time and, thus, be fully opposable to the other fingers. No doubt, this development made tool-making and tool use possible. Moreover, as some linguists claim, the erect posture gave rise to the subsequent evolution of the physiological apparatus for speech, since it brought about the lowering and positioning of the larynx for controlled breathing (Wilson 1998)—a phenomenon that is unique to the human species. During their first months of life, infants breathe, swallow, and vocalize in ways that are physiologically similar to gorillas and chimpanzees, because they are born with the larynx high in the neck (as are the other primates). At some point around the third month of life, however, the human larynx starts to descend, gradually altering how the child will use the throat, the mouth, and the tongue from then on. The new low position means that the respiratory and digestive tracts will cross above the larynx. This entails a few risks: food can easily lodge in the entrance of the larynx; drinking and breathing simultaneously can lead to choking. In compensation, the lowered larynx permits vocal speech by producing a chamber above the vocal folds that can modify sound. And this, in turn, prepares the child for the acquisition of language as a vocal system of signs.

Although other species, including non-primate ones, are capable of tool use, only in the human species did complete bipedalism free the hand sufficiently to allow it to become a supremely sensitive and precise manipulator and grasper, thus permitting proficient tool making and tool use in the species. The earliest stone tools date back to about 2.5 million years ago. By 1.5 million years ago, sites in various parts of eastern Africa have been discovered to contain not only many prehistoric stone tools, but also animal bones with scratch marks that could only have been left by human-like cutting actions. Shortly after *homo* became bipedal and a tool-maker, the evidence suggests that the human brain underwent rapid expansion. In the course of human evolution the size of the brain has more than tripled. Modern humans have a braincase volume of between 1,300 and 1,500 cc., having developed three major structural components that undergird the unique mental capacities of the species—the large dome-shaped cerebrum, the smaller somewhat spherical cerebellum, and the brainstem. Brain size does not determine the degree of intelligence of the individual; this appears to be determined instead by the number and type of functioning neurons and how they are structurally connected with one another. And since neuronal connections are conditioned by environmental input, the most likely hypothesis is that any form of conscious intelligence, however it is defined, is most likely influenced by upbringing. Unlike the early hominid adult skulls, with their sloping foreheads and prominent jaws, the modern human skull and the braincase—with biologically insignificant variations—retain a proportionately large size, in relation to the rest of the body (Figure 5.1).

The brain controls the hands in an asymmetrical fashion, called *handedness*. The motor cortex of the left hemisphere controls movements on the right side of the body, while the motor cortex of the right hemisphere directs movements on the left side of the body. More than 90 percent of human beings are right-handed because the left motor cortex, which directs the right hand, is dominant over the right motor cortex, which directs the left hand.

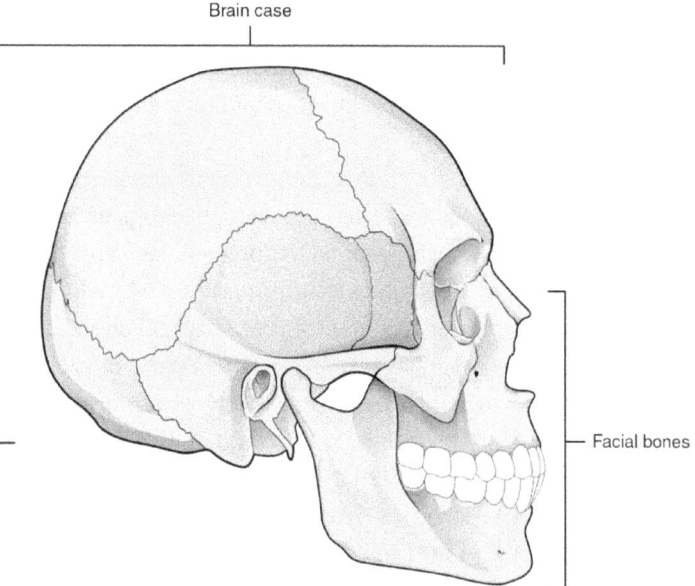

**Figure 5.1** Human braincase (Wikimedia Commons).

## 5.2 Haptic Signing

Since they were freed by bipedalism the hands and fingers evolved into versatile sign-making body parts. Two examples are counting and snapping. The use of the fingers for counting purposes, known as *dactylonomy*, goes back to antiquity and even prehistory (Schmandt-Besserat 1999). It appears as a semiotic counting strategy in ancient marketplaces and games (Neugebauer 1952: 9; Ifrah 2000: 48). In Pre-Columbian Maya culture, both the fingers and toes were used, providing the signs of their base-20 numerical system—in some Brazilian Native languages, the word for *twenty* is the same as the word for *feet* (Flegg 1989: 34). Interestingly, in some cultures, such as Native ones in California and Mexico, counting is based on the spaces *between* the fingers, rather than the fingers themselves (Ascher 1991). Finger-snapping also goes back to antiquity. It probably initiated as a means to signal the presence of something or to grab someone's attention—functions it still has today often in conjunction with verbal requests or commands. In ancient Greece, snapping was used by musicians and dancers to mark rhythm, as we do today as well (West 1994: 199). It has also been used as a substitute for hand clapping to acknowledge approval in various cultures.

An interesting example of a digital haptic sign is the one formed by raising the index and middle fingers of the right hand in the shape of a V (Figure 5.2).

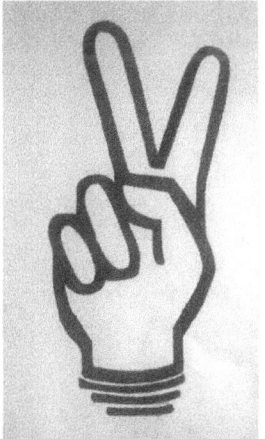

**Figure 5.2** Sketch of the V sign (Wikimedia Commons).

If asked what it means, people in contemporary urban cultures might answer that it stood for "victory" or "peace." The sign's link to the "victory" meaning goes back to the early 1940s during World War II, when it was apparently used by the Allied forces. British politician Winston Churchill used it in a 1943 recorded speech, which disseminated the sign broadly. The same sign underwent a reversal in meaning, signifying "peace," in the counterculture movement of the 1960s. The hippies used it deliberately as an entreaty for peace among all humans, thus turning the victory meaning of the sign on its head. Interestingly, the *Star Trek* program on American network television introduced a version of the sign in the same era—the Vulcan salute, signifying "Live long and prosper." This version, which appeared for the first time in the 1967 episode "Amok Time," was formed with the third and fourth fingers, instead of the second and third (Figure 5.3).

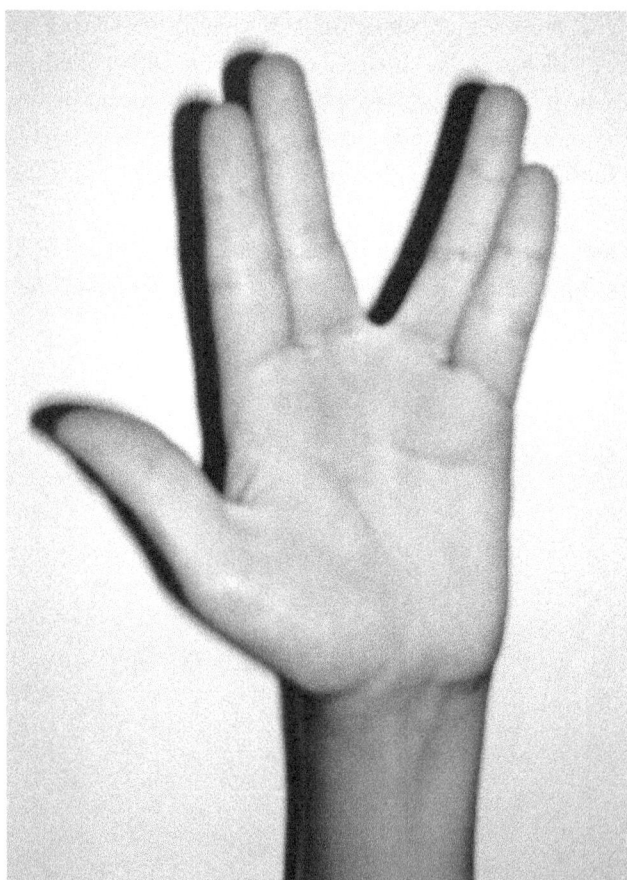

**Figure 5.3** Vulcan salute (Wikimedia Commons).

The meanings above are contemporary ones; but the same type of haptic sign reveals different meanings across time and cultures. When it is done with the back of the hand facing outward, it is perceived as an insult in some areas of Britain. In their comprehensive study of haptic signing, Morris et al. (1979) are unsure as to why and when the sign came to have this designation, pointing out that the taboo meaning is simply passed on from generation to generation without any conscious awareness of its source. In other cultures, the V-shape is a female archetype, alluding symbolically to a vessel, a metaphor of female fertility and motherhood across various ancient societies (Blackledge 2003; Danesi 2009).

As the examples above show, of all nonverbal codes, haptic signing appears to be especially susceptible to culture-specific meaning-making. Consider two other well-known examples—the OK sign and the thumbs-up sign. In most western cultures, the OK sign denotes approval, agreement, or an indication that all is well (Figure 5.4).

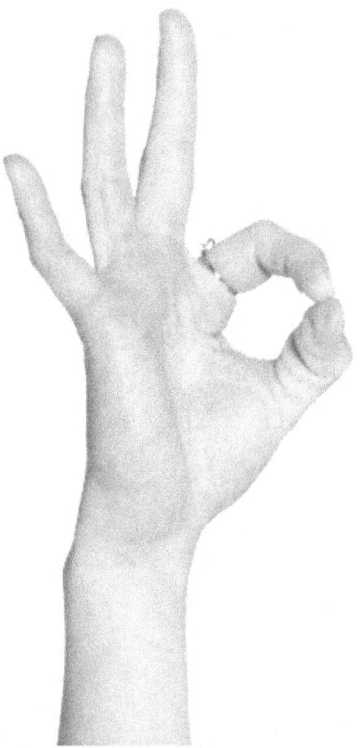

**Figure 5.4** OK sign (Wikimedia Commons).

Known also as a *ring sign,* its origin is traced back to ancient Greece, appearing in vases as a symbol of love—a meaning that continues in contemporary Naples and other areas of southern Italy. Its meaning as approval or consensus probably comes from the rhetorician Quintilian, who is recorded as having used it with this meaning. In some cultures, however, it conveys different connotations, including offensive ones. In Japan and France, it represents zero worth—a kind of *nada* gesture. In Turkey, Tunisia, and in various regions of Latin America, the same sign has vulgar or obscene connotations. In Brazil, it is synonymous with the middle finger sign in American culture, and thus an obscene gesture. In various Mediterranean cultures, it represents the evil eye and is used as a curse. In the digitally-connected global village, however, the western meaning of the OK sign has spread broadly, even in regions where it has traditionally had negative connotations, especially among digital natives. To avoid confusion, communicators use contextual cues, such as posture or facial expression, to clarify the meaning intended.

The thumbs-up sign in western cultures is used to indicate satisfaction of approval; its opposite, the thumbs-down sign, refers to dissatisfaction or disapproval (Figure 5.5).

**Figure 5.5** Thumbs-up sign (Wikimedia Commons).

While the exact origin of this sign is obscure, a number of possible scenarios have been put forth. The most common one traces it back to ancient Rome, where it was used in the context of gladiatorial combat to pass judgment on a defeated gladiator (up for "let him live" and down for "let him die"); but this origin scenario is uncertain, given that there is little archeological or philological evidence to support it. Morris et al. (1979) trace it instead to a medieval custom used to approve business transactions. Over time, the upraised thumb came to symbolize harmonious interactions more generally. Somehow, the same sign has become imbued with various other types of meaning that seem to have little connection to these origin scenarios. For instance, it is used as a hitchhiking request in modern societies. In areas of Iraq and Iran, it is an offensive sign, as it is in many parts of Asia. Like the OK sign, in these areas too, where global media are allowed, the same pattern of western meanings associated with the sign have started to penetrate common usage, especially given the use of the sign on websites and media platforms (such as Facebook), where the two oppositional signs (thumbs up-thumbs down), corresponding to "Like" and "Dislike" are used to indicate approval or disapproval of content. The number of "Likes" is thus perceived as a metric of social acceptance or of success, whereas the number of "Dislikes" indicates lack of success (Figure 5.6).

In sum, the number of haptic signs that are possible is limited only by the physiology of the hands and fingers. The ring finger (fourth finger on the left hand), for example, is not used as a sign autonomously because of the physical effort required to raise it. This shows that morphogenesis and semiosis are intrinsically intertwined—a phenomenon that mathematician René Thom (1975) called *semiogenesis*, which can be defined reductively as the natural evolution of sign forms guided by the anatomical and physiological structures of the body. A simple example is the genesis of potential phonemes in a language, which is constrained by the anatomy of the vocal apparatus, allowing for only certain sounds to be formed—around fifty to seventy in total.

**Figure 5.6** Like and dislike (Wikimedia Commons).

## 5.3 Tactile Communication

It was Darwin, again, who first identified the evolutionary importance of tactile communication, in his book on the emotions, pointing out that the anatomical structure of the hands was similar to analogous organs in other species: "What can be more curious than that the hand of a man, formed for grasping, that of a mole for digging, the leg of the horse, the paddle of the porpoise, and the wing of the bat, should all be constructed on the same pattern, and should include the same bones, in the same relative positions?" (Darwin 1872: 516). Remarkably, Darwin went on to observe that tactile contact in various mammalian species was an expression of sympathy (see Keltner 2009).

But, like Darwin's observations about facial expressions, this one too remained largely unstudied until the middle part of the twentieth century. An initial study emphasizing the importance of touching in interpersonal communication was provided by L. K. Frank (1957), followed by the work of Edward T. Hall (1963; 1964; 1966), which included tactile communication as part of a larger proxemic code of interaction—to be discussed in Chapter 7. Shortly after, Jourard (1966) investigated what parts of a person's body members of a given community would report as touchable or not. A number of investigators subsequently explored how variations in the ways in which people touch one another, as well as which body parts are considered touchable, are related to the social relationships existing between them (for example, Henley 1977). Psychology also began looking at the role of touch in childhood development, finding overall that it is one of the first senses to develop in the infant, playing a major role in neonatal cognitive growth (Leonard 2017). Given the growing awareness of the significant role of tactility in human interactions, Lynne Kaufman (1971) proposed the term *tacesics* as the specific study of tactile communication, to parallel Hall's term *proxemics*.

Tactile communication is common in greeting rituals. Consider handshaking, as a case-in-point, whose phatic meanings are guided by factors such as intensity (how delicate or strong the touch is), duration (how long or short), location (body area where the touching occurs), frequency (number of touches), and instrumentality (which body parts do the touching). Anthropologist Desmond Morris (1969) suggests that the western form of handshaking may have begun as a means to indicate that neither person in a greeting ritual was holding a weapon. It thus started out as a "tie sign," because of the bond of trust it was designed to establish. Subsequently, the sign became a symbol of equality among individuals, being employed to seal agreements of various kinds and eventually as a simple greeting protocol. But even in the latter, the original meaning is still resonant—refusing to shake someone's outstretched hand is interpreted as a "counter-sign" of aggressiveness or as a challenge. The archeological record actually supports this explanation, tracing the handshake as a sign of alliance-making to antiquity. A fifth century BCE wall sculpture of Hera and Athena shaking hands appears to corroborate this estimation (Figure 5.7).

In several myths, the two goddesses were rivals. By shaking hands, rather than bowing, the sculpture suggests that this act was meant to show that the two were equals, feeling sufficiently comfortable with each other not to bring weapons. This is actually one of several paintings and sculptures from ancient Greece as signs of agreement or pledges of trust.

In western countries, handshaking is the primary form of greeting strangers or in enacting contact among adults. Typically, children and even most adolescents do not shake hands, either among themselves or with adults. The exception is in Austria, where adults might shake children's hands as part of the greeting ritual. The initiator of the handshake can be anyone in most urban cultures; but in some, the initiator role is constrained by cultural variables, such as gender and age. In China, for example, the older person is

**Figure 5.7** Hera and Athena shaking hands, Acropolis Museum, Athens (Wikimedia Commons).

typically the individual who should be greeted with a handshake before others. But the handshake is not a universal greeting sign. In traditional Japanese society, for example, in place of the handshake, bowing the head, with hands by the sides, is the appropriate gesture, although people will greet non-Japanese individuals with a handshake, perhaps to show respect for others. In India, the respectful Namaste gesture—pressing the hands together with a slight bow—is traditionally used in place of handshakes (Figure 5.8).

However, today, handshaking is preferred in urban Indian settings, especially in the context of business dealings. Overall, the handshake is mainly a western greeting ritual, constrained usually to formal contact situations; in many informal ones, the fist-bump and high-five gestures are used in lieu of the handshake. These two gestures, together with elbow-touching, became widespread during the 2009 H1N1 pandemic and the Covid-19 pandemic in 2020.

Other forms of tactile communication used in both phatic and emotive rituals include patting someone on the arm, shoulder, or back to convey agreement or as a complimentary gesture; linking arms to indicate companionship; putting one's arm around the shoulder to indicate friendship or intimacy; holding hands to express intimacy; hugging to convey happiness; and so on. But the meanings of these forms vary considerably across the world (Montagu 1986). Anthropologists are unclear as to why tactile communication codes vary so widely. A plausible reason is the fact that touching is a highly emotional act, and may be perceived as very intimate in

**Figure 5.8** Indian Namaste greeting.

some cultures, less so in others. Actually, across the world, the intensity and frequency of touching increase according to the type of relationship people have with each other (Hertenstein et al. 2006). A relevant research study conducted by Jones and Yarbrough (2009) revealed seven main functions of touch that influenced relationships concretely: positive affect (emotion), playful, controlling, ritualistic, hybrid (mixed), task-related, and accidental touch. Each one conveys a specific set of feelings and emotive nuances, depending on context and culture. Suffice it to say that when we touch someone, or are touched by someone, the action triggers a complex array of meanings and feelings, some of which are patterned and predictable, others unexpected and sometimes even unwanted. In a high-contact culture, as in some Latin American societies, touch is part of interaction among friends; in low-contact ones, such as the American and Canadian ones, it is infrequent and often avoided.

## 5.4 Tactile Metaphors

As discussed previously, a useful tool of accessing the meanings of nonverbal behaviors is to analyze the metaphors (and other figurative strategies) that incorporate them as conceptual vehicles into common discourse. Tactile metaphors (metaphors using tactile-based vehicles) provide bimodal evidence of how we evaluate the importance of the hands and touching in everyday life. Below are examples of expressions using various aspects of haptics and tactility as metaphorical vehicles of understanding:

1 *These things go hand in hand*: meaning "close association": alludes to the use of both hands to carry out physical tasks, actions, etc.
2 *I have to hand it to you; you always know what to say*: giving praise or credit to someone is akin metaphorically to using the hands to give something to someone.
3 *Do not bite the hand that feeds you*: physically biting a hand that contains food will have a negative outcome; so too, being unfriendly to someone produces analogous negative results.
4 *At first hand, this seems worse than you might think*: the idea that the hand can hold all kinds of things, beneficial or not, is embedded in this metaphor.
5 *I can't grasp what you are saying*: using grasping to indicate knowledge of something brings out the importance of the hand as a prehensile instrument to carry out activities.

6 *I am touched by what you said*: this connects tactility to positive emotions and to the fact that touch conveys emotions powerfully.
7 *He lives from hand to mouth*: this alludes to how we first receive food in infancy and in social situations of poverty, extended to how we might waste resources and thus resort to living in a basic survival mode.
8 *Let's get in touch more often*: this makes reference to the fact that social contact is like physical contact—the word *contact* means literally touching each other (from Latin *contactus* "touched, grasped").
9 *I am out of touch with new trends*: being unaware of something is akin to not using physical touching to gain sensory information about something.
10 *Just hold on a little longer and you will succeed*: holding something with the hands to keep them safe extends metaphorically to ideas, events, etc..

Expressions such as these bring out the importance of touching to human life, etching it into language and, thus, into mindset. Metaphorical vehicles such as holding, handing, grasping, grabbing, seizing, wresting, touching, taking, picking, etc. reveal that we perceive the world through haptic and tactile modalities—physical and imaginary—which form the source of cultural symbolism at different levels. Some common words emerge through the metaphorical channel based on the hands and tactility, but are no longer recognized as such, indicating how deeply embedded this kind of image schema is in cognition. A few examples, will suffice:

- *manipulate*: from Latin *manipulus* "handful," from *manus* "hand;" this refers to controlling or influencing someone or a situation unfairly or unscrupulously in metaphorical analogy to how objects can be moved around by the hands.
- *mandate*: also from *manus*, plus *dare* "to give;" this refers to giving authority to someone to act in a certain way, metaphorically reflecting how the hands are used to pass something on to someone.
- *manage*: from Italian *maneggiare* "to handle," from Latin *manus*; it alludes to the success in surviving or attaining one's aims, reflecting metaphorically how the hands are used to do things practically.
- *comprehend*: from Latin *cum* "with" and *prehendere* "to grasp;" a word that connects physical grasping to mental grasping, alluding to the hands as primary means for sensing (grasping) the world around us.
- *perceive, conceive, receive,* etc.: words formed with Latin *capere* "to seize;" these are metaphorical extensions of grasping.

- *dexterity*, from Latin *dexter* ("right") refers to the belief that right-handedness is "right" as opposed to left-handedness—a concept traced back considerably in time.

It is truly remarkable how extensive the use of tactile metaphorical vocabulary is embedded in everyday language, perhaps indicating the primacy of nonverbal modes of communication, at least by allusion. Metaphors such as those above reveal a process that can be called *sense implication* (Danesi 2004). This is the ability of the brain to transform sensory, affective, or bodily experiences into conceptual strategies. This process produces what are called *root metaphors*. The number of these in the core vocabularies of languages throughout the world is immense. A few illustrative examples are given below:

- Vision metaphors: *flash* of insight, *spark* of genius, a *bright* mind, a *brilliant* idea, a *flicker* of intelligence, a *luminous* achievement, a *shining* mind, a *bright* fire in his eyes, *sparking* interest in a subject, words *glowing* with meaning.
- Touch metaphors: *seize* the opportunity, *grasp* an idea, *touch* a raw nerve, *pick through* those thoughts, *take* my advice, *give* me a hand.
- Taste metaphors: I can *taste* victory, *savor* the moment, a *bitter* thought, *sweet* love, their *spicy* affair, a *palatable* proposition.
- Hearing metaphors: to *hear* one out, to be all *ears*, to keep one's *ears* open, to be *deaf* to advice, out of *earshot*.
- Olfactory metaphors: to *smell* a rat, that idea *stinks*, your proposal *reeks*.

These are linguistic traces to the importance of sensory processes in understanding the world. As we use these words, there is an osmotic reflex in the body that comes out in how we gesture, as we shall see in the next chapter. When we say that we are *handing something to someone,* we put out hands instinctively forward in a giving formation, reflecting the body in the mind, as Mark Johnson (1987) has so aptly put it. They transform the physiology of touching, seeing, etc. into a "physiology of thought." The eighteenth/nineteenth-century Neapolitan philosopher, Giambattista Vico, claimed that the only way we have of understanding the mind is through sense implication: "The human mind is naturally inclined by the senses to see itself externally in the body" (in Bergin and Fisch 1984: 236).

The presence of haptic and tactile vocabulary in language fits in with the bimodality principle adopted in this book. In this case, the language is intertwined with manual communication, and the latter may be the source of verbality, as Stross (1976: 22) cogently explains:

> It is easy to imagine bipedal animals gesturing to attract attention or pointing out a particular object with a wave of the hand. Perhaps you can even visualize a group of prelinguistic humans imitating the shapes of things with hand gestures or pointing to parts of the body. Association of the gesture with the thing indicated would then have to be extended to situations in which the object was not present.

The connection of gesture to vocal language will be discussed in the next chapter. Suffice it to say here that the two are not separate evolutionary developments; they are interconnected in intrinsic ways, with one set of nonverbal signals and signs being transferred to the verbal channel, revealed by the use of osmotic gestures as we speak.

## 5.5 Handedness

On the basis of extended fieldwork among the Tinguian peoples in Mindanao, the Philippines, between 1910 and 1912, anthropologist Fay-Cooper Cole (1956) was likely the first to study and document the symbolic value of handedness in a specific social milieu. In Tinguian culture, the severed hand of a warrior rival was a symbol of victory, indicating the importance of hands in combat. The finger joints of the severed hand were then immersed in a drink to celebrate the "hand conquest" event. As brutal as this ceremony might seem, it is not unlike ceremonies and rituals found throughout the world, designating the importance of the hands, in combat and life generally. Mutilated hands are found on the walls of European caves dating back to Paleolithic times, probably indicating the same meaning of the hands as in Tinguian culture.

The meanings of hands and fingers have been depicted in various ways by artists throughout the ages. In the fresco of the *Creation of Adam* painted by Michelangelo on the ceiling of the Sistine Chapel, God extends his right index finger to touch Adam's outstretched left index finger to give him life (spiritual). The subtext is a clear one—the left is associated with human weakness, while the right is divine (Figure 5.9).

This handedness symbolism has remained in all kinds of religious ceremonies, from giving out communion at Christian services with the right hand, to a priest blessing someone with his right hand. Reversing the hands—

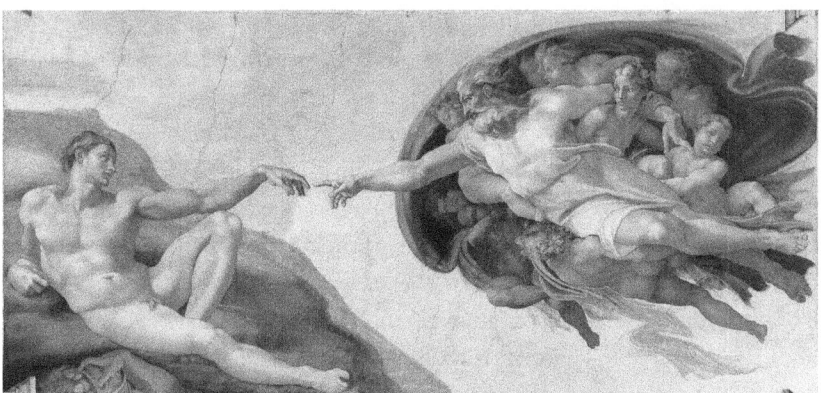

**Figure 5.9** Michelangelo Buonarroti, *The Creation of Adam, c.* 1508–12 (Wikimedia Commons).

using the left hand to carry out these practices—is perceived as aberrant or sinister (meaning "left" in Latin).

Handedness symbolism is found across societies. Handshaking is always enacted with the right hand—using the left one would seem anomalous at best, and conflictual at worst. In India, the right hand is perceived as the clean hand (spiritually) and thus the one to be used on most occasions, while the left hand performs tasks considered to be unclean. So, the right hand is prescribed for cooking and eating, no matter the handedness of the individual, whereas the left hand is prescribed for other kinds of activities. In the Balinese traditional shadow marionette plays, the narrator starts by taking the marionettes out one by one, placing the "good" characters on his right side and the evil ones on his left. In the end, the good marionettes always win, alluding to the magical, divine powers of the right hand.

This type of right-versus-left conceptual dichotomy is known more technically in semiotics and psychology as an *opposition*. The first in-depth psychological study of opposition was Charles Ogden's 1932 treatise, *Opposition: A Linguistic and Psychological Analysis*, in which he elaborated upon several key ideas discussed in 1923 by himself and I. A. Richards in *The Meaning of Meaning*. Ogden claimed that a small set of conceptual oppositions, such as *right*-versus-*left* and *yes*-versus-*no*, appeared to be intrinsically binary and found across cultures. These came to be called *polar*, since they could be envisioned as two poles on a conceptual scale. Other types of concepts showed *gradience* between the two poles (Danesi 2020). For example, in a polar opposition such as *white*-versus-*black*, various color concepts such as *gray, red, brown, blue, green, purple*, etc. could be located between the poles, a fact that clearly has both physical and conceptual resonance—gradient colors are distributed on the light spectrum, while *white* and *black* are not, forming instead conceptual endpoints on a color scale. Similarly, the polar opposition *day*-versus-*night* is filled-in with gradient concepts such as *twilight, dawn, noon,* and *afternoon*. Ogden argued that polar concepts are, by and large, universal, whereas gradient ones are culture-specific. This does not mean that such concepts cannot be intentionally put into an opposition for specific reason. The color *red* is a gradient concept; but in, say, a painting it can be put in opposition with another color such as *green* to emphasize some symbolic or thematic dichotomy, such as human blood versus the greenness of nature. Indirect evidence of Ogden's theory comes from the fact that languages of the world have terms for polar oppositions but not necessarily gradient ones. The *right*-versus-*left* opposition is present across the world, manifesting itself in representational, ritualistic, symbolic, and linguistic metaphorical ways. This comes from the fact that we have a right and left hand and that most people are right-handed.

The enigma of handedness was first described by Jean-Baptiste Lamarck in his 1809 book, *Philosophie zoologique,* in which he posited that when certain organs become specialized as a result of some need, then the specialization eventually becomes hereditary, passed on to progeny—hence the dominance of the right hand in humans as a Lamarckian trait, as it has come to be called. Whether verifiable or not, the same pattern of right-handed dominance appears in chimpanzees, as Robert Yerkes (1943) discovered. The neural source of handedness was first discovered by the nineteenth-century French physician Pierre Paul Broca (1861), who established that there existed an asymmetry between the brain and the body—a touch on the right side of the body, for example, is perceived in the left somatosensory area. He also discovered that language is located in the left hemisphere, which controls the right hand.

The relation between handedness and language is now known to be largely asymmetrical. In the majority of right-handers (almost 99 percent), speech is controlled by the left hemisphere of the brain, as it is in about 70 percent of left-handers. However, in some left-handers, both hemispheres of the brain are capable of controlling speech. The right hemisphere is specialized instead for the recognition of faces and the perception of spatial relationships in both right- and left-handers. However, in the latter, some hemispheric variation is also possible.

For whatever reason, left-handedness is seen as an exception in most cultures. Until very recently, left-handed people were often forced to switch to being right-handed, or at least switch to writing with the right hand. This has changed, fortunately, but the perception of dominance, physical and psychological, that is associated with the right hand continues to be an unconscious one to this day.

## 5.6 The Hands in Art

As mentioned, the hands have fascinated all kinds of artists across the ages, from the prehistoric *Cuevas de las Manos* (The Cave of Hands), discovered in Santa Cruz Province, Argentina, to M. C. Escher's *Drawing Hands* (1948), where two hands are shown drawing each other. The former is at least 9,000 years old, showing a group of hands reaching out for something or someone in a seemingly desperate way (Figure 5.10).

Similar paintings have been found in nearby caves. While the meaning of these drawings is unclear, many see them as ritualistic portrayals, probably akin to the Tinguian celebration of severed hands as indicating conquest. They may also represent the perception of the hands as critical in human

**Figure 5.10** *Cuevas de las Manos* (c. 9,000 years ago) (Wikimedia Commons).

life. Aristotle described the hand as the "tool of tools," and this may represent hunting tools (metaphorically) or even building tools. Whatever their meaning, the hands in the painting are signs of their importance and salience in human consciousness—a sense that is found throughout paintings ever since, such as Dutch artist Maurits C. Escher's *Drawing Hands* (1948), which is a lithograph that shows a sheet of paper on which two hands can be seen drawing one another paradoxically into existence (Figure 5.11).

This drawing can be read at many levels, but a pertinent one here is that it portrays the human hands as cooperative anatomical structures in human creativity. Without them, it is unlikely that painting itself as an art form would have come into existence—as the drawing suggests. Douglas Hofstadter (1979) has referred to it as an example of a strange loop—a structure that is found throughout reality.

Depictions of hands are found across the world and across times. Whatever their specific meanings and functions—ritualistic, representational, symbolic, etc.—they attest cumulatively to the importance of the hands in

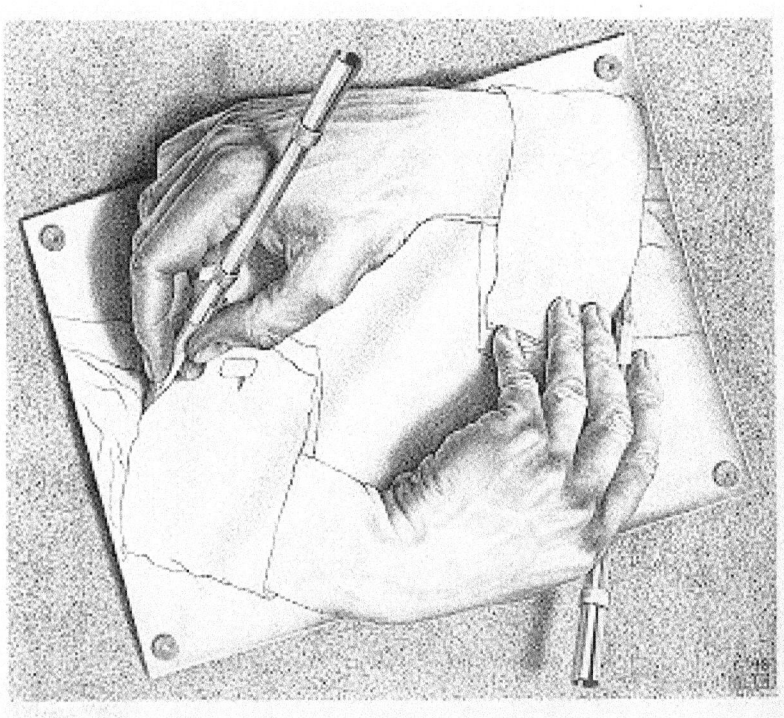

**Figure 5.11** Maurits C. Escher, *Drawing Hands*, 1948 (Wikimedia Commons).

**Figure 5.12** Leonardo da Vinci, *Study of Hands*, c. 1474 (Wikimedia Commons).

human life. One of the more luminous depictions of the hands as symbols of emotional states, as Darwin had noted, is the *Study of Hands* sketch by Leonardo da Vinci (Figure 5.12).

As in many of da Vinci's drawings and paintings, the gender of the hands is somewhat ambiguous, although the anatomical structure is closer to that of a female hand than it is of a male hand. At the bottom of the sketch, one hand is folded underneath another lightly sketched one, a kind of "ghost hand," suggesting the presence of someone else (perhaps a younger person) as a participant in this portrayal of the hands as empathy tools. In fact, from the muscles of the fingers to the wrinkles of skin, one can read a host of human emotions in them, from affection to embracing. In da Vinci's era, the hands were becoming increasingly a subject of interest to artists. An example is Albrecht Dürer's *Hands of the Apostle Praying*, which convey the spiritual power of the hands (Figure 5.13).

There is controversy among art critics as to the meanings of this sketch, although there is some consensus that it is designed to impart the power of prayer. For the present purposes, it is sufficient to note that it highlights the

**Figure 5.13** Albrecht Dürer, *Hands of the Apostle Praying*, 1471–1528 (Wikimedia Commons).

sense of spirituality that the hands evoke when configured in this way, emphasizing unity and union. It is remarkable that the Indian Namaste gesture (discussed above) is virtually identical to this prayerful configuration. There is evidence that in the Talmud, praying in Hebrew culture was conducted with the hands folded. The Dürer sketch encompasses this meaning powerfully—as an act of spiritual submission and as a means to convey empathy and kindness.

The human hand also appears in all kinds of myths and legends. In Greek mythology, the Dactyls were entities born from the fingerprints of the goddess Rhea as she gave birth to Zeus. From such legends, the practices of chiromancy and palmistry emerged throughout the world (Harwood 2011).

## 5.7 Epilogue

The hand is both a physical organ adapted for grasping and a sign system with many cultural functions. We are blessed by clerics with their right hand;

we salute each other by raising the right hand; the laying-on of hands is used by both clerics and medics as curative acts; oaths are taken in court by raising the right hand; deals and agreements are completed by shaking hands; like other paired organs (eyes, feet, legs) each hand is dominantly controlled by the opposing brain hemisphere, so that handedness reflects individual brain functioning, and thus is often interpreted as a sign of personality; and so on. Moreover, as the artworks based on the hand show, the hand can express love, hate, doubt, judgment, rejection, acceptance, and virtually every other sentiment of which humans are capable.

This chapter began with an allusion to Darwin and his emphasis on touch as a primary mode of sympathy exchanges among mammals. As Keltner (2009) has argued, there is now research which reveals that "sympathetic environments—those filled with warm touch—create individuals better suited to survival and reproduction, as Darwin long ago surmised." The studies have been showing that the young of rat populations who receive high levels of tactile contact from their mothers, "in the form of licking, grooming, and close bodily contact, later as mature rats show reduced levels of stress hormones in response to being restrained, explore novel environments with greater gusto, show fewer stress-related neurons in the brain, and have more robust immune systems" (Keltner 2009).

As discussed throughout this chapter, tactility is a major form of NVC. This raises several questions that are of critical importance in today's non-touching cyberspace communicative environments: Is the lack of touch between people in social media creating emotional problems? Do the simulated touch modalities that are emerging to replace physical touch playing the same kinds of key emotional functions of actual touch? So far the answer seems to be in the negative to both questions (for example, Greenfield 2015), although there is now ongoing research that will provide more substantive answers to these questions.

Simulating and even reproducing the capacities of the human hand are now, actually, a central part of robotics. In 2001, surgeons in the city of New York were able to operate on a patient in Strasbourg, France, by manipulating remote-controlled arms and equipment via the Internet. Robot systems in Strasbourg copied the movements and carried out the surgery successfully. This event is no longer exceptional; it is now routine. It shows the phenomenon of extending the human body via technology, which will be discussed in Chapter 9. Robotic body parts can nowadays replace real parts that have been injured or lost. The wearer controls them by thinking, sending nerve signals connected to the neurology of thought to skin sensors which control the robotic body parts. Haptic technologies, as they are now called, are designed to create (or recreate) the experience of touch via forces, vibrations, or motions, passed on by some device to a user; or they can be used to create virtual objects in computer simulations. They have also made it possible to deconstruct human haptics and tactility into their component kines and kinemes by simulating them. There are three systems in humans—cutaneous (based on the skin and how it perceives tactility), kinesthetic (the sense of self-movement), and haptic (as described in this chapter). The technologies allow researchers to reconstruct these artificially and thus to gain an indirect understanding of the meanings and functions of tactility.

In effect, haptic technologies are touch-substitutes; they are gaining widespread use in virtual reality systems, in medicine, and other areas, creating a kind of synesthetic reality, extending and amplifying human anatomy considerably, as Marshall McLuhan would often point out (McLuhan 1972). Systems now use haptic interfaces for modeling and design, including holograms that can be both seen and felt with artificial hands that can control objects and manipulate them like the biological hand. However, artificial touching will never be able to impart sympathy and other emotional modalities that human hand touching achieves all the time and this, it would seem, is critical to our survival.

# 6

# Gesture

## Chapter Outline

| | |
|---|---|
| 6.0 Prologue | 121 |
| 6.1 Functions of Gesture | 123 |
| 6.2 Gesticulants | 130 |
| 6.3 Gesture and Vocal Language | 133 |
| 6.4 Gesture in Non-Human Primates | 136 |
| 6.5 Gesture and Dance | 141 |
| 6.6 Epilogue | 144 |

## 6.0 Prologue

The previous chapter dealt with the hands as vehicles in haptic signing and tactile communication. In this chapter, the focus is on the hands (and arms) as used in *gesture* and gesticulation. Although there is much overlap between haptic, tactile, and gestural signing, the latter is distinctive in the fact that it not only accompanies verbal speech, but can also substitute or replace it completely, as is the case of the sign languages of communities of the hearing-impaired. Like other nonverbal sign systems, gesture can be unwitting (involuntary), witting (voluntary, culture-specific), or a mixture of the two. An example of the former is shielding one's eyes with the hands to obstruct a strike or blow. This action is instinctive, suggesting an evolutionary origin. On the other hand, the come-here, or beckoning, gesture, whereby the index finger is held up and flexed repeatedly to beckon someone forward is guided in its uses and meanings by cultural rules, and is thus specific to certain cultures.

In the United States, the beckoning palm can be used in place of the finger gestures, with the same meaning but with (arguably) more emotive force. Both are accomplished by up-turning the palm. Now, its culture-specific status can be seen by the fact that in Japan and the Philippines it is normally seen as an insult, and in the latter society may even be subject to legal sanctions or penalties.

Gesture also serves communicative functions in non-human primates. Chimpanzees raise their arms in the air as a signal that they want to be groomed; they stretch out their arms to beg or invite; and they have the ability to point to things (Beaken 1996: 51). These gestures are purposeful and regulatory of the actions of other chimps. But the number of gestural forms of which chimpanzees are capable is limited when compared to human gesturing, which encompasses varied social and symbolic functions, including the types of gestures used by religious groups during periods of imposed silence, those used by traffic personnel to direct traffic, and those used by musicians to conduct an orchestra, among an infinitude of others. Some gestures can have quite specific meanings, such as those for good-bye, for catching someone's attention, for showing anger, and so on.

This chapter will look at gestural signing and communication. It will also look at the relation of gesture to language origins and the use of gesture to teach primates human language. As in other chapters, a selection of topics has been made in order to limit the chapter to a viable length. The focus is on major themes and research findings. Gesture spans the entire range of communication and is integrated with many aspects of vocal language as will be discussed (Armstrong, Stokoe, and Wilcox 1995; Golden-Meadow 2003; Kendon 2004). For example, using the index finger together with adverbs such as *there, here,* etc. is a common gestural reinforcement of the adverbial forms, reinforcing the location function of the words. The term gesture can refer to any body part that can be moved directionally (hands, lips, nose, tongue, etc.). But it is largely used to indicate hand movements and actions, that both communicate or represent something. Some gestures have an iconic function, rather than an indexical one (as with the pointing finger) employed instinctively to represent the shape of, say, a round object, with the hands moving together in clockwise (the right hand) and counter-clockwise (the left hand) directions. Many other gestures, however, are used for carrying out interactional protocols such as greeting, affirmation, negation, etc.

## 6.1 Functions of Gesture

As the twentieth-century linguist Edward Sapir (1949: 555) astutely observed, gestures are "an elaborate and secret code that is written nowhere, known to none, and understood by all." This statement encapsulates the intuitive perception in people that gesture is understandable by virtually everyone, no matter what language they speak. While this is certainly true to a great extent, of all the kinesic systems, gesture is the one that is actually more culture-specific than the others—an aspect of NVC that was noticed by Darwin already in the nineteenth century. As Paul Ekman (2009: 3449) remarks:

> While Darwin proposed that facial expressions of emotion are universal, he also proposed that gestures are culture-specific conventions. This has proven to be correct. The same hand movement, for example the first finger touching the thumb to form a circle in the North American 'A-OK' gesture, has a radically different meaning in other countries. Totally different gestures may be used to signal the same message, as in the example of 'good luck' signalled by crossed fingers in North America and thumbs inserted into the fist in Germany. And there are messages for which there is a gesture in one country and no gesture in another country.

Generally, gestures can be grouped into *descriptive, emphatic, suggestive,* and *cuing* categories—other classifications will be discussed below. The first type (also known as iconic) is used to clarify or enhance a message. It often involves using the hands to draw outlines or indicate actions in terms of their size, shape, movement, etc., such as moving the hands laterally apart to indicate growth or size increase. Emphatic gestures are used to underscore something—for example, a clenched fist suggests some strong emotion, such as anger or conviction. A suggestive gesture is designed to elicit a certain thought or mood—for instance, an offering hand might accompany words of advice or the imparting of some thought, whereas a shoulder shrug might indicate perplexity or sarcasm. The open palm gesture is another suggestive one. Its meaning depends on the position of the palm—an upward palm implies giving or receiving; a downward palm can mean secrecy or stability; an outward-oriented palm suggests halting or negation; a perpendicular palm tends to imply limits comparisons, or conflict. Cuing gestures are used to elicit (cue) a desired response—for instance, raising one's hands and clapping them invites an audience to also clap their hands.

As in all forms of signing, context plays a major role in what a gesture means. Consider the common gesture of pointing the index finger. If it accompanies an utterance such as *look over there*, then it has a reinforcement function, directing the interlocutor's attention to something in the immediate environment. It is a locational indexical sign that relates referents to sign-users in spatial contexts, used with words such as *this, that, here* or *there*. The indexicality can also be formulaic or metaphorical, as can be seen in the use of this gesture in expressions such as: *Here is my point; There is no reason for saying this;* etc. which are accompanied typically by an instinctive pointing gesture. The movement of the hand either in front or behind the head, on the other hand, is more technically a temporal index, accompanying such adverbs such as *before, after, now,* or *then*. If pointing at someone while saying *He is my friend*, then it is an identification index, designed to relate the participants involved in a specific situation or context to each other. If the gesture involves drawing the outline of a circle, then it is an iconic sign, as mentioned, that is, a sign referring to something circular or abstract by pointing to it in the mind. This type of gesture accompanies expressions such as *You're talking in circles* or *This is a roundabout way of talking*.

As the foregoing discussion implies, semiotically, gestures have three main functions, identified first by Charles Peirce (1931–58)—iconic, indexical, and symbolic. An iconic gesture is one whose physical form is made to resemble the referent or referential domain, such as the circular motion of the hand to stand for something that has a circular shape. As mentioned, the pointing finger is an example of an indexical gesture. When we point to something, we are in fact relating it to our location (or that of others) as pointers. If we point to ourselves, then we are referring indexically to the Self; pointing it at someone else is an indication of a Self-Other relation. Making the sign of the cross is a symbolic gesture in Christianity. Although it represents the figure of a cross on which Christ was crucified iconically, it is interpreted historically and conventionally as a sign standing for the religion that was founded after Christ's death.

As mentioned, gesture languages have been devised to replace vocal languages, called sign languages. In American Sign Language (ASL), for instance, the sign for "catch" is formed with one hand (in the role of agent) moving across the body (an action) to grasp the forefinger of the other hand (the receiver). ASL kinemic forms are made by one or both hands, which assume distinctive shapes and movements. Figure 6.1 shows the signs that correspond to alphabet characters in sign language.

**Figure 6.1** The alphabet in sign language (Wikimedia Commons).

As Goldin-Meadow (2003: 94) has aptly observed, "sign languages assume the structural properties characteristic of spoken languages." Interestingly, sign languages exist in hearing communities as well. One of the best-known examples of this type of sign language is the one used by the Plains people of North America, which functions as a means of communication between tribes with different vocal languages. The gestures used represent things in nature, ideas, emotions, and sensations. For instance, the sign for a white person is formed by drawing the index and third fingers across the forehead, indicating a hat. Special signs also exist for each tribe for particular topological referents (rivers, mountains, etc.). The sensation of cold is communicated by means of a shivering gesture in front of the body; the same sign is used for winter and year, because the Plains peoples count years in terms of winters. Turning the hand in a slow, relaxed fashion means vacillation, doubt, or possibility; a quicker movement is the question sign (Mallery 1972).

Gestures are also used for sacred ritualistic or symbolic purposes. For example, as mentioned, in Christianity the sign of the cross is a gesture that aims to recreate the central event of Christianity—the Crucifixion. In Buddhism, the gestures known as *Mudras* are used during ceremonies to represent an array of embedded meanings, including meditation, reasoning, doctrine, protection, request, enlightenment, unification of matter, and spirituality. The devil's hand, with the index and little finger raised, on the other hand, belongs to the domain of mysticism, magic, and superstition. In some cultures, it represents a horned figure intended to ward off the evil eye and in others a sign of cuckoldry.

Gestures have been studied by philosophers and orators since antiquity (Kendon 1982). For example, the Roman rhetorician Marcus Fabius Quintilianus discussed how gesture could be used to reinforce oratory—prefiguring the current work on gestures during speech. One of the first scientific studies of gesture was undertaken in 1644 by English physician John Bulwer, who discussed and analyzed the formation and communicative functions of dozens of gestures. Bulwer's illustration of common gestures (captioned in Latin) is worth reproducing here since it is one of the first on record (Figure 6.2).

In the nineteenth century an Italian antiquarian, Andrea de Jorio (1832), published an extensive scientific treatment of gestures and their role in everyday communication in Naples, a city that is known popularly and anecdotally as a "gesture culture" by many other Italians. De Jorio showed that there was an intrinsic connection between gesture, symbolism, and Neapolitan culture. One of the examples he used is instructive—namely, the *fare le corna* gesture—the horn gesture, which is also a symbol for the devil's hand (as discussed briefly in the previous chapter).

De Jorio (1832: 92–4, 113) traced its origin to ancient Neapolitan culture, where it had the following meanings—most of which continue to this day in that culture:

1 *Marital infidelity*. De Jorio writes that this meaning comes from referring to a victim of infidelity traditionally by pointing to an animal with horns. According to De Jorio, the Greeks used the same gesture with the same meaning.
2 *Threat*. When the hand is kept in a horizontal position, the sign indicates a threat to take out one's eyes. De Jorio points out that this

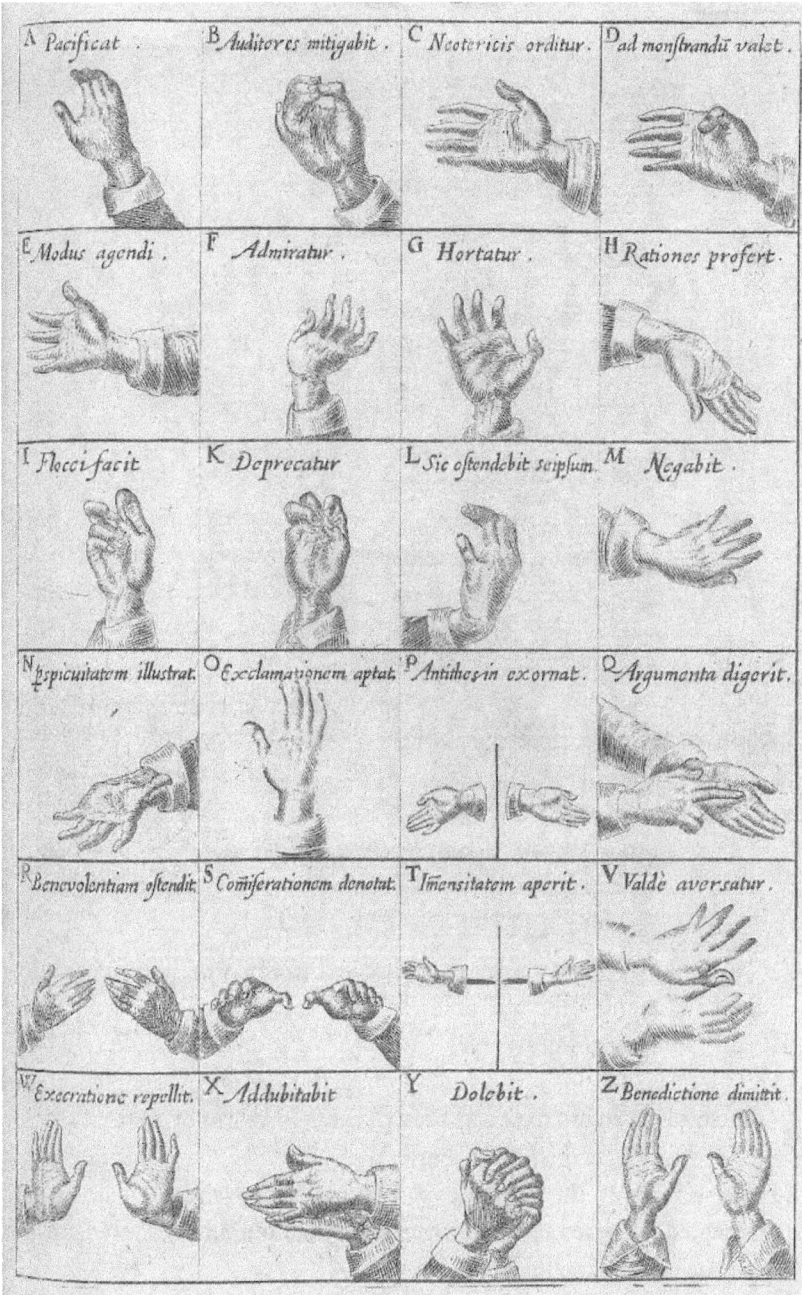

**Figure 6.2** Common Hand Gestures, John Bulwer, 1644 (Public Domain).

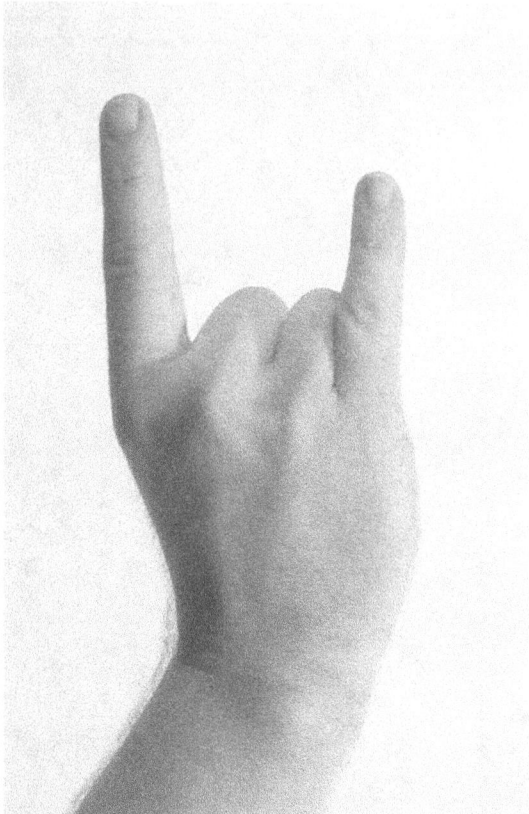

**Figure 6.3** The sign of the horns (Wikimedia Commons).

particular form of the gesture, directed towards the face of another person, implies the threat to scratch that person's eyes out used commonly in antiquity.

3 *Protection.* De Jorio notes that when the gesture is directed at the person who might have cast the evil eye, it is a form of gestural amulet as protection against the evil eye.

4 *Curse.* This is the opposite of the previous—when the horns are directed at someone, with fingers stretched out and an irate face, the gesture implies an imprecation.

Today, this gesture has become widespread, beyond Naples and even Italy. Roger Axtell (1991: 119) writes that "most Texans will recognize this gesture (fist raised with index finger and little finger extended) as a University of Texas rallying call because it mimics the horns of the school's symbol and mascot, the famous Texas Longhorn steer." He adds that in Africa, it can mean the levying of a curse (as it does in Naples). And in Brazil and Venezuela, the same gesture is considered a good luck sign to ward off evil (also as in Naples). "For still another interpretation," Axtell adds, "consider this. When I was a child in my home state of Wisconsin, my buddies and I used this very same gesture, but to us it meant neither the evil eye or good luck. Instead we were saying B.S. or, putting it more literally, 'You're full of horse manure.'" (Axtell 1991: 54).

Classifying and studying gestures according to communicative function and as related to vocal speech has become a central topic of interest within several disciplines, including semiotics, linguistics, anthropology, and psychology. There are two main kinds of gestural communicative functions—vocal-language-related (called co-speech gesture) and vocal-language-independent. An early investigation of these functions was the one by David Efron (1941), who described how gestures relate to the content of speech—an approach adopted later by Ekman and Friesen (1969a, 1969b) among others.

A pioneer in the research of co-speech gesturing, Adam Kendon (1972; 2004) has established precise structural correlations between gestures and words during speech. He called co-speech gestures *lexical*, since they are intended to amplify or modulate the lexical content of the speech act with which they co-occur. The contrasting view is that such gestures do not reflect lexical content but serve the pragmatic functions of speech (for example, Gillespie et al. 2014). It is more correct to say that lexical gestures serve both purposes—pragmatic and lexical. In fact, it is almost impossible (in the present author's view) to separate the two functions, given that vocabulary is used in speech acts to serve specific pragmatic intentions. Another way to connect the two functions is as *informative* versus *communicative*. The former refers to those co-speech gestures that provide visual information about the content or intent of the utterance. They do not alter the content of the message—they highlight the informational content of the message. A communicative gesture is one that is produced meaningfully and intentionally as a way of emphasizing, reinforcing, or complementing verbal speech. For example, pointing to a lectern as a symbol of authority during some utterance is a communicative gesture.

As Kendon (2010: 51–4) has shown, a common communicative function of gesture is to ensure smooth turn-taking in conversations, along with "features of voice, semantic and grammatical organization, and aspects of visible action that might serve as signals by which the participants might achieve smooth coordination of turns" (Kendon 2010: 52). As we saw (Chapter 3), turn-taking also involves patterns of gaze direction. As Kendon (2010: 53) observes, "it becomes clear that participants do pattern their movements and gaze directions in a fashion that is highly coordinated with their speech and in ways that are consistent with the hypothesis that such movements are often relied upon by co-participants as cues." Other kinemic supports to speech include head-nodding and haptic signing (discussed previously).

The second main category—vocal-language-independent gesture, rather than co-speech gesture—involves the use of gesture for specific communicative purposes, in lieu of speech. It includes gestures such as the greeting gesture with the right hand, the signaling gesture for the bill at a restaurant, crossing fingers for good luck, the waving gesture for phatic protocols such as greeting or saying goodbye, the gestures used in mime and pantomime, etc..

The research on child development is strongly suggestive of a link between the types of gestures used and the acquisition of verbal language. One major study in this area is Meltzoff and Moore's (1977), which examined how gesture and vocal language developed in tandem, via imitation of adult gesturing and speaking. The researchers argued that gestures directly transformed thoughts into gesture forms, which accompanied attempts at vocal speech. Children will typically point to objects of which they do not know the name. After learning the appropriate verbal labels, they tend to eliminate the relevant gesture—a fact that supports a gesture-to-language cognitive flow of acquisition. But gesture does not disappear with the growth of control over verbal language, with language-dependent (lexical) gestures becoming increasingly prominent in verbal interactions. If we adopt an evolutionary paradigm for the sake of argument, then it can be hypothesized that the instinctive ability to use the hands for grasping and pointing was achieved by our hominid ancestors after they developed they ability to walk upright. This liberated the hands from the requirements of locomotion, allowing early humans to make tools, to use fire, and for signaling. Vocal language came later. And the two reveal to this day an intrinsic interconnection that comes out saliently in childhood development.

## 6.2 Gesticulants

In 1992, linguist David McNeill discussed and illustrated, in his book *Hand and Mind*, based on ten years of research, the systematic connections between co-speech gestures and the content of utterances. He followed this up in 2005 with an in-depth treatment of gesture as a co-current system with vocal language.

In his fieldwork, McNeill videotaped a large number of people as they spoke, gathering a substantial amount of data on how gesture complements vocal language. To separate language-independent gesture from the co-speech one, he adopted the term *gesticulant,* introduced by Adam Kendon in 1972, to refer to the latter. McNeill's findings suggest that gesticulants are integrated semantically and cognitively to verbal communication, exhibiting images that cannot be shown overtly in speech, as well as images of what the speaker is thinking about. Speech and gesticulation thus constitute a single integrated communication system in which both cooperate to express the person's meanings. They might also reveal how cognition unfolds through both verbal and gestural images.

McNeill subdivided the gesticulants into five main categories:

1 *Iconic:* hand movements that mirror or simulate in form what is being said. For example, McNeill found that when someone was describing a scene in which a character bent a tree back to the ground, the speaker's right hand performed a movement of gripping something in the air and pulling it back. This action was a manual depiction of tree bending. Common examples are the circular hand movements when talking about roundabout reasoning; moving the hands far apart when talking of something large; moving both the head and hands in an upward direction when saying *Let's go up*; etc.
2 *Metaphoric:* hand movements that depict the vehicles or image schemas of metaphorical utterances. For instance, McNeill observed a speaker who was talking about a cartoon, simultaneously cupping his hands and putting them forth as if he were offering it as an object to his listener. This type of gesticulant is common when conduit metaphors are involved—*presenting an idea, putting forth an argument, offering advice,* and so on.
3 *Beat:* hand actions that resemble the beating of musical tempo, whereby speakers flick a hand or fingers up and down, or back and forth, to accompany the rhythmic pulsation of speech. Beats mark the introduction of new concepts in an utterance. They are used commonly when "making points"—*first . . . second . . . and lastly.*
4 *Cohesive:* repeating hand actions to emphasize that the separate parts of an utterance hold together.

5 *Deictic*: hand actions that indicate something that had been mentioned earlier in the conversation, such as waving a hand near the ear and shoulder to indicate that something has passed.

McNeill's gesticulant categories are subtypes of illustrators, discussed in Chapter 2 (Efron 1941; Anderson 1999; Ekman 2003). These can be defined generically as instinctive co-speech hand and arm movements that illustrate the content (literal and metaphorical) of vocal utterances. As such, they provide a basis for studying how gesture and language suggest each other in normal discourse. As Frutiger (1989: 112) has observed, accompanying gestures reveal an inner need to support what one is saying orally: "If on a beach, for example, we can hardly resist drawing with the finger on the smooth surface of the sand as a means of clarifying what we are talking about."

This type of research also has implications for language acquisition in childhood, since gesticulants develop along with vocal speech in an integrated fashion, with each gesticulant matching a so-called "growth point" in verbal acquisition (McNeill et al. 2008). McNeill (1992: 200) defined this as follows:

> The growth point is the speaker's minimal idea unit that can develop into a full utterance together with a gesture. The content of the growth point tends to be the novel departure of thought from the presupposed background. It is the element of thought that stands out in the context and may be the point of greatest relevance. The concept of the growth point unites image, word and pragmatic content into a single unit.

The growth point is used as evidence that gesticulants and speech content occur at the same point, literally, during acquisition. Jan de Ruiter (2006) provided corroborative evidence by witnessing the same pattern of growth points in aphasics, who replace words with gesticulants at first but, by continued growth point association, develop the ability to synchronize the two modalities. Work by Morsella and Krauss (2004), however, presents contrasting evidence that gesticulation and speech are not coincident cognitively, but rather that the primary role of gesture in speech is to facilitate lexical retrieval. This type of work can actually be traced to Adam Kendon (1980), who showed that gesticulation and speech involve a sequential organization of the gesticulant, which he called the *stroke*:

1 *Preparation*: phase introducing the stroke, with the hands preparing for the hand movement;
2 *Retraction*: if initiated, the stroke may be withdrawn for some reason with the hands moving back in a rest position;

3 *Gesticular:* phase composed of the preparation and the stroke.
4 *Gesture unit*: which is "demarcated as extending from the moment the excursion of the limb to the moment when the limb is in rest again.

Research has shown that there is, in fact, a synchronization of the stroke with the co-occurring speech, creating a "gesture-speech ensemble" (Kendon 2004: 127). The gist of such research is that speech and gesture are intertwined in specific ways and that gesture itself may guide speech, or at least, reinforce it. The work corroborates, overall, the bimodality principle adopted in this book—namely, that verbal and nonverbal communication are integrated physically, cognitively, and emotionally, with one reflecting the other.

## 6.3 Gesture and Vocal Language

The foregoing discussion leads to the topic of the relation between vocal language and gesture, both structurally and in terms of how both may have originated in tandem, given that they are processed by regions in the cortex that are responsible for mouth and hand movements, which border each other (Corballis 2010). Termed *gestural theory*, this view of language origins actually goes back to the eighteenth and nineteenth centuries, starting with the work of philosopher Abbé de Condillac (Danesi 1993). To be able to connect the two modalities—vocal speech and gesture—Kendon (2003) proposed a continuum between the two, from less linguistic (and more gestural) to fully linguistic (and less gestural). Gestures that can be placed on different relative locations on the continuum include gesticulations, pantomimic gestures, emblems, and the gestures used in sign languages.

The gestural hypothesis is supported anecdotally by the common occurrence that when vocal communication is not possible between speakers of different languages, the interlocutors instinctively resort to gesture to carry out the communicative event (as best as can be achieved in this way). So, if one were to describe, say, an automobile, not knowing the appropriate word in some language, one would tend to use the hands to portray a steering wheel and the motion used to steer a car, accompanying this gesture, perhaps, with an imitative motor vocalization. This type of event suggests that gesture is a fundamental mode of nonverbal communication, felt to be less culture-dependent than vocal language and, thus, by inference a predecessor of the latter. Many gestures are indeed instinctive, including the use of the index finger to point to things, representing the shape of objects with the hands, and so on. But, as discussed, this is not a general principle.

The earliest version of gesture theory, which has become a point of reference for all subsequent ones, was formulated by the eighteenth-century philosopher Jean-Jacques Rousseau (1966). Rousseau became intrigued by the origins of language while seeking to understand what he called the "noble savage." He proposed that the natural cries that early humans must have shared with the animals, and the gestures that they used in tandem, led to the invention of vocal language. He explained the evolutionary transition simply in this way: When the gestures proved to be too cumbersome, their corresponding cries replaced them. Rousseau also proposed what certainly must have been a radical idea for his era—that metaphor was not a mere stylistic variant for a more basic literal mode of expression, but rather, a cognitive remnant of a previous, and hence more fundamental, stage in the evolution of the rational mind, constituting the verbal-mental counterpart of physical gestures (Rousseau 1966: 12):

> As man's first motions for speaking were of the passions, his first expressions were tropes. Figurative language was the first to be born. Proper meaning was discovered last. One calls things by their true name only when one sees them in their true form. At first only poetry was spoken; there was no hint of reasoning until much later.

But this view left a huge evolutionary gap: How did gesture develop into speech systematically, not just in terms of single gesture-metaphor correlations? And even in the case of the latter, how did it come about? It was in the early part of the twentieth century that Richard Paget (1930) attempted to fill-in the gap by relating gesture to movements in the buccal articulatory organs, known as *mouth-gesture* theory. Paget claimed that manual gestures were copied unconsciously (osmotically) by positions and movements of the lips and tongue. The continual apposition of gestures and imitative vocal movements led eventually to the replacement of the former by the latter (Paget 1930: 24):

> Human speech arose out of a generalized unconscious pantomimic gesture language—made by the limbs as a whole (including the tongue and lips)—which became specialized in gestures of the organs of articulation, owing to the hands becoming continually occupied with the use of tools. The gestures of the organs of articulation were recognized by the hearer because the hearer unconsciously reproduced in his mind the actual gesture which had produced the sound.

But, even though Paget's theory does indeed plausibly explain how gestures may have been transformed into vocal sounds, and although it has been shown to be compatible with brain and vocal tract evolution (Hewes 1973; 1976), it ignores a whole range of rudimentary questions: What feature of the brain made the transition from gesture to vocalism possible? Why has gesture survived as a communicative subsystem? How did syntax develop out of the oral substitutes for gestures? It could well be part of a larger form of osmosis triggered during work activities. The term osmosis is used here in reference to the unconscious assimilation of behavior apprehended in relation to cognitively meaningful stimuli. As the Russian neurologist Luria (1970: 80) outlines: "There is every reason to believe that speech originated in productive activity and arose in the form of abbreviated activities which represented work activities." Many grunts too could have become words during such osmotic activities, as Stross (1976: 22) explains:

> Groups of early humans, straining with the intense and common effort necessary to move a fallen log or other such occupation, came to emit spontaneous grunts which were partly consonantal and which would eventually be used to signal common exertion in much the same way that today we use "heave" or "pull" in group lifting or pulling efforts. Eventually the grunts used for coordinating the efforts of many persons in a rhythmic way came to be associated with the work performed and then to stand for the work itself in symbolic communication.

Several types of evidence are now used support gesture theory: (1) gesture and vocal language depend on the same neural systems; (2) gesture precedes and then complements vocal language in childhood development; and (3) non-human primates can use gestures for some forms of communication with humans (discussed below). Of course, various other language-origin scenarios have been put forth, which need not concern us here, given that the focus is on gesture. Actually, the most plausible one is offered by Kendon (2017), whereby the two modalities—gesture and vocalism—evolved together, much like mouth-gesture theory. As a particular gesture is used pragmatically, the other organs seem to accompany it in tandem, with the vocal organs activated simultaneously. There is also evidence today from neuroscience that gesture lessens the cognitive-semantic load on the brain during interactions (Willems and Hagoort 2007). The brain first processes the meanings of gestures, extracting the grammatical relations in them in a connected or distributed fashion throughout the brain (Hickock, Bellugi, and Klima 2001). But visual stimuli that carry different information—such as the features of a drawing—are converted into neuronal activities that are involved in motor commands for reproducing the drawing.

## 6.4 Gesture in Non-Human Primates

Gestures are not unique to humans—they are used by non-human primates, a fact that links the two species communicatively (Corballis 2009). This led in the middle part of the twentieth century to the formulation of an intriguing question: If primates can use gesture, can this modality be used to teach them human language? Since gorillas and chimpanzees are incapable of full vocal speech because they lack the requisite vocal tract anatomy, the experimenters chose a sign language, such as American Sign Language, as the means for answering this question at first. Later, they used other non-vocal means such as lexigrams, or symbols representing words, a technique producing *Yerkish*, which requires the primates to use a keyboard to punch keys with the lexigrams on it. Yerkish was developed by psychologist Ernst von Glasersfeld (1974) and used by Duane Rumbaugh and Sue Savage-Rumbaugh to train a chimp called Lana (Rumbaugh 1977; see also Bettoni 2007). In addition to determining whether primates can learn human language, the experiments have also made it possible to address other evolutionary questions: What kinds of things can animals do without language, and can they do them better after language training? Can the results of the experiments be applied to human children who may be having difficulties in acquiring language? What is in the minds of primates, and can this be discovered via the experiments? Is human language truly unique?

One of the first primates taught human language with ASL was a female chimpanzee named Washoe, whose training by Allen and Beatrix Gardner (Gardner and Gardner 1969; 1975) began in 1966 when Washoe was almost one year of age. The Gardners fashioned Washoe's environment to resemble one in which a human infant with non-hearing parents would be reared, using communicative strategies that paralleled those that the children of such parents would likely be exposed to. For example, Washoe was taught the ASL sign for *toothbrush* through repeated usage, associating it with the relevant object. Washoe was also constantly encouraged to use gestures expressing certain needs or desires, such as the ASL *give-me* and *come-here* gestural kinemes. The Gardners used instrumental reward teaching throughout. For example, they taught the word *more* by tickling Washoe.

A sign was deemed to have been acquired by Washoe if observed by three independent observers as having been applied meaningfully to an appropriate context without prompting, and used at least once a day for fifteen consecutive days. The signs so learned were added to a checklist that was used to record the learning process. Washoe learned to use a few hundred ASL signs in just over 4 years, using them spontaneously in rudimentary sentences such as *Washoe sorry, Baby down, Go in, Hug hurry,* and *Out open please hurry,* which resembled the early speech of children, which is at first *holophrastic* (one-word) serving three basic functions: (1) naming an object; (2) expressing an action or a desire for some action; and (3) conveying emotional states. Gradually, the holophrases evolve into a so-called *pivot* grammar, in which two main classes of words, called the *pivot* class and an *open* class, allow the child to express thoughts in terms of a rudimentary syntax. In Washoe's sentences, the pivot signs included *down, in, hurry,* etc., while the open ones were the larger lexical concepts. Remarkably, she also developed the ability to ask questions—*Time eat? What that? Where go?*

There was great enthusiasm over Washoe's development. A widely cited example of her creativity is the one when she saw a duck, an animal for which she had not learned a word, and for which she apparently devised the expression *water bird* for this purpose. Remarkably, when she was later given an infant chimpanzee to raise, named Loulis, it became obvious to the Gardners that she tried to teach him how to sign as well, which the baby chimp eventually learned to do, albeit to a limited extent.

The Washoe project is remarkable on several counts, of which the use of gesture as a primary form of communication stands out. In one recorded episode, Washoe was observed looking at herself in the mirror, when she was asked what she was seeing. Her answer was truly amazing: *Me, Washoe,* showing consciousness or awareness of self and, thus, reflective thinking. Washoe also seemed to enjoy playing with dolls, bathing them and talking to them, implying a human-like sense of imagination. She showed a sensitivity to socialization, brushing her teeth before partaking of tea parties and (amazingly) empathy for humans. One of her caretakers missed coming to work with Washoe because of a miscarriage. The effect this had on Washoe is truly astounding, as recounted by Fouts and Mills (1998: 190):

> Washoe greeted Kat [the caretaker] in just this way when she finally returned to work with the chimps. Kat made her apologies to Washoe, then decided to tell her the truth, signing *My baby died.* Washoe stared at her, then looked

down. She finally peered into Kat's eyes again and carefully signed *Cry*, touching her cheek and drawing her finger down the path a tear would make on a human (Chimpanzees don't shed tears). Kat later remarked that one sign told her more about Washoe and her mental capabilities than all her longer, grammatically perfect sentences.

So, did the Gardners' work with Washoe prove that primates can learn human language? Are primates and humans only separated by linguistic upbringing? If such upbringing is removed from humans, do they resort to a more primate-like form of communications and life, as seems to be the case with feral children? These questions remain largely unanswered. However, the publication of the Washoe experiments ignited scientific interest in both sign language and the acquisition of its gestural modalities by primates, since the experiments raised profound questions about the biological-emotional roots of language.

In the 1970s, a research team, headed by Herbert S. Terrace of Columbia University, also used ASL to train a chimp named Nim Chimpsky, in reference to linguist Noam Chomsky, who had been critical of primate language research efforts (Terrace 1979; 1983; Terrace et al. 1979). Nim acquired 125 signs and seemed to understand basic notions of syntax: for example, he put *more* before another word (*chocolate, tickle*) consistently to indicate quantity, as did Washoe. However, analysis of the videotapes of Nim show him using sentences such as *Give orange me give eat orange me eat orange give me eat orange give me you*, which are not consistent with ASL syntax. Terrace himself admitted that Nim showed none of the kind of linguistic competence needed for him to construct a human grammar. Nevertheless, in forty-four months of training, Nim Chimpsky learned to communicate effectively with his trainers, perhaps because, like Washoe, he was reared in a home environment by human surrogate parents.

Unlike the Gardners, Terrace ended up being skeptical about the ability of primates to acquire language, as a "doubly articulated" system, in which signs which develop for naming objects and states are then combined syntactically to produce meanings that appear to be understood uniquely by humans. In response Roger Fouts, who was a part of the Washoe Project, critiqued Terrace's work as poorly conducted because it was based mainly on conditioning rather than on social-emotive exchanges with Nim.

ASL was also used by Francine Patterson of Stanford University in the same time frame to teach language to a female gorilla named Koko (Patterson 1978; Patterson and Linden 1981; Ward 1999). Patterson went a step further than the other experimenters by claiming that Koko could form many types of sentences and, most amazingly, could understand and produce puns, jokes, and even lies. Patterson also reported that Koko had acquired an active vocabulary of more than 1,000 signs, which is similar to the number of lexical items acquired by a three-year-old child (Law 2017). Patterson simultaneously exposed Koko to spoken English early on, and it seemed that Koko was able to comprehend around 2,000 words of spoken English, in addition to the ASL signs.

As with other primate language experiments, the extent to which Koko mastered and demonstrated competence in human language continues to be disputed. Patterson also reported that Koko made several complex signs of her own that suggested a higher degree of cognition than is usually attributed to non-human primates. For example, Koko was seemingly able to refer to objects that were not present. Like Washoe, Koko was also able to recognize herself in a mirror and to use language deceptively or for humorous effects. Patterson also reported that Koko invented new signs for novel thoughts using human techniques such as analogical portmanteau. For example, she combined the signs for finger and bracelet, which she knew, to refer to a ring, which was an unknown object at the time—hence *finger-bracelet*.

Criticism of the Koko experiments was that there were no objective observers and so the whole interpretive process was that by Patterson herself, who may have seen improbable concatenations of signs as meaningful. Some also noted that Koko was likely being prompted by Patterson's unconscious cues to display specific signs, called the Clever Hans effect. Nevertheless, the overall experiment was truly remarkable and, while it did not answer the question of how gesture and language are intertwined phylogenetically, it was very suggestive of a connection.

Researchers David and Ann Premack (1976; 1981), took a different approach. Rather than using ASL, they used plastic tokens that had images on them of various referents to teach vocabulary to a chimp named Sarah, who showed the ability to associate the tokens to referents correctly. Moreover, Sarah was eventually able to use the tokens creatively and to associate the tokens with certain intents and ideas, such as negation and even counterfactual thoughts (*if-then*). Overall, the Premacks claimed that Sarah had demonstrated aspects of linguistic behaviors and human cognitive growth that were similar to those of children acquiring language in human context.

Researchers Duane and Sue Rumbaugh used Yerkish to teach chimpanzees and bonobos in a laboratory (Rumbaugh 1977). In one case study, they had apparently taught two chimps to engage in a conversation. For example, one of the chimps was allowed to observe a trainer hide an item of food in a container. The chimp knew through previous training how to press a key on a computer keyboard with the symbol for the food item in question, which could be seen by a second chimp. The second chimp was then able, on the basis of the first chimp's keyboard signal, to locate the food item. Another chimp, named Kanzi, apparently learned by eavesdropping on the keyboard lessons given by one of Rumbaughs to his adoptive mother. One day, Kanzi was asked: *Can you make the dog bite the snake?* Kanzi had never heard this sentence before. In response, he rummaged among toys present in the room, until he found a toy dog and a toy snake, putting the snake in the dog's mouth, in imitation of a biting gesture (Savage-Rumbaugh 1976; Savage-Rumbaugh, Rumbaugh, and Boysen 1983; Savage-Rumbaugh et al. 1983). This type of learning behavior is truly remarkable, corroborating the work of the Gardners in particular. Jensvold and Gardner (2000) similarly found that chimps learn to apply their learning to new situations. In their experiments, a researcher would bring up a specific topic and then ask a chimpanzee a relevant question on the topic. Jensvold and Gardner claim that the chimps were able to understand and expand upon simple questions, in ways that are similar to how children respond to questions. Some experimenters have even tried to teach chimps to articulate actual words. Keith and Cathy Hayes, for example, were apparently successful in teaching a chimp named Viki how to utter a few words, such as *mama, papa, cut,* and *up* (see Urban 2002).

What is even more extraordinary is that teaching non-human animals language may be possible in species other than the primates. For instance, Epstein, Lanza, and Skinner (1980) were able to get the same kind of behaviors from two pigeons, named Jack and Jill. The pigeons were put in adjoining cages with a transparent wall between them. Jack was in a position to peck a key labeled *What color?* as a cue for Jill to look behind a curtain with three lights—red, green, and yellow—that were not visible to Jack. After ascertaining which light was illuminated, Jill pecked one of three keys—R, G, or Y—which Jack could see. Jack then responded by pecking a key labeled *Thank you*, whereupon Jill was given a food reward.

Despite the enthusiasm with such experiments, the question of whether or not non-human animals can learn human language remains an open one. In some cases, the trainers may have read much more in the behaviors of their subjects than was really there. The Gardners had hired a hearing-impaired ASL user to help train Washoe. Later on he made the following comment (cited in Pinker 1994: 37):

Every time the chimp made a sign, we were supposed to write it down in the log. They [the Gardners] were always complaining because my log didn't show enough signs. I watched really carefully. The chimp's hands were moving constantly. Maybe I missed something, but I don't think so. The hearing people were logging every movement the chimp made as a sign. Every time the chimp put his hand in his mouth, they'd say "Oh, he's making the sign for drink," and they'd give him some milk. When the chip scratched himself, they'd record it as the sign for scratch. Sometimes the trainers would say, "Oh, amazing, look at that, it's exactly like the ASL sign for give!" It wasn't.

This might have been an isolated incident, however. All told, the experiments are important and relevant not only for attempting to fathom the minds of non-human primates, but also for understanding how gesture is related to verbal and cognitive development in humans. The underlying question that this whole line of experimentation begs is the following one: If the primates had a vocal apparatus similar to that of humans, would they have been able to transfer the gestural forms they learned to it, and thus speak? This answer remains necessarily elusive.

## 6.5 Gesture and Dance

As a system of coordination of hands, arms, head, and other bodily parts, dancing is a form of NVC, which emerges in the rites and celebrations of early human cultures. It can be characterized as *total body gesture*, serving ritualistic, ceremonial, sacred, aesthetic, or other functions. Nine-thousand-year-old paintings in India and 5,000-year-old Egyptian tomb paintings depicting dancing figures indicate that dancing emerged as a form of nonverbal communication early on in human history (Schafer 1951).

As Hanna (2010: 93) observes, dancing involves all faculties and is akin to an autonomous language with a complete grammar:

> Human dance is a form of thought, emotion, and action. Compared with other animal nonverbal communication, dance serves a wider variety of purposes with greater complexity in open lexical, semantic, and syntactic systems. Humans have a greater potential for motor variety, control and learning, and also for creative manipulation of patterns within rules, so that individuals and groups can select a variety of styles and structures. Although nonhumans may be trained to perform human-like dances, there is no evidence that they can create meaning and transmit to other animals

dance sequences that are physically, affectively, or symbolically complex. Nor is there data that nonhumans reflect upon dance and leave something representing it that lingers beyond their lifetime, e.g., drawings, sculpture, notation, or film of dance.

Dancing is common to all peoples and cultures. Its main functions can be summarized as follows:

1. It is a body-gestural means of expressing emotions, moods, ideas, or telling a story.
2. It may have an aesthetic function; that is, it can give pleasure.
3. It can be part of communal rituals. In some traditional cultures, spirit dances continue to be part of village life, designed primarily to exorcise evil spirits.
4. It can be a form of recreation.
5. It can be part of ceremonial occasions, such as weddings, symbolizing union, among other things.
6. It can be part of courtship rites or a means of attracting partners through the dance itself.

Some researchers see dancing as a residue of movement for survival—it is harder to attack moving prey. This notion goes back to Darwin, who articulated it in his 1871 book, *The Descent of Man*, in which he remarked that: "the perception, if not the enjoyment, of musical cadences and of rhythm is probably common to all animals and no doubt depends on the common physiological nature of their nervous systems." This animal mechanism can be seen in other species, as for example the so-called male Eleonora cockatoo, which is capable of beat induction, that is of synchronizing his body to the movements of beating. Dance-like actions can also be observed in monkeys and even in fiddler crabs, which sway their claws back and forth in dance-like displays and frogs, which gesture rhythmically with their legs. There is little doubt that the cockatoo, the crab, or the frog are moving to rhythmic urges, for some survival function, such as mating or foraging (recall the example of bee dancing). And it is true that their gestures appear to unite species in a "dance." But humans alone seem to be capable of acquiring dance rhythms for pleasurable reasons alone—a theme that seems to be central in Edgar Degas' famous *Dance Class* painting (Figure 6.4).

The imaginary scene depicts the abandonment to rhythmic structure that characterizes a dance class—in this case under the tutelage of Jules Perrot, a famous Parisian ballet master. The effortlessness with which the dancers

**Figure 6.4** Edgar Degas, *The Dance Class*, 1874 (Wikimedia Commons).

appear to dance, and the sense of aesthetic importance that the movements elicit, are found nowhere else in the animal realm. The painting also suggests that dance in humans is voluntary, not necessarily instinctive. The coordination of gestural components—from the hands to the head—suggests as well how dancing may be a precursor to syntax as a phenomenon of "combinatory meaning," rather than just composite meaning (as Hanna above proposes). The basis of ballet is the fact that combinatory patterns of the arms, legs, head, and torso produce an emotive message for its own sake (not tied to any evolutionary prerequisite).

In sum, dance as total body gesture implies that gesture may indeed be a default form of communication based on osmotic responses to rhythm.

Repetitive movements seem, in fact, to characterize life—examples are the circadian rhythms, the regularity of seasonal change, etc. The dance may be a semiotic mirror of such regularities. Jordania (2011: 99) has cogently argued, in fact, that the sense of rhythm is a central part of human evolution, claiming that it was crucial for the survival of early hominids.

## 6.6 Epilogue

As discussed throughout this chapter, gesture is a mode of NVC aiding, substituting, or reinforcing vocal speech, and it is central to many cultural and symbolic activities, such as dancing. It a key component for understanding how human communication unfolds bimodally—verbally and gesturally. Research shows that gesture emerges around six months in infancy to facilitate interactions with adults. As children grow, their use of gesture becomes increasingly sophisticated and integrated with vocal speech. But throughout life, unwitting gesticulation remains instinctive in many interactions. When children tell a lie, they tend to cover the mouth with one or both hands immediately afterwards—a gesture that is used unwittingly later in life as well.

Like other forms of NVC, many gestural forms are high on a universality scale. Take the role of the palms in communication as a case-in-point. Research has shown that the open palm is associated with truth, honesty, allegiance, or submission in most cultures across the world (Cooperrider, Abner, and Goldin-Meadow 2018). When people aim to convey honesty, they will typically hold one or both palms out to the other person, saying something like *to be perfectly honest* or *to be open with you*, to accompany the gesture. When someone hides the palms (usually behind the back), as do children when they are lying, the person is generally trying to hide something or is not being open about something. At that point the body's lie detector system kicks in and a recognizable incongruence manifests itself with reactions such as fidgeting, sweating, and the like. Most people find it difficult, if not impossible, to lie with their palms exposed. Rubbing the palms together—to use another example of a cross-cultural gesture—is a way of communicating positive expectation. This is why people who throw a pair of dice in gambling rub their hands first. It is also the reason why masters of ceremonies tend to rub their palms as they announce to the audience *we are looking forward to our next speaker*. The speed at which a person rubs the hands signals the degree of expectation they bring to the situation—the greater the rubbing the more the expectation. For Cooperrider,

Abner, and Goldin-Meadow (2018), this gesture bears many implications for the study of NVC generally:

> During communication, speakers commonly rotate their forearms so that their palms turn upward. Yet despite more than a century of observations of such palm-up gestures, their meanings and origins have proven difficult to pin down. We distinguish two gestures within the palm-up form family: the palm-up presentational and the palm-up epistemic. The latter is a term we introduce to refer to a variant of the palm-up that prototypically involves lateral separation of the hands. This gesture—our focus—is used in speaking communities around the world to express a recurring set of epistemic meanings, several of which seem quite distinct. More striking, a similar palm-up form is used to express the same set of meanings in many established sign languages and in emerging sign systems. Such observations present a two-part puzzle: the first part is how this set of seemingly distinct meanings for the palm-up epistemic are related, if indeed they are; the second is why the palm-up form is so widely used to express just this set of meanings. We propose a network connecting the different attested meanings of the palm-up epistemic, with a kernel meaning of absence of knowledge, and discuss how this proposal could be evaluated through additional developmental, corpus-based, and experimental research. We then assess two contrasting accounts of the connection between the palm-up form and this proposed meaning network, and consider implications for our understanding of the palm-up form family more generally. By addressing the palm-up puzzle, we aim, not only to illuminate a widespread form found in gesture and sign, but also to provide insights into fundamental questions about visual-bodily communication: where communicative forms come from, how they take on new meanings, and how they become integrated into language in signing communities.

Another case-in-point is clenching the hands together in a central, raised, or lowered position (depending on whether the person is standing or sitting) to convey confidence. However, it can also communicate frustration if the clenching is robust to the point of turning the knuckles white. The palm-in-palm gesture (behind the back) is the most common of the gripping-clenching gestures—one hand grips the other wrist or arm as if to prevent it from striking out. The further the hand is moved up the arm, the angrier is the person likely to be. The folding and crossing of the arms send out specific kinds of signals. Folding them generally implies that the person has negative thoughts about the interlocutor and is thus paying less attention to what they are saying. Folding both arms together typically undergirds an attempt to hide from an unfavorable situation. It is also a negative sign in some situations, indicating that the person disagrees with what someone is saying. If the arms are gripped tightly it reveals a negative but restrained attitude. A variant of this sign is the partial arm gesture, with one hand holding the other near or at the elbow. This shows lack of self-confidence or humility. It is used typically by someone about to receive an award.

Whatever the function of such gestures, they seem to reveal a propensity to coordinate the body's movement to thoughts, feelings, rhythms, etc. Although vocal language is our primary mode of communication, the evolutionary link between speech and gesture is still clearly noticeable, as argued throughout this chapter. Gesture may also be connected to the evolution of drawing. The ability to draw the outlines of rudimentary figures emerges approximately at the same time as the first words. If a drawing instrument is put in a child's hand at this point in life, he or she will instinctively make random scribbles on a surface, much like the child would use gesture to represent something. As time passes, the scribbling becomes more and more controlled; shapes become suggestive of undeveloped figures that, with adult prompting, are soon labeled in some way (as "suns," "faces," and so on). At first, children do not appear to draw anything in particular, but instead spontaneously produce forms, which become refined through practice into precise, repeatable shapes. They draw for the pleasure of it, without larger or more explicit associations of meaning.

This type of early behavior may actually be a clue as to the origin of writing. A plausible scenario would be the following anecdotal one. Visual art (as discussed previously) goes back some 30,000 years and was probably the result of "iconic gesturing" being transferred by means of some sharp cutting tool to a cave wall—producing the vivid images of animals which cover the roofs and walls of caves all over the world—or to an object—producing the small sculptures of animals and female figures found at archeological sites. As the hand movements used to make such representations by our sapient ancestors became more abbreviated, they evolved into more condensed and abstract visual symbols. This led eventually to communication by means of pictographs—the first tokens of writing (Schmandt-Besserat 1992).

# 7
# Proxemics

## Chapter Outline

| | | |
|---|---|---|
| 7.0 | Prologue | 147 |
| 7.1 | Proxemic Analysis | 148 |
| 7.2 | Interpersonal Zones | 152 |
| 7.3 | Proxemics and Discourse | 155 |
| 7.4 | Perceived Proximity | 158 |
| 7.5 | Epilogue | 160 |

## 7.0 Prologue

The physical zones people maintain between themselves when speaking and interacting constitute a form of NVC that is based in part on universal mechanisms involving territoriality and partially on coded meanings. This can be confirmed anecdotally by observing situations wherein the zoning code that dictates how far apart interlocutors should be during an interaction is broken. For example, if a stranger were to initiate contact by standing right next to someone else, the likely reaction of that person would be a negative one, showing this (perhaps) by moving back away from the stranger. Anthropologist Edward T. Hall was the first to study this phenomenon scientifically, calling it a "silent language," as mentioned previously (Hall 1959). In the late 1950s, Hall started investigating the relevant body-to-body patterns that characterize F2F interactions, investigating and measuring the zones people maintain between themselves unconsciously. He called his approach *proxemics* (from Latin *proximus* "near"), defining it as follows: "the interrelated observations and theories of humans' use of space as a specialized elaboration of culture" (Hall 1966: 3).

Proxemics is the subject matter of this chapter. As in other chapters, a selection of topics and research findings has been made in order to keep the treatment within the confines of a textbook. Proxemic behavior is guided by both biology and culture. Everyone is able to detect the presence of others in the space around them with their sensory apparatus, and this has effects, ranging from feelings of protection to those of aggression, that are not unlike those of other animals. Goffman (1963) refers to this inner system of sensing as the detection of "co-presence," whereby humans emit "silent information" about themselves. Kendon (2010: 56) elaborates on this principle of interaction as follows:

> Once two or more individuals become able to detect each other by means of their unaided senses, they may be said to be *co-present*. In these circumstances, each is unavoidably a source of information for the other. Insofar as each acts upon the information each gains from the other, interaction can be said to take place. The *distance* that separates people when they are co-present will have a crucial influence upon the kinds of information that each can gather from the other. How people organize themselves spatially in interaction situations is thus a fundamental aspect of such situations and plays a crucial role in their structuring.

Proxemics aims to understand the meanings of the *distances* or *zones* that characterize interactions. It includes not only the physical zones that characterize F2F interaction, but also the spatial organization of the settings in which interaction takes place and by extension the broader organization of space as it manifests itself in architectural and city-building practices. As Hall (1963: 103) put it, proxemics aims to investigate "how man unconsciously structures microspace—the distance between humans in the conduct of daily transactions, the organization of space in his houses and buildings, and ultimately the layout of his towns."

## 7.1 Proxemic Analysis

As a soldier during World War II, Hall noticed repeatedly that people maintained distances between themselves during conversations that mirrored rank and relationship—two "buddy" soldiers would talk to each other at a closer distance than they would when talking to a superior. He came to the conclusion, anecdotally at first, that the size of the distance, or *zone*, fit a social pattern—the closer the interacting bodies were to each other, the less formal the relationship between the speakers; the farther away, the more formal. Moreover, he came to realize that many (if not most) breakdowns in communication and in relationships were attributable to infractions of these zone patterns.

While this may seem intuitively obvious to us today, no one before Hall had ever looked at this socio-communicative phenomenon closely and systematically, analyzing its kinemic structures and their meanings. As he began to study the zones, Hall came to the overall conclusion that the unconscious differences in the ways that people of diverse cultures perceive interpersonal zones, and the ways they behave within them, played a powerful role in influencing the outcomes of face-to-face interactions. To conduct his research, Hall measured and assessed these critical interpersonal zones with great accuracy, finding that they varied according to age, gender, social power dynamics, etc., and that they bore emotional effects—for instance, a distance of under six inches between two people was perceived virtually across the world as an "intimate" distance; while a distance at from 1.5 to 4 feet was the minimum one perceived to be a safe social distance. Intruding upon the limits set by these "hidden dimensions" caused considerable discomfort. For example, if a stranger were to talk at a distance of only several inches away from someone, that person would be considered rude or even aggressive in most cultures (as mentioned briefly above). If the "safe" distance is breached by some acquaintance, on the other hand, it might be interpreted as some kind of intentional infraction.

Overall, Hall identified four proxemic zones: *intimate, personal, social,* and *public*. The first two fall under the broad category of *microspace;* the *social* and *public* fall respectively under *mesospace* and *macrospace*. The latter includes public spaces, settlements, cities, and beyond: its features are called *fixed,* which includes such things as walls and territorial boundaries; *semi-fixed,* which includes mobile elements such as curtains and screens; and *dynamic,* which are objects that can move about in certain spaces, such as vehicles. Within the zones there are three reactive modes—*infra,* which is rooted in our "biological past" (Hall 1966: 95), and is thus based on our innate sense of territoriality; *pre,* which is rooted instead in sensory reactions (tactile, visual, etc.) to space and to people in spaces that are conditioned by culture-specific codes of space; and *micro,* which involves specific reactions to different zones.

The study of the interpersonal behaviors within the different zones is the target of proxemics, including bodily orientation, posture, gazing, and haptic-tactile behavior. For example, in the intimate zone, eye contact is more frequent and direct, but it is less so in other zones; leaning forward is common in intimate and personal zones, but not in social and public ones; the degree of touching is higher in intimate zones, but less so in other zones; and so on. Posture in each zone correlates to social role, as does sitting or standing. If someone is standing up at the front of an audience, that person is perceived as more important than those sitting down in terms of the event. Speeches, lectures, classes, musical performances, etc., are perceived in this way. Officials, managers, directors, etc., sit behind a desk to convey importance and superiority. Only their superiors can walk behind the desk to talk to them. To show "friendliness," the person behind the desk will have to come out and sit with his or her interlocutor in a different part of the room.

Hall identified a set of factors shaping proxemic behavior and the size of the zones people maintain between each other:

1  postural identifiers (standing vs. sitting);
2  gender identifiers (male vs. female);
3  sociofugal-sociopetal orientation (face-to-face, back-to-back);
4  kinesthetic factors (distances of body parts, within or beyond physical reach);
5  tactility factors (permissible touch patterns within each zone);
6  eye contact factors (gazing, looking away, looking directly into the eyes);
7  thermal factors (whether radiated heat is detected or not)
8  olfactory factors (detection of odor or breath);
9  vocal factors (loudness of voice, tone of voice).

Hall called the description of the factors as *proxetic* (in analogy with *phonetic* description in linguistics and *kinetic* description in kinesics), and the analysis of how these relate to each other meaningfully as *proxemic* (in analogy with *phonemic* analysis in linguistics and *kinemic* analysis in kinesics). The relevant *proxemes* (meaningful zone units) are determined by comparing them to each other within the broader framework of an interaction. As mentioned, what is especially interesting from the overall perspective of nonverbal communication study is that proxemic behavior meshes with other kinds of nonverbal behaviors, from tactility to eye contact. As discussed throughout this book, this implies that the various modalities of communication are not separate or autonomous, but integrated with each other.

Carrying out research on proxemic communication involves several phases such as (Hall 1959; 1963; 1964; 1966; 1968; 1974; 1983): (a) measuring the size of the zones maintained; (b) determining the social relation between interlocutors in correlation with these seizes; (c) recording and mapping the nonverbal behaviors (tactile, gestural, etc.) that characterized each zone against the social relationships of the interlocutors; (d) correlating the discourse level (formal, informal, etc.) to the zone structure; and (e) assessing and analyzing how the previous factors coalesced to define the outcome of the interaction. Hall also claimed that proxemics revealed how we come to penetrate each other's thoughts, extending the objective of proxemics as "the study of the ways in which man gains knowledge of the content of other men's minds through judgments of behavior patterns associated with varying degrees of proximity to them" (Hall 1964: 41). Research has largely confirmed the validity of the zones and their effects on communicative behaviors (Segaud 1973; Loof 1976; Pinxten, Van Dooren, and Harvey 1983). It should be noted that Hall never claimed that proxemics was a branch of any existing science, even though it certainly overlaps with disciplines such as psychology, anthropology, and semiotics. The classification of proxemics as a branch of semiotics started with Umberto Eco (1968: 344-9) and O. Michael Watson (1970; 1974; Watson and Anderson 1987).

The evolutionary source on which proxemic behavior is *territoriality*, defined by biologists as: (1) a survival mechanism that permits an animal to gain access to, and defend control of, critical resources (food, nesting sites, etc.), and (2) the instinctive need of an animal to procure a safe boundary around itself. The zoologist Konrad Lorenz (1952) was among the first to study territorial patterns among species, which, he claimed, were as important to an animal's survival and sense of security as were its physiological attributes developed from its morphogenetic evolution. Lorenz suggested that aggression in animals, including humans, is the result of an innate territorial imperative—a theory that became popularized in Robert Ardrey's 1966 book, *The Territorial Imperative*. The main implication was that, in order to maintain a safe boundary for protection and sanity, we will become aggressive and enter into conflicts to ensure it; as such this was used by some to explain the origin of war in human history. Hall also saw the psychological and social implications of territoriality, seeing it as the likely source for the zone patterns he observed in his research. It would explain, for instance, why microspace (the immediate physical zone around a human being) is so imbued with emotional resonance, constituting a territory that is fiercely protected, and why emotional intensity decreases as the interactional space between people expands. As psychoanalyst Jacques Lacan (1977: 16–17) observed, territorial boundaries mirrored "all the successive envelopes of the biological and social status of the person."

## 7.2 Interpersonal Zones

To reiterate, Hall described four main zones that define interpersonal interactions: intimate, personal, social, and public (Figure 7.1). For American culture, he found these to have the following dimensions:

1 *Intimate* (0 in.–1.5 ft.): reserved for family members, close friends, lovers, and all children (no matter their relationship to the individual);
2 *Personal* (1.5 ft.–4 ft.): reserved for informal conversations with friends, to interact with associates, or even for group discussions among acquaintances;
3 *Social* (4 ft.–10 or 12 ft.): reserved for strangers and new acquaintances;
4 *Public* (12 ft.–plus): reserved for events such as speeches, stage performances, and the like.

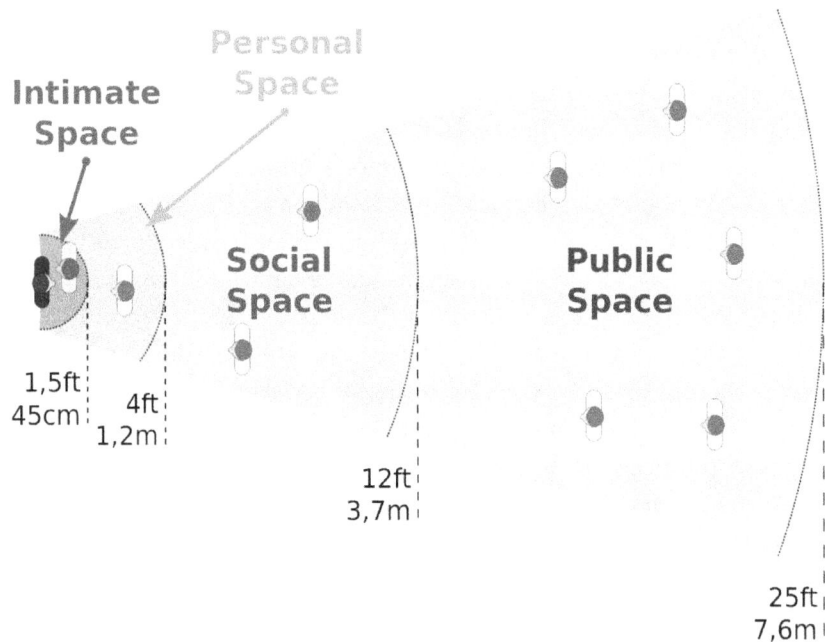

**Figure 7.1** Interpersonal zones (Wikimedia Commons).

Hall did not claim that his measurements precisely translated human behavior, but were rather a means to determine how interpersonal zones vary from culture to culture. He further subdivided the zones into *close* and *far* distances (within each zone). In the intimate zone, the close phase (0 in.-6 in.) is emotionally charged, reserved for romance, comforting, and protecting those with whom people are closely familiar, such as the core family, and the far phase (6 in.–18 in.) is the zone in which extended family members and intimate friends interact under normal conditions. In the personal zone, the close phase (1.5 ft.–2.5 ft.) is reserved for close friends, and the far phase (2.5 ft.–4 ft.), which is around one arm's length, for extended family members. Within the social zone, the close phase (4 ft.–6 or 7 ft.) is typical of casual interaction among acquaintances, while the far phase (7 ft.–12 ft.) is the maximum distance for social interaction to take place meaningfully, such as among colleagues and occasional acquaintances. In the public zone, the close phase (around 12 ft.–15 ft.) is the distance at which passers-by can be included, while the far phase (beyond 15 ft.) is the zone that allows for strangers to interact safely. Any of these distances can be breached or modified at various points in interactions—for example, greeting a stranger is performed at the public distance, but the interaction can eventually evolve to reduce the distance into a social one. The diagram in Figure 7.2 shows the social actors within the four zones.

The intimate-personal zone is violated in urban centers where crowds tend to form—as for example, in subways, in elevators, etc. So, the intimate-personal meanings of these zones are also breached—while most people

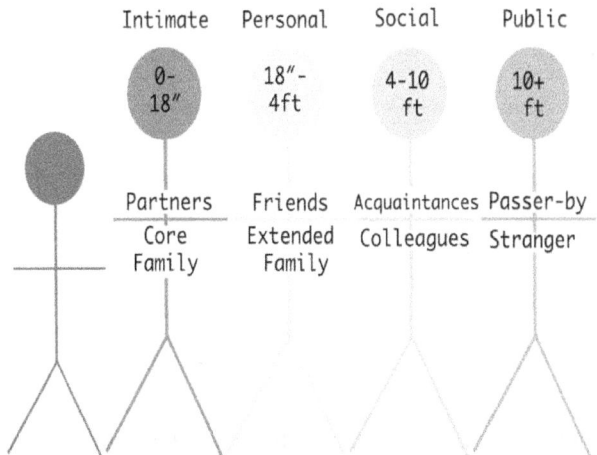

**Figure 7.2** Actors in the four zones (Wikimedia Commons).

would sense the physical proximity of strangers on subways or elevators to be uncomfortable, it is still accepted as a fact of modern-day city life. The situation is now felt as impersonal, and the factors above are adapted accordingly—for example, eye contact tends to be avoided and any non-accidental physical contact is perceived as an unwanted advance or threat. This suggests that we carry our personal space with us wherever we might be—it is a psychological-semiotic space that constitutes a form of self-definition and self-awareness (Richmond 2008). It is a residual territorial mechanism that is likely based in our evolution—located in the amygdala of the brain, which is involved in all forms of emotional responses. Body spacing and posture, as they unfold in a particular zone, are unconscious reactions to sensory fluctuations or shifts, as Hall called them, such as subtle changes in any one of the above factors—tone and pitch of voice, eye contact, etc.

The actual physical distances of the zones are called *horizontal*, and the associated social behaviors are called *vertical*. So, for example, looking up at or down on the other person generally coincides with social status (Richmond 2008). Needless to say, the regions of intimate-personal zones vary horizontally across cultures. For instance, personal zones with respect to strangers exceed 3.9 ft. (120 cm) in Romania, Hungary and Saudi Arabia, but have been found to be less than 2.9 ft. (90 cm) in Argentina, Peru, Ukraine, and Bulgaria (Sorokowska, Sorokowski, and Hilpert 2017). These horizontal factors then influence vertical ones—for instance, in cultures where the zones are less than they are in others, the tendency is to react in more emotively expansive ways, with increased eye contact and even touch. As Kendon (2010: 54) observes, the zones are shaped by behavioral and sensory factors:

> Hall has pointed out that the degree and kind of detail that can be perceived in another's behavior varies with distance, and whereas at very close distances information may be transmitted via the senses of touch and smell, at greater distances sight and hearing become the only senses that can be employed and at very great distances only sight is available. Hall has further suggested that such changes in available information will have consequences for the kinds of actions that interactants can engage in. He has suggested, for instance, that whereas at close distances, where small noises can easily be detected, rapid feedback from listeners is possible, at greater distances this ceases to be available, and speech styles and gesture styles may shift accordingly.

As in other areas of NVC, a key source of insight into how we perceive interpersonal zones is to examine the metaphors used that incorporate image schemas based on distance, such as the following examples:

1  *Keep your distance*. *Proxemic translation*: Do not enter my intimate-personal space.
2  *We drifted apart*. *Proxemic translation*: We are no longer in intimate space.
3  *We are getting very close*. *Proxemic translation*: Personal or intimate space is being opened up to those previously not in it—usually with a romantic implication.
4  *His words were invasive*. *Proxemic translation*: The language used was inappropriate for people who are in the same zone.

Albert Mehrabian (1972) called this category the "approach metaphor," since it reveals how we perceive the approach of others towards us in an interaction. In effect, such metaphors reflect our understanding of proxemic behaviors—that is, they represent in language the ways things in the world are, including what boundaries mean in interactive settings, helping us analyze the role proxemic codes play in human societies. It is through metaphor that we can talk about our experiences related to proxemic behaviors.

## 7.3 Proxemics and Discourse

In line with the bimodality principle, Hall suggested that each of the interpersonal zones matches a discourse register, corresponding more or less to the typology proposed by the linguist Martin Joos in his classic 1967 book, *The Five Clocks: A Linguistic Excursion Into the Five Styles of English Usage*, in which he argued that people move unconsciously up and down the discourse register scale in regular daily conversations. Register is a style of speech determined by degree of formality established between speakers according to context, communicative purpose, and social status. The implication that verbal registers can be matched to proxemic zones in a coincident way is a relevant vertical feature of interactions. Simply put, in the intimate zone, the register used is also intimate, whereas in the more distant formal zones the register is also formal. One of the features that stands out in mapping discourse style and zone structure is what Hall called *sensory shifting*. In formal interactions, the speech register may shift at some point from being highly formulaic to one that aims to establish a sense of friendliness, as the conversation goes on. In other words, the shift to a more informal register occurs in tandem with the desire to enact a less formal conversation. Hall noted that this discourse shift was coincident with the shift in sensory modality, shown by nonverbal features such as eye contact, posture, body orientation, etc.

Joos identified five main types of register, which can be mapped against proxemic patterns:

1. *Frozen* or *Static:* based on fixed and relatively stable speech formulas including clichés, aphorisms, culturally-relevant quotations, and so on. Examples are oaths ("I solemnly swear to tell the truth"), the Pledge of Allegiance, the expressions used in some specific situations: "Please fasten your seatbelts for takeoff;" "Please turn off your cellphones during the movie;" etc. The wording is similar, or even identical, every time and (generally) the speech act does not require a response. The zones maintained between people while this register is used correspond to the social and public ones (depending on situation).

2. *Formal:* marked by highly formal style. It is used, for example, at business meetings, in lectures, courtrooms, and the like: "I would like to call this meeting to a close;" "Has the jury reached a verdict?" etc. It is also the style used in formal phatic (contact) situations: "My name is Jennifer Richards. Glad to make your acquaintance." The zones that people maintain as they use this register match the social proxemic zone or even the public one, according to level of formality expected.

3. *Consultative:* largely informal (or lower formal), characterizing situations where advice, help, or assistance might be needed. It also typifies speech between a superior and a subordinate, between expert and apprentice, teacher and student, lawyer and client, and so on: "Please, listen very carefully;" "Let's not make any assumptions." The social zone applies in this case.

4. *Casual or Informal:* between friends and peers; it is usually replete with slang items, incomplete sentences, and colloquialisms: "I'm off!" "Get your act together!" The personal zone applies to this situation.

5. *Intimate:* used among individuals who have a close relationship, including core family members, close friends, and romantic partners: "Are you upset at me?" "Come off it!" The corresponding proxemic zone is, needless to say, the intimate one.

Registers and zones form an overlaid communicative system, reflecting and guiding each other according to situation, time of day, relationships among interlocutors, etc.. Joos' book was truly significant for the era in which it appeared, dovetailing with the early spread of research in proxemics in the 1960s. The discourse-proxemic system is perceived as a holistic one by interlocutors, with each one providing cues that are synchronized (Xu Lin 2007). If either system is breached, then reactions tend to be negative or defensive. Violation of phatic speech registers, for instance, is a major source of misunderstanding in intercultural dialogue. As Ye (2004) has pointed out, the Chinese discourse system draws a sharp distinction between strangers (*shēngrén*, literally "uncooked person") and old acquaintances (*shúrén*, literally "cooked person") activating different cultural discourse-proxemic scripts. Children are taught from an early age to greet *shúrén*, but this behavior is not expected in children or in adults when they interact with *shēngrén*. Ye (2004: 221) presents an interesting example from the Chinese film *The Story of Qiuju* to explain how the Chinese *dǎ zhāohu* differs from English greetings:

> Throughout this film, dǎ zhāohu never takes place between strangers, not even in the situations where "greetings" are expected by Anglo cultural norms. A telling example is at the beginning of the film when the protagonist Qiuju takes her injured husband to see a physician at a country clinic. There was no exchange such as "hello" or "how are you" between doctor and patients when they come into each other's field of vision. The doctor simply asked "Zěnmele?", which means "What happened (to you)?".

The traditional Chinese greeting is never purely formulaic, but involves a gambit to start a short conversation, which may be purely phatic as regards its function. Typically, this takes the form of a question whose answer is obvious in the context of the speech event, and is thus largely rhetorical.

As mentioned, Hall was keenly aware of the relation between discourse and proxemic patterns. For this reason he divided cultures into two basic categories: *contact* and *non-contact*. In the former, physical touching between acquaintances is not only allowed but is also necessary for establishing interpersonal relationships. Discourse tends to be less formal than in other cultures. For non-contact cultures, touching and intimate speech is reserved for only the most intimate acquaintances. British linguist Richard D. Lewis (1996) later expanded upon Hall's ideas, positing three specific types of cultures:

1 *Linear-active* (non-contact). Speakers in such cultures tend to remain reserved in the exchange of information. They keep their distance during formal and many informal (non-intimate) interactions, and speech is also somewhat distant. Examples of such cultures include North American and most Northern European ones.
2 *Multi-active* (contact). Speakers in these cultures stay closer to each other, readily expressing emotions openly, and are engaged in frequent

tactile communication. They may interrupt conversations and display impatience openly. Examples of such cultures include Mexican, South American, and some southern European ones.

3  *Reactive* (non-contact): Speakers in such cultures value decorum and factual information. They are normally patient listeners who constrain body language and maintain the appropriate register throughout interactions. Examples include most Asian cultures.

While some of these observations may be disputed, especially since they are in constant flux, the overall premise is valid. A study that has examined this premise across several cultures is the one by Sorokowska, Sorokowska, and Hilpert (2017). Using data collected from nearly 9,000 subjects in forty-two countries, the researchers found that the discrepancies in verbal and nonverbal interactive behaviors were due to various factors, including rules of contact or non-contact. The researchers also noted an intriguing correlation between climate and proxemic behaviors: "Our study indicates that individual characteristics (age and gender) influence interpersonal space preferences and that some variation in results can be explained by temperature in a given region … which might be used as a reference data point in future studies."

The gist is that if cultures fall into the same broad category—contact versus non-contact—then nonverbal behaviors constitute indexes of the perceptions of interactions that people in each type of culture possess. Greeting rituals, for instances, tend to be similar in Northern Europe and in the United States, both non-contact cultures, consisting of minimal contact protocols—often just a handshake. However, within these cultures there are differences: Americans tend to keep more open space during conversations (roughly 4 ft.) compared to Europeans, who tend to stay from 2 to 3 feet apart. Hall noted that awareness of the proxemic codes operative in different kinds of culture improves cross-cultural understanding, even though the feelings that native cultural rules engender are almost impossible to eliminate. So, in addition to learning another culture's verbal language, the implication is that people should also learn its silent (proxemic) language.

## 7.4  Perceived Proximity

While the main discussion of nonverbal communication from a cybernetic perspective is deferred to the final chapter, in this section a cybernetic theme connected to proxemics will be broached briefly—cybernetics is the science of communication and automatic control systems in machines and living things. Research in human-computer interaction (HCI) has shown differences in proxemic perceptions according to technological device and process. For instance, touch-based screens, rather than mouse-based ones, appear to have a stronger proxemic pull, allowing users to feel more engaged in the content of a message. This type of simulated (or extended) tactility has become a major area of research in *extended* NVC—that is, NVC carried out virtually with the computer and its components being perceived as extensions of physical and cognitive processes.

While physical proximity is not possible in virtual, computer-mediated communication (CMC), makers of computers and cybernetic theorists claim that *perceived proximity*—or simulated proxemic communication—can be realized and that over time such proximity is felt as if it were real-world physical proximity albeit in a vicarious way, as studies now indicate (Olson and Olson 2000; O'Leary et al. 2008) The findings suggest that various psychological, cultural, and situational factors influence how close we feel to an interlocutor, regardless of distance, medium, or mode of interaction—F2F or CMC. The clues to proxemic relation in CMC come from the type of discourse and devices used (including emojis and gifs), which indicate if the interaction is intimate, personal, social, or public.

Bailenson et al. (2001) conducted an interesting experiment examining the relationship between mutual gazing and sense of perceived proximity in a three-dimensional virtual environment in which a subject was immersed interacting with an embodied agent. The researchers wanted to investigate the nonverbal exchanges that occurred between the human subject and the embodied agent. They found that the subjects did not treat the agent as mere artificial animation—they were influenced by the three-dimensional environment and thus obeyed the same kind of proxemic rules of real-world F2F interaction in response to the agent's behavioral representations. The female participants were a little more affected by the gaze cues of the agent than the men, adapting their personal zone range accordingly. However, the men also recognized the agent's gaze behavior, even if their adjustments were lesser in response. Both genders demonstrated, overall, less variation in their proxemic behaviors when the agent displayed a mutual gaze than when the agent did not.

The implications of this study are significant. First, the human subjects reacted proxemically as if the agent were human, suggesting that once an interactional-proxemic code has become habitual it is applied unconsciously, even in response to artificial situations. Second, this has implications for HCI research and design, since people seem to relate to humanoid representations in ways that parallel how they react to real human beings. Once some iconic representation resembles a humanoid figure it is processed in the mind as if it were real, albeit vicariously. As Anacleto and Wells (2015) found, this applies to wearable computer devices, through which users sense the same pattern of meanings of proxemic zones in real spaces. The control devices included those that involve such modalities as closeness to the body, sensory linkages, controllability, and so on. When strangers accessed the wearer's intimate data space, the wearer became uncomfortable, on the other hand when intimate relations accessed the same data space, the wearer indicated pleasure.

A comprehensive review of the relevant studies by Rios-Martinez, Spalanzani, and Laugier (2015) has also shown that robots can be designed to react proxemically to spaces, with software that allows the robot to measure the distances between itself and humans according to proxemic science. Also, the experiments suggest that humans react to robots proxemically as if they were human.

## 7.5 Epilogue

As discussed in this chapter, proxemic behavior is likely a residue of territoriality mechanisms in human evolution. The emotional reactions connected to the zones people maintain between each other are located largely in the amygdala, where strong reactions to personal space violations have been detected: it has been found, for instance, that these are absent in subjects whose amygdala has been damaged, but it is activated consistently when people with intact amygdalae are physically close (Kennedy et al. 2009). In other words, the neuroscientific studies have linked the amygdala with the pattern of emotional reactions that typify proxemic situations: "Our findings suggest that the amygdala may mediate the repulsive force that helps to maintain a minimum distance between people. Further, our findings are consistent with those in monkeys with bilateral amygdala lesions, who stay within closer proximity to other monkeys or people, an effect we suggest arises from the absence of strong emotional responses to personal space violation" (Kennedy et al. 2009: 1227).

Territoriality might explain why proxemic behaviors are universal, albeit shaped in their details and degrees of connotation by cultural rules—that is, they vary from culture to culture but their basis in a territorial imperative is constant. Hall believed that proxemics could be extended to explain even the organization of towns and of living spaces, because they are artifactual surrogates of an innate sense of territoriality. Walls, streets, buildings, etc. are arranged in ways that delineate someone's territory or personal space. Hall identified four main kinds of territories:

1 *Bodily*: the personal space or zone that people maintain around themselves.
2 *Primary*: spatial structures, such as homes, that define safe living spaces.
3 *Secondary*: any structured environment to which entry is reserved for specific individuals—for example an office, a school, a church, etc.
4 *Public*: any open space into which anyone can enter and leave—a park, a shopping mall, etc.

The territories can overlap or crisscross socially and psychologically. For example, a musical band might rehearse in the home of one of the members. For the latter, it constitutes a primary territory, whereas for the others it constitutes a secondary territory.

While the primary evolutionary function of animals inhabiting and defending a territory is to enhance survival, there are many occasions that arise where cooperation is required—a fact that might explain why animals might share territories. However, within the shared territory, instinctive cohabitation rules emerge as to how the territory is to be apportioned and to how the animals within it must react and interact with each other. This instinctive cooperation agreement sustains biological life; but humans have transformed such territorial patterns into sign systems that have liberated them from the territorial imperative (to varying degrees). Humans have the capacity to redesign aspects of their territories if the need should arise, as well as to modify proxemic behaviors within them. This became obvious during the COVID-19 crisis that led to provisional new forms of proxemic behavior based on distancing measures designed to impede the virus from being transferred from person-to-person, as well as suspending certain haptic forms of behavior such as handshaking.

# 8

# Extended Nonverbal Communication

## Chapter Outline

| | |
|---|---|
| 8.0 Prologue | 163 |
| 8.1 Extension Theory | 165 |
| 8.2 Spatial Codes | 168 |
| 8.3 Dress Codes | 171 |
| 8.4 Simulated Nonverbal Communication | 175 |
| 8.5 The Tetrad | 179 |
| 8.6 Epilogue | 184 |

## 8.0 Prologue

In the previous chapter, it was mentioned that Hall viewed proxemics more widely than as just part of F2F interaction; he extended it to the study of the broader organization of space, beyond interpersonal zones and, thus, as a research tool for understanding how humans have extended "the organization of space in houses and buildings, and ultimately the layout of towns." This type of study aims to discern how physical and cognitive capacities can be extended beyond the body's natural resources through technology—an idea that was elaborated in great depth by the late Canadian communications theorist Marshall McLuhan (1951; 1962; 1964).

The crux of McLuhan's view is that humans have designed many of their tools, objects, inventions, devices, etc., to enhance their sensory, bodily, expressive, or intellectual capacities. In this framework, for example, an ax extends the ability of the human hand to break wood; the wheel of the human foot to cover greater distances with less effort; the telescope of the eyes to see further; and so on. So, as Hall suspected, cities and houses can be seen as architectural extensions of territorial proxemic structures; in the same vein, clothing can be seen as an extension of bodily skin; virtual reality devices as extensions of various nonverbal modalities (tactility, visuality, gesture, etc.); and so on. This chapter will deal with some of these extensions, focusing on the nonverbal aspects that they amplify. The approach can thus be called *extended nonverbal communication* (ENVC) for the sake of convenience. It aims to investigate how artifacts and devices, such as buildings and computers, extend specific aspects of NVC.

Extension theory has never been applied systematically to the study of NVC, as far as can be told, although Hall's description of cities and houses as extended proxemic structures would certainly fall under this rubric. There is also evidence that Hall and McLuhan influenced each other in this area of investigation, as evidenced by the considerable correspondence between the two, as Everett Rogers (2000: 117) has pointed out:

> Marshall McLuhan, the Canadian media guru, and Edward T. Hall (1959), the American anthropologist who wrote *The Silent Language* and founded the field of intercultural communication, exchanged over 133 letters during the period between 1962 and 1976. Their correspondence provides insight into the evolution of such important ideas as the conception of the media as extensions of man, media technological determinism, and McLuhan's dictum that the medium is the message. Although these ideas are usually attributed to McLuhan, who wrote about them in two important books, *The Gutenberg Galaxy* (1962) and *Understanding Media: The Extensions of Man* (1965), Hall had considerable influence in their development.

In the Hall-McLuhan paradigm, technology is viewed as an artificial surrogate for biology and social interaction. Consider, for instance, the automobile. In this framework, it is defined as an extension of the body's locomotive resources and a protective shell around the body in traffic that is perceived as inviolable as the body itself. To accommodate this artificial body with amplified locomotion qualities, it became part of social life, interacting with real bodies in a synergetic way and, in the process, leading to the re-structuring of the environment to accommodate it. In the 1920s, many low-income families in the United States could finally afford to buy an inexpensive car. As a result, the number of passenger cars in the country jumped from fewer than 7 million in 1919 to about 23 million in 1929. This made the construction of roads and highways for automobile use a necessity, leading to new technologies for building road infrastructure, creating at the same time a need for novel businesses catering to an emerging automobile culture, including gas stations, roadside restaurants, and auto clubs. As a consequence, the automobile is felt to be an extension of one's body and personality and part of a social system of interaction. Proxemic structure applies between cars in various ways—for example, the closer a car is to another, the more a reaction of space invasion emerges.

## 8.1 Extension Theory

Extension theory claims that humans have the capacity to extend or amplify their biology through artifacts. For example, a specific biological faculty such as locomotion is extended by the wheel, which was designed initially to allow people to move faster and go farther with less physical effort. This then led to other related technologies, from the making of wheel-carts to bicycles and automobiles (Figure 8.1).

Each invention or technology is designed to extend or amplify something in particular—the ax extended a biological organ, the hand, while computers have extended human memory, allowing for infinite storage and easy retrieval of stored information. McLuhan argued, in effect, that we create tools, at first, to extend ourselves—to hear across greater distances, to access information more quickly, to store it more permanently, and so on. Once

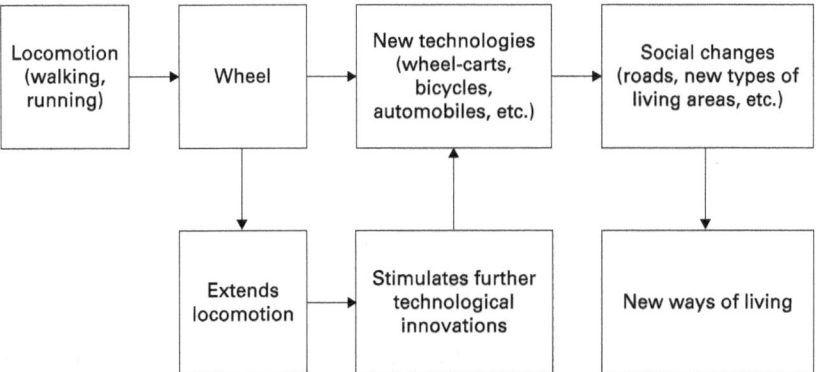

**Figure 8.1** Extension theory (author's drawing).

we have the tools for doing so, we extend them further and further to create sophisticated technological systems. As a consequence, human evolution is guided more and more by technology, rather than by strictly biological processes. We are, in effect, makers of our own worlds, or as he aptly remarked, we live in "a man-made environment that transfers the evolutionary process from biology to technology" (McLuhan 1968: 85).

For McLuhan, the term *tool* involved not just mechanical technologies, but other kinds as well—for example, words are tools of intellect, since they allow the brain to store information more effectively than the instincts, symbols compress information so as to make it easy to store it more efficiently, and so on. He identified several main extension tools:

1 *Physical*: the wheel has extended the locomotive capacities of walking, the telescope of vision, etc.;
2 *Intellectual*: writing has extended the ability to record and preserve knowledge efficiently, drawing of visualizing the world more permanently, etc.;
3 *Symbolic*: numeral systems have extended our ability to count up to infinity, science symbols have extended out ability to compress information so that it can be used efficiently over and over, etc.;
4 *Mechanical*: automobiles have extended locomotive capacities, print reproduction technology the dissemination of texts, etc.;
5 *Mnemonic*: the computer allows for greater storage and retrieval of information, enhancing memory, devices such as diaries also allow for memory extension, and so on.

As we invent new and more powerful technologies, so too do we change our modes of knowledge-making, of understanding the world, of transmitting information, of interacting socially, of communicating, and so on. In the print age, brought about by the invention of the printing press in the 1400s, written materials such as books were the main tools for recording and disseminating knowledge, extending the oral medium of transmission considerably, since print materials can be distributed farther than oral events. As the print age gave way to the electronic age, and then to the digital age, the tools for knowledge-making and communicating also changed, extending the reach of print considerably. These technologies are thus extensions of previous technologies. As McLuhan (1970: 180) put it, "When the evolutionary process shifts from biology to software technology the body becomes the old hardware environment. The human body is now a probe, a laboratory for experiments."

Extensions can be condensed into three general categories:

1 tools and technologies that extend the human body (body extensions);
2 tools and technologies that extend cognitive, communicative, and emotional faculties (cognitive-communicative extensions);
3 tools and technologies that extend institutions (social extensions).

Examples of each type are given in Table 8.1.

Extensions always have positive and negative effects. While they enhance biological, mental, communicative, and institutional structures beyond the limits of biology, they may also may lead to "amputations," as McLuhan called them. So, for instance, the ax made it possible to cut wood more

**Table 8.1** Extensions

| Body Extensions | |
| --- | --- |
| Tool | Extension |
| knife | the ability of the hand to cut substances |
| clothing | the ability of the skin and hair to protect the body from the elements |
| hammer | the ability of hands to modify the environment |
| telescope | the ability of eyesight to see farther |
| wheel | the ability of the legs and feet to go farther and more quickly |
| Cognitive-Communicative Extensions | |
| Tool | Extension |
| alphabet | the ability to condense and store information economically and efficiently; it also extends sound into sight, since it allows units of sounds in words (phonemes) to be represented visually |
| computer | the ability of the brain to carry out logical tasks and to store information |
| Internet | intellectual and communicative faculties so as to be able to reach out to everyone anywhere, the ability to communicate instantly removing the time and space constraints of all previous communicative extensions |
| Recent Social Extensions | |
| Tool | Extension |
| Facebook | the ability of people to remain connected socially through cyberspace, which is itself an extension of real space |
| Twitter | the ability of people to follow each other in some task |
| YouTube | the ability of people to put themselves on display through a visual medium |

effectively, but it also became a weapon of killing, literally allowing humans to amputate each other more effectively. The automobile extended the body's locomotive abilities, but it has also led to the loss of physical locomotion capacities that might have evolved biologically more so than they have—that is, it has led to the amputation of walking regularly and the healthy aspects connected with it.

McLuhan's most elaborate presentation of the notion of extension is in *Understanding Media: The Extensions of Man* (1964). In it, he suggested that our mass media and mass communications societies have reconfigured the ways in which we understand things—hence his phrase "the medium is the message." In themselves, media bear no meanings; but they create a new environment for them to ferment and coalesce. He used the example of a light bulb to illustrate this point. A light bulb has no meaning or content in the way that, say, a book has chapters, a newspaper has sections, or a television channel has programs. Nevertheless, it enables people to see in the dark and thus creates a physical environment in which they can carry out activities involving sight. These would not be possible without the bulb. As he remarked: "a light bulb creates an environment by its mere presence" (McLuhan 1964: 8).

## 8.2 Spatial Codes

Hall's assessment of architecture and city design as extensions of proxemic dynamics would fall into several categories above. This can be called, simply, *extended proxemics,* which, as Jerry Moore (1996: 789) has pointed out would involve studying "ritual communication, thresholds of human sense perceptions, and constructed spaces." Such study would focus on *spatial codes*, culturally-elaborated systems of meaning.

Spatial codes fall into three main categories—*public*, *private*, and *sacred*. Public spatial codes are those that regulate proxemic behaviors at public sites such as offices and malls; private spatial codes are those that regulate how people interact in private spaces such as homes; and sacred spatial codes are those that regulate interaction at those locales that are considered to have metaphysical, mythical, or spiritual value, such as churches or sacred sites. Spatial codes are the reason why, for example, one must knock on the door of a friend's house to announce one's presence, but not need to do so on the door of a retail store; they are also the reason why one may sit and wait for someone in a foyer, atrium, or lobby, but why one does not normally wait for someone in a public washroom (usually); they are also the reason why one can walk on a public sidewalk, but not on someone's porch without permission; and they are the reason why when one enters a sacred place like a church or chapel, one behaves differently than when one enters a bank or a stadium.

The fact that social groups build and design their abodes and public edifices of their villages, towns, and cities in characteristic ways is an indication that these are meaningful proxemic structures. A building is hardly ever perceived by the members of a society as simply a pile of bricks, wood, straw, etc., put together to provide shelter. Rather, its shape, size, features, and location are perceived to be signs or sign vehicles that refer to a range of culture-specific proxemic meanings. Buildings are, in effect, artificial extensions of those who inhabit them. This applies as well to public spaces, which are felt to be extensions of a "communal body." This is why societies are often described as being "healthy," "vibrant," "beautiful," "neat," "organized," "disorganized," etc. And this is why when someone defaces a public place, that individual is felt to have violated the entire community. Conflicts between groups or nations are often triggered by acts against the communal body.

Spatial codes also assign tasks and functions to specific locales, as well as how to behave and appear in them, including dress, language, etc. They give coherence and purpose to social activities and routines, producing recognizable effects on how people experience places—the space in one's home feels more personal than the space in a bank; at a party, a feast, or a traditional ceremony people assume the social personae that they are either assigned or expected to play, including what clothes to wear, etc. The end result is that public events are experienced as a communal bodily experience.

In the same way that public spaces are perceived to be parts of a communal body, private spaces are felt typically to be extensions of the Self. A home is thus a Self-code, a shelter system providing protection from weather and intruders, but also an extension of character, as indicated by its layout, design, material objects, etc.. It is felt, therefore, to be an extension of the body's protective armor and the personality of the inhabitant. When one steps inside, one feels as if one has entered into one's own body. When people build and decorate their homes, they are primarily engaged in making images of themselves to suit their own eyes and to present themselves through them to others.

Sacred places are sites where it is believed that people can secure some form of contact with, or proximity to, the divinities. The spatial codes that relate to these places are emotionally powerful. In a Catholic church, for example, a confessional is felt to be a very intimate enclosure. Therefore, it cannot be lit or be made amenable to social interaction. It signifies a space in which one is expected to look into the dark depths of the soul. The altar area is perceived as more sacred and therefore less traversable than the area containing the pews. Every culture has its designated sacred spaces—the word *church* comes from New Testament Greek *ekklesia*, meaning "those called out," that is, those called away from their daily life to form a new and spiritually deeper relation with the divine.

Many species have the ability to construct appropriate shelters within their habitats to protect themselves from the elements and to procure a safeguard against intruding enemies: for example, beavers build dams of stick, mud, brushwood, or stone to widen the area and increase the depth of water around their habitats; marmots (groundhogs) make burrows in the ground where they can hibernate safely during the winter; birds build nests for their young to survive; and the list could go on and on. Humans too build shelters, but these are hardly just "survival structures." As in all human extension systems, they are a blend of biology and culture. Thus, while building styles and practices may vary according to available technologies in a culture, the primary proxemic-extensive functions of buildings remain the same the world over—protection against intrusions and avoidance of discomforts caused by an excess of heat, cold, rain, or wind. But, this function is extended connotatively in specific ways. Temples, churches, and mosques, for instance, are designed to allow people to practice their faith. Fortresses and castles are designed with defense in mind and to display the political and social power of the inhabitants. Palaces, villas, and skyscrapers are also shelters, but they too display power and wealth (Preziosi 2010). In large urban centers, more people live in mass housing structures and go to work in large buildings; they spend their incomes in large shopping centers, send their children to different kinds of schools, go to specialized hospitals and clinics when sick, linger in airports on the way to distant hotels and resorts. In a phrase, architectural structure has effects on the perception of Self and how people interact with each other proxemically.

The foregoing discussion was meant to emphasize that buildings and cities are much more than agglomerations of materials. As Hall intimated, architecture imposes order on space. It is based on the same proxemic principle of F2F interaction—when things are organized right, they feel right. In China, this principle has been given expression in the form of the "art of placement," which interprets the forces of nature and of the cosmos to enhance well-being through architectural design. Traced to the *I Ching*, the art of *Feng-Shui*, as it is called, is a mixture of geometry, geography, architecture, and proxemic meaning. The orientation, layout, and placement of objects within an area are also considered to be part of how people should perceive themselves and interact with each other.

In sum, building and city design extend proxemic structure in an artificial way, reflecting the same kinds of cultural values, beliefs, and emphases that characterize interactions in interpersonal zones. In ancient Greece, religious and civic citadels were oriented in such a way as to give a sense of aesthetic balance to the inhabitants—streets were arranged in a grid pattern and housing was integrated with commercial and defense structures. In the Renaissance, the design of cities around piazzas was in sharp contrast to the narrow, irregular streets of medieval cities. Renaissance city planners stressed wide, regular radial streets forming concentric circles around a central point, with other streets radiating out from that point like spokes of a wheel. To this day, the downtown core is known as *centro* (center) in Italy, reflecting this Renaissance view of the function of circular structure in city design. After the Industrial Revolution, the concept of the grid started to gain a foothold on city designs. The grid conveys rationalization, efficiency of movement, and precision. This is evident in New York City's plan of 1811, which divided Manhattan into identical rectangular blocks that were even named in terms of the grid system—1st and 7th, 2nd and 31st, and so on. Since the middle part of the twentieth century, many new grid-type designs have emerged. As the human population continues to grow unfettered in the twenty-first century, more and more of the land around central cities will be filled by people. The suburbs will spread out so far that some metropolitan areas will run together with no rural areas between them. Such a continuous stretch of metropolitan areas is now called a *megalopolis*. A megalopolis has already formed between Boston, New York City, Philadelphia, Baltimore, and Washington, DC. As climate change, over-population, and frequent pandemics threaten, entire urban communities may eventually be enclosed in plastic domes in the future.

## 8.3 Dress Codes

Another target of research in ENVC is clothing, which can be defined as an extension of the body's protective system (including skin and hair) and as a means to enhance persona. Clothes are used all over the world not only for protection and modesty, but also for the purpose of constructing socially meaningful messages about oneself. They may also be worn to make ideological, political, and other kinds of socially relevant statements. In effect, clothes constitute a nonverbal meaning-making system, revealing how extension theory operates. Concretely, *dress codes* are systems of clothing signs that cohere to provide information on what dress means or, more specifically, what it extends and how it shapes Self-presentation (Barthes 1967; Rubinstein 1995; Davis 1992; Craik 1993; Hollander 1988; 1994).

The human body has been subject to varying interpretations across history and across cultures—as the source of pleasure, as the source of moral corruption, as a temple, as an enemy of the spirit, and so on. Because clothes are worn on bodies, they are perceived as extensions of such meanings. As the anthropologist Helen Fisher (1992: 253–4) has observed, in the jungle of Amazonia, Yanomami men and women wear clothes for sexual modesty. A Yanomami woman, she explains, would feel as much discomfort and agony at removing her string belt as would a North American woman if one were to ask her to remove her clothes. Similarly, a Yanomami man would feel just as much embarrassment if his genital covering would drop down as would a North American male caught literally with his pants down. When a young Zulu woman falls in love, she is expected to make a beaded necklace resembling a close-fitting collar with a flat panel attached, which she then gives to her boyfriend. Depending on the combination of colors and bead pattern, the necklace will convey a specific type of romantic message: a combination of pink and white beads in a certain pattern would convey the message *You are poor, but I love you just the same* (Dubin 1987: 134).

To reiterate, denotatively clothes are human-made extensions of the body's protective resources, perceived as additions to protective bodily hair and skin thickness. As Werner Enninger (1992: 215) aptly observes, this is why clothing styles vary historically according to geography: "The distribution of types of clothing in relation to different climatic zones and the variation in clothes worn with changes in weather conditions show their practical, protective function." But, clothes also take on a whole range of connotations in specific social settings that extend the meanings of clothes considerably. These meanings coalesce into dress codes that inform people how they should dress (ideally) in social situations. To someone who knows nothing about Amish culture, the blue or charcoal *Mutze* of the Amish male is just a jacket. But to the Amish, the blue *Mutze* signals that the wearer is between sixteen and thirty-five years of age, the charcoal one that he is over thirty-five. Similarly, to an outsider the Russian *kalbak* appears to be a brimless red hat. To a rural Russian, however, it means that the wearer is a medical doctor.

It is relevant to note that dress codes, like other types of codes, can be used to lie about oneself: con artists and criminals can dress in three-piece suits to look trustworthy; a thief can dress like a police officer to gain a victim's confidence, and so on. To discourage people from deceiving others through clothing, some societies have even enacted laws that prohibit misleading dressing, defining strictly who can dress in certain ways. In ancient Rome, for instance, only aristocrats were allowed to wear purple-colored clothes.

In the 1830s Darwin (1871) traveled to the islands of Tierra del Fuego, off the southern tip of South America. There he saw people who wore only a little paint and a small cloak made of animal skin, in spite of the cold rain and the sleet. He gave the people scarlet cloth, which they took and wrapped around their necks, rather than wear it around the lower body for warmth. Even in the cold weather, the people wore clothing more for decoration than for protection. Darwin had discovered, in effect, that dress is a code that is connected to the social or communal body as a means of extending character and values. No one knows exactly when people first wore clothes. Estimates trace the origin of clothing to 100,000 years ago. Archeological research suggests that prehistoric hunters in colder climates may have worn the skin of a bear or a reindeer in order to keep warm, but cave drawings and other ancient images (such as in small sculptures) also suggest that these became signs of personal skill, bravery, and strength. By the end of the Old Stone Age, people had invented the needle, which enabled them to sew skins together. They had also learned to make yarn from the threadlike parts of some plants or from the fur or hair of some animals. In addition, they had learned to weave yarn into cloth. At the same time, people had begun to raise plants that gave them a steady supply of materials for making yarn. They had also started to herd sheep and other animals that gave them wool. These new tools and technologies made it easier and more practicable to extend clothes into the social domain of meaning.

At the level of connotative meaning, clothes allow for the presentation of Self (Goffman 1959). Confident people often show more independence in choosing their style of dress than do those who are shy or unsure of themselves. The confident individual is likely to try new clothing styles. A shy person may seek security by following current styles. Others may be unconcerned about their dress and care little whether they dress in style or not. Other people may wear plain clothes because of strong moral beliefs, seeing fashionable dress as superficial decoration. The hippies, on the other hand, dressed to emphasize liberation from the past in the 1960s, using their unisex clothing as symbolic of the break. Motorcycle gang members wear leather jackets, boots, and various items such as brass knuckles to convey toughness. Like language, a dress code can be endearing, offensive, controversial, delightful, disgusting, foolish, charming.

In all societies, certain items of dress have special cultural meanings. Consider headgear, the social functions and meanings of which vary widely, depending not only on climate, but also on customs. For instance, a Russian farmer wears a fur hat to protect himself from the cold, but is also aware that it identifies his rural origins. A South American cowboy wears a felt gaucho hat as part of his traditional costume, while the American cowboy wears a wide-brimmed hat for protection from the sun; but in both cases, the hat is an identifier of social class and, to some extent, of worldview (as distinct from the worldview of, say, urban citizens). The members of a nation's armed services wear a hat as part of their uniform, but, along with the uniform, it conveys the meaning of protective strength. The hats of coal miners, firefighters, and matadors indicate the wearer's occupation, and the connotations that each one bears. To the Amish, the width of the hat brim and the height of the crown can communicate whether or not the wearer is married. It is interesting to note that throughout the centuries, the desire of people to be fashionable has resulted in many kinds of unusual hats. During the 1400s, many European women wore a tall, cone-shaped hat called a *hennin*. This hat measured from 3 to 4 feet high and had a long, floating veil. The Gainsborough hat became popular with both men and women in the late 1700s. It had a wide brim and was decorated with feathers and ribbons. Hats are, and have always been, props in dress codes, communicating various things about the people who wear them. Most people wear a hat that they believe makes them look attractive. This is why much protective headgear today, such as fur hoods and rain hats, is both attractive and stylish. Even the caps of police officers and military personnel are designed to improve the wearer's appearance.

The human being is the only animal that does not go nude, so to speak, without social repercussions (unless, of course, the social ambiance is that of a nudist camp or some other context where nudity is expected). Nudity is the oppositional counterpart (pole) of clothing. As a result, what is considered exposable of the body will vary significantly from culture to culture, and from era to era, as will what body part is sexualized (Foucault 1976). The nude body has thus always constituted a nonverbal sign system. This is why visual artists have always had a fascination with the nude figure.

## 8.4 Simulated Nonverbal Communication

As mentioned in Chapter 1, the advent of computer-mediated-communication (CMC) as a daily medium of interaction, especially on social media, raises several questions with regard to NVC: How have nonverbal aspects of F2F communication become transformed artificially in CMC? How have gesture and facial expression, for example, been transferred via artificial simulation to CMC? These types of question are an intrinsic part of ENVC analysis which, in this case, looks at how nonverbal modes of F2F communication are simulated and experienced in virtual systems of interaction by extensive technologies and devices.

Simulated nonverbal communication is an attempt to reproduce features of actual NVC through artificial simulative (iconic) devices and systems. Consider as simple, yet illustrative, cases-in-point the "smiley" and "face with tears of joy" emojis (Figure 8.2).

These are artificial icons of facial expressions that represent the smile and the smile with tears of F2F communication in outline form, with mouth, eye, and eyebrow configurations simulative of the relevant microexpressions. But they are not just straightforward denotative forms—that is, forms standing directly for corresponding facial expressions. Like any sign, they convey the same connotative meanings connected with smiling and crying in F2F interactions. The various facial emojis are, in fact, based on simulated microexpressions involved in facial forms (Chapter 3) (Table 8.2).

*Smiley*                              *Face with tears of joy*

**Figure 8.2** Smiley and face with tears of joy emojis.

**Table 8.2** Emoji facial expressions

| Emoji | Meaning/Function |
|---|---|
| | Smiling face with open mouth and cold sweat |
| | Smirking face |
| | Winking face |
| | Flushed face |
| | Unamused face |
| | Crying face |
| | Worried face |
| | Angry and pouting faces |
| | Frowning face and anguished face |

As Pereira-Kohatsu et al. (2019: 4564) have aptly noted, such iconic substitutes have various functions, from reinforcing the meaning of a message to even subverting it:

> Emoji can be used as a supplemental modality to clarify the intended sense of an ambiguous message, attach sentiment to a message, or subvert the original meaning of the text entirely in ways a word could not. Emoji carry meaning on their own, and possess compositionality allowing for more nuanced semantics through multi-emoji phrases.

Since emojis are pre-constructed and largely standardized visual characters, they constitute a visual-pictographic nonverbal sign system. As such, their interpretation is largely guided by cultural rules. For example, each of the smileys was intended to avoid cultural-ethnic neutrality identifiers—for example, the yellow color removes recognizable facial features associated with race or ethnicity; roundness attenuates specific details of facial structure that would otherwise suggest personality or identity; etc. But, almost right after their spread into common usage, new emojis were constructed that embedded culturally based meanings. So, now, various smileys in different shades and facial configurations have emerged to reflect racial and ethnic diversity in humans (Danesi 2016). Like F2F facial expressions, emojis have assumed many of their communicative functions. Phatic speech, for instance, is a crucial aspect of bonding rituals and a means for putting forth what the sociologist Erving Goffman (1959) termed a "positive social face" during interactional situations. So, a smiley used at the beginning of a text message provides a phatic basis on which to present such a face and to imbue the tone of the message with positivity, thus ensuring that bonding between the interlocutors is maintained. It lubricates the communicative exchange by implying a sense of empathy between the interlocutors. The phatic function can also be seen in the tendency to end a message with a relevant emoji that summarizes the content of a message, such as another smiley, a heart emoji, etc. The emotive function, on the other hand, involves adding tone, silent commentary, and perspective to the message. The use of an ironic face emoji, for example, may involve criticism or simple state of mind, but the fact that the criticism unfolds in a visual way, seems to skirt around the more negative emotions that ironic or sarcastic words would elicit in regular messaging.

Like F2F communication, research has shown that facial emojis are often misinterpreted, mainly because the emojis are filtered through cultural codes of meaning. So, while an addresser may select a facial emoji with a specific emotive intent, it may not elicit the same feeling or sense in the addressee. In China, the smiley face has hardly the same sense that is has in most western cultures; it is used typically to convey mockery or disgust, given that the expression of the eyes in the emoji is still, which is interpreted as suppressing a real genuine smile.

As another example, consider emoji gestures as substitutes of haptic and tactile communication in F2F contexts (Figure 8.3).

Again, while these are visual-iconic substitutes for physical gestures, the emojis have also been filtered connotatively. The halting gesture might

| Pointing | Handshaking | Halting |

**Figure 8.3** Emoji gesture forms (public domain).

indicate "Stop and think," or else "Do not do this." It could also have specific gesticulant functions, accompanying texts such as "You really need to stop doing this," or "Look out for what's coming." Inferring the actual meaning intended comes in part from the text's content, but also from the connotative meanings that the actual F2F gesture has always encoded—transferred to the emoji icon. The pointing emoji has obvious simulated indexical functions—indicating that something is important in the text, or that the reader should look in another direction, physically and metaphorically. And the handshaking one is used to indicate that some agreement has been reached or some pact negotiated, either concretely or metaphorically.

Another domain of research for ENVC is in the field of *virtual reality*—a term that has been used since the late 1950s, when the first attempts to create a simulacrum of reality through early computer technology became realizable. Shortly after, in 1960, cinematographer Morton Heilig wanted to stimulate a movie audience's senses with a "Sensorama" machine—a chair that could tilt, allowing the viewer to stare at a wide-angle screen which showed three-dimensional films accompanied by sound and odor emitters. Heilig was unable to get funding for developing his machine, but it stimulated further research into VR technology. In 1961, the Philco Corporation developed the "Headsight"– a video screen put on a head mount, linked to cameras, producing a viewing angle when a user turned the head. In 1965, Ivan Sutherland created a graphics accelerator instead of a camera for his "Ultimate Display" device, connected to a computer, which displayed graphics and allowed head movements to change the view. By 1979, the United States military adopted the emerging VR technology for flight simulation. In the 1980s, pilots could navigate through highly detailed virtual worlds in simulation machines designed to reproduce actual flight patterns and effects. In 1989, the sensory glove was invented to explore the different possibilities of real hand movements in virtual spaces. Since then VR has become a burgeoning field of computer research.

Computer-generated virtual worlds are extensions of real worlds, in the Hall-McLuhan sense. They are created by mathematical models and computer programs that deconstruct not only how the physical environment can be artificially remade, but also how people act and behave in artificial worlds. VR differs from other computer simulations in that it requires special interface devices that transmit the sights, sounds, and sensations of the simulated world to the user. These devices also record and send the speech and movements of the users to the simulation program. In effect, the human subject is immersed in a totally made-up world, a kind of representational space where the subject is interacting with the representation of reality, rather than reality itself. To see in the virtual world, the user wears a head-mounted display (HMD) with screens directed at each eye. The HMD contains a position tracker to monitor the location of the user's head and the direction in which the user is looking. Using this information, a computer recalculates images of the virtual world to match the direction in which the user is looking and displays these images on the HMD. Users hear sounds in the virtual world through earphones in the HMD. There are now tactile devices such as driving simulators that give the user the impression of actually driving an automobile, predicting actual motion with feedback on the driver's action, via visual and audio cues, allowing the driver to modify the activity of driving itself.

The use of avatars in simulated environments now allows users to interact with them, providing a means to study NVC in a simulated way, as we saw with the research on perceived proxemics in the previous chapter. VR also plays key roles in various other areas of research, such as robotics, and in applied areas such as medicine (as already discussed).

## 8.5 The Tetrad

To explain the effects of extenions, McLuhan devised four laws of media—amplification, obsolescence, reversal, and retrieval—which form what has come to be known as the *tetrad* (McLuhan and McLuhan 1988). As discussed throughout this chapter, a new technology or invention will at first amplify some sensory, intellectual, or other human psycho-biological faculty. While one area is amplified, another is lessened or rendered obsolescent, until it is used to maximum capacity whence it reverses its characteristics and is retrieved in another medium. A well-known, and now classic, example given by McLuhan is that of print technology (mentioned above). Initially, it amplified the concept of individualism because the spread of print materials encouraged private reading, and this led to the view that the subjective interpretations of texts was a basic right of all people, thus rendering group-based understanding obsolete until it changed from a single printed text to mass produced texts, leading to mutual readings, albeit displaced in time and space. This allowed for the retrieval of a quasi or secondary communal form of understanding—that is, reading the same text connected readers in an imaginary way.

The notion of the tetrad is a synthetic model to represent the operation of the four laws. It provides a framework for determining the changes that tools, artifacts, and new media bring about in tandem. For example, applying the four laws to the Internet will show how that medium amplifies, obsolesces, retrieves, and reverses various features of both previous technologies and the interconnected social and psychological effects (Figure 8.4).

An example that McLuhan himself thought was a crucial one of how the tetrad worked was in the domain of formal education, predicting that it would eventually take place in what he called a classroom "without walls" in contrast to the traditional "walled-in" classroom. The classroom of the future, he claimed as early in the 1960s, would be a technologically shaped one designed to open up the learning experience beyond the constrained environment of the traditional setting. In the era of the Internet and social media this has certainly come about, as students and teachers alike communicate among themselves and with others online on a routine basis. But in order for the new learning-teaching environment to make sense, the tetrad implies, accurately, that many of the pedagogical practices of the traditional walled-in classroom are being constantly retrieved in various ways. So, in this case, the tetrad highlights what has happened to these practices with the introduction of computers and social media into classroom pedagogy (Figure 8.5).

The different quadrants in a tetrad are organically intertwined, thus explaining how the human brain deals with the new media and how it adapts to them naturally in a specific environment—the education one in this case. In a phrase, learning patterns are not, and never have been, universal; they are shaped by environments, the era in which education occurs, and devices that are used to deliver content. The importance of this tetrad became quite evident during the COVID-19 pandemic. Without technological extensionality, education would have crumbled for a period of time.

| AMPLIFIES | OBSOLESCES |
|---|---|
| • Networking among denizens of cyberspace<br>• Decentralization of information sources<br>• Speed and range of information searches<br>• Access to the Global Village<br>• Access to connected intelligence systems<br>• Virtual communities<br>• e-systems (e-trade, e-books, etc.)<br>• Self-publishing<br>• Access to materials and information of all kinds | • Previous restrictions of time and space in communications<br>• National boundaries<br>• Face-to-face communication<br>• Single-source propaganda<br>• Privacy<br>• Copyright<br>• Censorship<br>• Print monopolies<br>• Retail merchandising<br>• Paper print technologies<br>• Reading print materials such as books for various purposes such as leisure |
| REVERSES INTO | RETRIEVES |
| • Obsession with information itself<br>• Information overload<br>• Loss of affect<br>• Disorders of a new kind (addiction to technology)<br>• Loss of values associated with literacy<br>• Loss of sense of importance associated with traditional academic humanistic disciplines | • Writing and reading in new ways<br>• Tribalism<br>• Secondary orality<br>• Local activism<br>• New forms of interaction that actually retrieve the need to form cliques and groups |

**Figure 8.4** Internet tetrad.

The four laws were devised as components in a larger model, called *media ecology theory*, or the study of media, technology, and communication as they affect human evolution. McLuhan first used this term in *Understanding Media* (1964). The term *ecology* in this model alludes to the physical, psychological, and social environment in which a new medium, as an extension of previous media, is used. A collaborator of McLuhan's, the late Neil Postman defined it as follows: "if in biology a 'medium' is something in which a bacterial culture grows (as in a Petri dish), in media ecology, the medium is 'a technology within which a culture grows';" and thus it

| Amplifies | Obsolesces |
|---|---|
| • Networking with students and other teachers<br>• Decentralization of methods and materials used<br>• Speed and range of activities<br>• Access to the Global Village and educational sites within it<br>• Access to connected intelligence systems that involve a school subject<br>• Virtual communities of other teachers, educators, writers, scientists, etc.<br>• e-systems (e-trade, e-books, etc.)<br>• Self-publishing (as on YouTube and Facebook)<br>• Access to relevant materials and information of all kinds | • Previous restrictions of time and space (thus making the "walled-in" classroom archaic)<br>• National boundaries (whereby a subject, such as literature or mathematics, is seen as something that transcends traditional nationalistic views)<br>• Face-to-face communication (except for the dialogue that takes place in the physical classroom)<br>• Privacy<br>• Copyright (which is now a major issue in the educational use of published materials) |
| Reverses Into | Retrieves |
| • Obsession with multimedia pedagogy and materials<br>• Information overload (whereby choosing what to learn or teach becomes problematic)<br>• Disorders of a new kind (alienation due to disembodied forms of communication)<br>• Over-specialization of skills<br>• Desire for success beyond any reasonable limit | • Writing and reading as values that are re-emphasized (albeit not necessarily retrieved in their entirety)<br>• Tribalism (whereby teachers and students now feel part of a tribe)<br>• Orality (the need for dialogical interaction between students and teachers and among students themselves)<br>• Local activism (as seen by teachers debating the value of curricula based on previous educational philosophy) |

**Figure 8.5** Education tetrad.

investigates "how media of communication affect human perception, understanding, feeling, and value; and how our interaction with media facilitates or impedes our chances of survival" (Postman 2006: 5). Media ecology claims that changes in communication technologies lead to significant social change (Hakanen 2006).

One of the first areas to which McLuhan applied the tetrad was writing. Many historians trace the origin of writing systems to ancient Sumer and Egypt, where two of the earliest systems (hieroglyphic and cuneiform) emerged, both of which developed phonemic signs over time—signs standing for sounds rather than referents directly. Most also agree that the Phoenician alphabet is the oldest verified phonemic script, that is, a script in which symbols stand for sounds. This changed how we interpret writing. In hieroglyphic and other pictographic scripts we process the written texts created with them by stringing together the meanings of the images that the different pictographic forms encode. In a sense, we visualize the meanings of the forms, rather than "hear" the words that they implicate. In other words our cognition is shaped visually. We become inclined to see the meaning in writing rather than process it phonically. Alphabets induce the latter form of cognition, namely a visually based one.

When we read phonetically, a layer for reconstructing what a written word stands for is added to the process—we must first realize that the written form is made up of phonemes, and then after reconstructing the word phonically we must then relate it to a referent. This intervening layer adds a level of abstraction that needs to be developed through learning. This is why in alphabet-using cultures, children must be taught how to read the words as sound-structures not as images of the world directly. Of course, even in pictographic cultures, learning is involved, but the image-based nature of the forms is less problematic than it is in the former cultures. Now, as McLuhan noted, phonetic writing has taken humans out of oral culture, replacing the form of thinking associated with that culture, which is holistic and communal, with individualist linear thinking (Figure 8.6).

This tetrad makes it obvious that literacy introduced new ways of deciphering and understanding the forms with which information is encoded. A similar kind of tetrad could be easily drawn up for emoji writing, which is a retrieval of pictography, at the same time that it makes phonetic-alphabetic writing obsolescent, and yet reverses into it by blending with it. McLuhan used the concept of *sensorium*, or the notion that our senses are activated differentially by diverse media, to explain how the extensions operated. In the case of a new medium, such as alphabetic writing, the sensorium is reconstituted, away from orality and more towards "reading." This produces what is commonly called the literate mind. In oral, pre-literate societies the main senses involved in the processing of information were hearing and touching. People lived in an acoustical-tactile sensorium through which they understood the world. With the advent of alphabets and the literate mind, the sensorium in which people lived and thought became highly visual and abstract. The print age favored the latter type of cognition, putting value on reading versus listening. In the modern-day world, which is often called "post-literate," there is a retrieval of many of the sensory patterns

| AMPLIFIES | OBSOLESCES |
|---|---|
| • Linguistic memory | • Orality |
| • Atemporal access to previous knowledge | • Concept of subjective knowledge |
| • Analytical capacities | • Extroversion, since orality involves listening to a story-teller together with others |
| • Introspection, since reading is a solitary activity | • Communal understanding |
| • Favors innovative thinking | • Mythic-heroic thinking and story-telling |
| • Linear structure of processing information | • Episodic history, consisting of episodes connected to the gods or heroes |
| REVERSES INTO | RETRIEVES |
| • Obsession with oral cultures (cliques, special groups, etc.) | • Tribalism based on different values of writing and reading |
| • Disorders of a new kind (dyslexia) | • Secondary orality (dialogical interaction in smaller groups) |
| • Dependence on literacy for success | • New forms of episodic and mythical thinking |

**Figure 8.6** Writing tetrad.

of the pre-literate world, blending with the visuality of the literate one, as evidenced by emoji writing and multimodal forms of representation. To cite McLuhan again: "Until writing was invented, man lived in acoustic space: boundless, directionless, horizonless, in the dark of the mind, in the world of emotion, by primordial intuition, terror. Speech is a social chart of this bog" (McLuhan and Fiore 1967: 48).

## 8.6 Epilogue

The concept of the sensorium overlaps somewhat with the notion of "embodied cognition," traced initially to Maturana and Varela's book, *Autopoiesis and Cognition* (1973). Rosch, Thomson, and Varela (1991: 172–3) defined the term "embodied" as follows:

> By using the term embodied we mean to highlight two points: first that cognition depends upon the kinds of experience that come from having a body with various sensorimotor capacities, and second, that these individual sensorimotor capacities are themselves embedded in a more encompassing biological, psychological and cultural context.

Without going into the many points of contact between Hall-McLuhan extension theory and embodied cognition theory, suffice it to say here that they are based on a similar premise—extensions of the human body allow it to do more than it was programmed to do by biology. But this notion actually goes back to antiquity, as can be seen, for instance, in the story of Prometheus. In Greek mythology, Prometheus was a Titan and a friend and benefactor of humanity. He and his brother Epimetheus were given the task of creating humans and animals, providing them with the endowments they would need to survive. Epimetheus gave the various animals gifts of courage, strength, swiftness, and feathers, fur, and other protective coverings. Prometheus then fashioned humans in a nobler form and enabled them to walk upright. After he went to heaven and stole fire from the gods to give to humanity, he incurred the wrath of Zeus, who thus had Prometheus chained to a rock, where he was constantly preyed upon by an eagle until he was freed by the hero Hercules. The moral of the story is a relevant one—fire was the technology that endowed humans with sapience and liberated them from their animal heritage. Without it, they would have remained at the level of instinctual life. Technology, in other words, liberated humans from the constraints of biology, allowing them to live through a world of their own making.

The ancients likely believed their myths to be true (at least partially). But mythic thinking and language persist in our references to machines, revealing that we do indeed see them unconsciously as human surrogates. Ascribing human qualities to computers has become so widespread that it is only a small step to believing that they are indeed forms of artificial life (to be discussed further in the next chapter). For this reason, some AI researchers are now claiming that machines and humans are undergoing a convergent evolution. However, there is a caveat here, implied in the myth of Prometheus, which has a final chapter to it—the story of Pandora. Zeus sent the beautiful Pandora to Earth to counteract the blessing of fire, which, to reiterate, Prometheus had stolen. The gods gave Pandora a box, warning her never to open it. Her curiosity overcame her, however, and she ended up opening it, releasing innumerable plagues and sorrows into the world. Only Hope, the one good thing the box had contained, remained to comfort humanity in its misfortunes.

Because of extension, the biological laws of natural selection play an increasingly diminished role in our thrust forward. Indeed, through genetic engineering and other powerful medical technologies we may even be altering the course of biological evolution itself. As an example, consider the wheel again. It would be unlikely that nature will intervene in human life in the future to give us extra limbs to increase our locomotion capacities (like a centipede, for example); we no longer need this intervention since we have invented the wheel to allow us to do the same thing and perhaps even better. Through space travel technologies (meta-extensions), our ability to go farther and farther into all kinds of spaces has become a truly remarkable achievement.

There are several subthemes that come out of any consideration of McLuhan's four laws. One is that any new technology initially brings about fear of losing the security of the previous systems of social life and, thus, of a dangerous radical break with the past. In other words, fear of change is connected with the introduction of new technologies. As he put it: "When new technologies impose themselves on societies long habituated to older technologies, anxieties of all kinds result" (McLuhan 1962: 44). A second one is that technology is what we make of it. It does not have to come about as if guided by some necessary natural impulse; we invent what we feel is important and adaptive. In a sense, the laws of natural selection have ceded to the laws of technological selection. A third one is that communication, verbal and nonverbal, is shaped by our own communication tools and technologies..

The spread of computers has retrieved a form of magic that induces us to believe that our machines are able not only to replace us but also to become more intelligent than us, since they not only simulate how we communicate but may even enhance it. McLuhan warned against this deceptive belief, since the computer, like the book, is a human invention, and thus cannot replace the mind that made it. As he put it: "Computers can do better than ever what needn't be done at all. Making sense is still a human monopoly" (McLuhan 1972: 109).

# 9

# Human–Machine Communication

## Chapter Outline

| | |
|---|---|
| 9.0 Prologue | 187 |
| 9.1 Cybernetics | 188 |
| 9.2 Machine Intelligence | 191 |
| 9.3 Human–Robot Communication | 195 |
| 9.4 Epilogue | 198 |
| 9.5 Final Remarks | 200 |

## 9.0 Prologue

Today, the term "communication" has been extended beyond human-to-human communication (HHC) to encompass human-to-machine communication (HMC), given that all kinds of devices that are programmed to react to voice commands and to carry out activities are proliferating across the world. Moreover, the increasing use of robots and machines in all areas of everyday life has led to an extension of principles and patterns of HHC to HMC. In a phrase, today humans are faced with a communicative situation that has never occurred in the past—interacting with machines. In real-world situations, the human body is involved in interactional settings. The eyes, the hands, the face, etc., are all "at the ready," so to speak, to enact exchanges of information, conveying states of mind through various configurations, as discussed throughout this book. The question now becomes: What kinds of nonverbal structures and cues are involved, if any, between humans and machines? What does this new communicative situation imply for the future of *human* communication itself? These questions constitute the subject matter of this chapter, which extends the analysis of HHC into the domain of human-machine communication (HMC). The branch of science that studies this extension is called *cybernetics*—a field which, as Guddemi (2020) has argued, was in part inspired by notions such as metacommunication, developed by Bateson, as we have seen, who saw commonalities between different systems of communication, human and nonhuman.

Today, the many changes to human life brought about by research in Artificial Intelligence (AI) technologies, which are powerful extensions of human intelligence (in the McLuhanian sense discussed in the previous chapter), have reshaped everyday life and put it on a new developmental path. There are even algorithms that can simulate one's past communicative history (conversations, activities, etc.) via an analysis of the person's social media uses, leading to the concept that we now have an "algorithmic self" in addition to a real-life self. Software called Affective Computing (AC) has been developed with the capacity to detect emotional states in people on the basis of the algorithmic analysis of facial expressions, muscle tension, postures, gestures, speech tones, pupil dilation, etc. The relevant technology includes sensors, cameras, databases, deep learning software, etc. The aim is to construct robots that can decode emotional states or influence them. Such research can also be included under the rubric of HMC.

## 9.1 Cybernetics

Cybernetics is the science dealing with communication and control in living organisms, machines, and organizations as analogous systems. The term comes originally from the Greek word *kybernetikos*, meaning "good at steering," in reference to the craft of helmsmanship. It was introduced in its technical meaning of "science of communication in different systems" by mathematician Norbert Wiener in his 1948 book, *Cybernetics, or Control and Communication in the Animal and Machine*. The same term was actually used in 1834 by the physicist André-Marie Ampère to denote the study of government within human systems knowledge. Ampère had probably taken it from Plato, who had also used it to signify the governance of people. Modern-day cybernetics also studies a form of governance—the structure of control mechanisms that govern communication systems. Wiener subsequently popularized the social implications of cybernetics, drawing comparisons between machines (robots and computers) and humans, in his best-selling 1950 book, *The Human Use of Human Beings: Cybernetics and Society*.

Wiener developed cybernetics by observing that people and machines carried out similar functions in orderly ways, seeking stability in the enactment of these functions. So, while the material-physical forms of the different systems, organic-versus-non-organic (software), may be different, the principles according to which they operate and are organized reflect the same type of structure. An example is the *servomechanism*, a mechanical device which was first used in military and marine navigation equipment, but which today has been extended to regulate the information that flows between signal-senders and signal-receivers. In artificial mechanical communication systems, it controls the performance of the systems automatically. In organic systems, it regulates codes that allow organisms to adapt the flow of information according to their needs.

Servomechanisms are part of *feedback* mechanisms, which involve the structured circling of information to a control device (such as thermostat or the human brain) in order to adjust the functioning of the system via a looping structure. For instance, when a human being's body temperature is too high or too low, the body feeds this information back to the brain. The brain then reacts to produce symptoms that alert the person to the change; the person can then take measures to adjust the temperature. A household thermostat functions in the same way, albeit in a more mechanical way, using feedback from the temperature in the environment according to a calibrated device so as to adjust the operation of a furnace to maintain a fixed temperature.

Technically, feedback is the mechanism in any communication system that regulates any communicative-control process (P) involved between inputs and outputs, providing information on the status of the process. Feedback is realized by means of two basic kinds of loops (Figure 9.1).

The top one describes the body temperature system, since it gives feedback from the output (increase in body temperature); the one below describes devices such as thermometers which monitor temperature changes. Servomechanisms and feedback structures are designed to provide stability to a system. So, in effect, artificial mechanisms such as thermostats serve the same purpose that organic mechanisms in the nervous system carry out in coordinating information to determine which actions will be performed. Their functions and physical make-up may differ, but their underlying structure and function are isomorphic. In sum, there are two main types

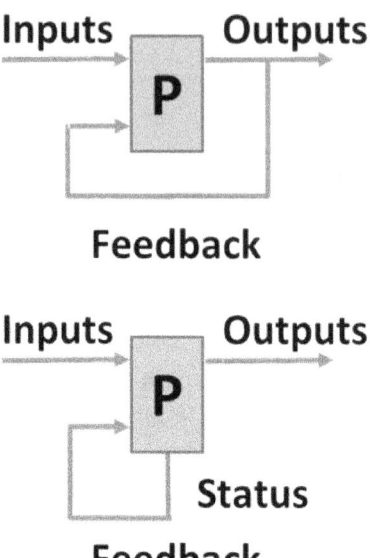

**Figure 9.1** Feedback (Wikimedia Commons).

of feedback. In an electronic-mechanical heating system, as just discussed, the feedback mechanism is the thermostat which controls the system, keeping it in balance—when a certain temperature is reached, a device in the thermostat sends information to the temperature-regulating system to shut down or start up. This self-correcting process is an example of what Wiener called *negative feedback*, whereby changes in output are fed back to the input source so that the change is reversed. In *positive feedback*, an increase in output is fed back to the source, expanding the output, thus creating a snowballing effect. An example is the screeching sound that occurs when a microphone is brought too close to its loudspeaker.

Cybernetics has concrete implications for the study of NVC, since servomechanisms and feedback systems include gazing cues, facial expressions, gesticulants, etc., which inform interlocutors to adjust aspects of an interaction. Understanding these mechanisms may also be the crux for enhancing HMC, given that nonverbal cues are highly regulatory of interactions, as Jokinen (2009: 227) aptly argues:

> Understanding how nonverbal aspects of communication support, complement, and in some cases, override verbal communication is necessary for human interactions. It is also crucial for designing and implementing

interactive systems that aim at supporting flexible interaction management using natural language with users. In particular, the need for more comprehensive communication has become obvious in the ubiquitous computing context where context-aware applications and automatic services require sophisticated knowledge management and adaptation to various user needs. Interactions with smart objects, services, and environments need to address challenges concerning natural, intuitive, easy, and friendly interaction.

Mechanical systems communicate via electronic (or other artificial) signals; nonhuman animals communicate via natural signals based on their specific biology, with some signage in various species; and humans communicate via systems of signals and sign systems that underlie all communicative subsystems such as the following: (1) gesture (hands and bodily actions); (2) vocal organs (oral language); (3) writing (pictographic, alphabetic, etc.); (4) visuality (painting, sculpting, etc.); (5) mechanical means (radio, computers, etc.); (6) audio media (singing); (7) body signals (gazes, facial expressions, etc.). The key to the cybernetic study of HMC, therefore, is to understand such systems, deconstructing them and then restructuring them in machines so that the relevant information can be exchanged across systems—human and mechanical—meaningfully or at least purposefully.

The term *information* comes up in any cybernetic discussion of communication, as discussed briefly in Chapter 1. In cybernetics, it can be defined simply as input data that can be received by humans, animals, or machines in both differential and common ways so as to generate some output. As discussed, Claude Shannon (1948) was the first to characterize information load as inversely correlated to its occurrence—the more probable a signal, the less load it carries with it; the less likely it is, the more load it carries. Now, since different species and machines process information differentially, the question becomes: What kind of information exchange between humans and machines will allow for constructive interaction? This question is at the core of research in Machine Intelligence (MI), considered a branch of cybernetics.

## 9.2 Machine Intelligence

Machine Intelligence aims, essentially, to model, simulate, and perhaps even reproduce human intelligence. It raises the question of what intelligence is, and whether it can exist in different forms in species and machines. One of the first to raise this question was mathematician Alan Turing (1950), who showed with a test that one could program a computer in such a way that it would be virtually impossible to discriminate between its answers and those contrived by a human being. The Turing Test can be condensed as follows. Suppose someone is in a room which hides on one side a programmed computer and, on the other, a human being. The computer and the human being can only respond to the person's questions in writing on pieces of paper which both pass on to the observer through slits in the wall. If the observer cannot identify, on the basis of the written responses, who is the computer and who the human being, then the person must logically conclude that the machine is "intelligent." It has passed the Turing Test. In other words, the test aimed to show that intelligence is what we humans say it is—we cannot escape our own understanding and, so, by implication we will interpret other intelligences—animal or artificial—in terms of our own intelligence.

Generally, in animals intelligence is defined as the ability to take purposeful actions to maximize stability and adaptability; it is part of the animal's survival mechanisms (Russell and Norvig 2003). In the case of Machine Intelligence, the mechanisms are not designed for survival but for the production of intelligence artificially and thus requires human programmers who transfer their own understanding of intelligence to the design of machines. But, once constructed, there is the possibility that machine intelligence can function independently in unexpected ways and even surpass human intelligence—a possibility traced back to a comment made by mathematician John van Neumann, and cited by Stanislaw Ulam (1958: 5): "[The] ever accelerating progress of technology and changes in the mode of human life, which gives the appearance of approaching some essential singularity in the history of the race beyond which human affairs, as we know them, could not continue." A few years later, another mathematician, Irving Good, predicted that eventually an ultraintelligent machine would ignite an intelligence explosion (Good 1965: 31):

> Let an ultraintelligent machine be defined as a machine that can far surpass all the intellectual activities of any man however clever. Since the design of machines is one of these intellectual activities, an ultraintelligent machine could design even better machines; there would then unquestionably be an 'intelligence explosion,' and the intelligence of man would be left far behind. Thus the first ultraintelligent machine is the last invention that man need ever make.

The implications of machine intelligence were thus obvious already in the middle part of the twentieth century, when computers were becoming continuously more sophisticated. Among the first attempts to construct artificial intelligence was the field of Machine Learning (ML)—a term coined by Arthur Samuel in 1959, who defined it as the "field of study that gives computers the ability to learn without being explicitly programmed." ML has become an ever-expanding field within AI, aiming to create algorithms that can learn to do new things from huge amounts of data, independently of human intervention. The earliest example of ML actually goes back to the 1956 Dartmouth workshop which introduced the first program that learned to play checkers by competing against a copy of itself. Other programs have since been devised for computers to play chess and backgammon, as well as to recognize human speech and handwriting.

ML algorithms are based on mining the relevant information for carrying out some cognitive or communicative tasks, which are then converted into knowledge network systems to produce representations in the software that approximates human learning. In some instances, the algorithm attempts to generalize from certain inputs in order to generate an output for previously unseen inputs, thus emulating inductive learning in humans. In other cases, the algorithm operates on inputs where the desired output is unknown, attempting to discover hidden structure in the data—emulating human deductive learning. This whole line of research has, remarkably, led to the construction of robots which appear to acquire human-like skills through the autonomous exploration of new input and through interaction with human teachers.

Research in ML involves both "shallow" and "deep" approaches. The former uses statistical analysis to determine the sense of, say, an ambiguous word on the basis of the words surrounding it in a text. Collocation theory in linguistics is used in such an approach. A collocation is a sequence of words that typically co-occur in speech more often than would be anticipated by random chance. Collocations are not idioms, which have fixed phraseology. Phrases such as *crystal clear, cosmetic surgery*, and *clean bill of health* are all collocations. Whether the collocation is derived from some syntactic (*make choices*) or lexical (*clear cut*) criterion, the principle underlying collocations—frequency of usage of words in tandem—always applies. And it is this principle that undergirds certain kinds of shallow algorithms. First, the algorithm identifies a key word in context and then determines the frequency of combination of other words with the key word in order to disambiguate the meaning of the phrase.

Deep approaches combine statistical methods with tags for ambiguities in textual structures. Known as *ontological modeling*, this kind of knowledge extraction and disambiguation involves parsing options within knowledge networks. In some cases, more than 50,000 nodes may be needed to disambiguate even simple stretches of text. Using so-called similarity matrices, a deep-approach algorithm can then match meanings of words in syntactic phrases and assign a confidence factor using statistical inference. Evidence that such approaches are productive comes from the fact that Google and military departments of the government have been developing ML algorithms to make them as effective as possible.

ML research led early on to development of a new field within AI, called Natural Language Programming (NLP). A famous early NLP program was developed by Joseph Weizenbaum in 1966, which he called ELIZA. It was designed to mimic a dialogue that might unfold with a psychotherapist. ELIZA's questions such as "Why do you say your head hurts?" in response to "My head hurts" were perceived by subjects as being so realistic that many believed that the machine was actually alive. But, as Weizenbaum remarked a decade later, ELIZA was a parodic imitation of psychoanalytic speech; it had no consciousness of what it was saying.

As mentioned, work in such areas of AI led, already in the 1950s, to the speculation that machines could be built to surpass human intelligence—a theory and research paradigm that now comes under the rubric of Artificial General Intelligence (AGI) defined by Sirius and Cornell (2015: 14) as follows:

> AGI describes research that aims to create machines capable of general intelligent action. The term was introduced in 2003 in order to avoid the perception that the field was about creating human-level or human-like intelligences, which is covered by the term "Strong AI." AGI allows for the inclusion of nonhuman as well as human models of general intelligence.

A goal of AGI is reverse engineering of the brain which, if realizable, would likely produce only an object that imitates neural functions rather than reproduce them in any human way. The main reason is that animal brains are shaped by environmental information, machines by artificial input. Can automated reasoning systems become "autopoietic" in the biological sense, that is, capable of reproducing and maintaining themselves by creating their own parts and eventually further components? As Maturana and Varela (1973: 16) observed in their classic book (mentioned earlier), autopoiesis "takes place in the dynamics of the autonomy proper to living systems." Autopoietic systems are self-propagating and self-contained, and are contrasted to "allopoietic" systems, such as an automobile assembly line, which involves assembling raw materials into an automobile (an organized structure) that is something other than itself (the assembly line). Human intelligence and communication is fully autopoietic; machine intelligence is (currently) largely allopoietic. McGann (2000: 358) explains the difference as follows:

> An autopoietic system is a closed topological space that continuously generates and specifies its own organization through its operation as a system of production of its own components, and does this in an endless turnover of components. Autopoietic systems are thus distinguished from allopoietic systems, which are Cartesian and which have as the product of their functioning something different from themselves. Coding and markup appear allopoietic.

It is unclear how machine intelligence can ever *experience* input in a human way, since it is largely allopoietic. And if it did, what would it make of a truly autopoietic change in its software and thus its intelligence? So, to conclude, for true *meaningful* HMC to be possible the question of what a machine understands is of primary importance, or else dialogue is *meaningless*. And if an AI system should become a true super-intelligence, what would it mean?

## 9.3 Human–Robot Communication

Robots are machines possessing the artificial capacity to carry out activities that are defined by human programmers. Like other algorithms, robot algorithms are based on data which is converted into knowledge network systems to produce knowledge representation, so that the algorithms can generate an output for previously unseen inputs. The algorithms mimic inductive learning. The relevant question for the present purpose regards the possibility and meaning of human-robot-communication, which is a specific type of HMC—the difference being that in the case of the former the machine is an iconic representation of the human body, making it verisimilar to another human being and, thus, enhancing the perception that there is meaningful interaction.

One of the first mentions of robots (called automatons) is in Homer's *Iliad,* in which the god of metalwork, Hephaestus, created an army of robot servants. The modern term comes from the Czech word *robota*, meaning "drudgery," used for the first time with its modern designation by Czech writer, Karel Capek in his 1921 play, *R.U.R.*, in which he criticized technology and social conformity by creating a race of manufactured robots who take over the world. One of the first true robots, named Elektro, was constructed in 1937 by the Westinghouse Electric Corporation. Elektro was humanoid in appearance—it could walk and move its arms and head by voice command, speak around 700 words (through a record player built into it), and smoke cigarettes. But Elektro did not have advanced AI, and thus could not learn to adapt to its environment and perform new tasks through deep learning mechanisms.

A typical robot today is programmed with a set of algorithmic instructions that specify precisely what it must do and how to do so. The instructions are stored in the robot's computer control center, which, in turn, sends commands to the motorized joints, which move various parts of the robot, constituting servomechanism and feedback systems. A basic design principle is called "degrees of freedom," which refers to the different ways that the robot can move—up and down, in and out, side to side, tilt, rotate, etc. Robot algorithms enact the degree of freedom required in a certain situation, using camera images of the environment to determine possibilities of movement. Satellite navigation systems are also used today, allowing the robot to move around and to perform actions such as picking things up, moving them around, etc.

Research on data-mining techniques is now central to the construction of robots or any automata system. By compiling and sifting through large quantities of data on the Internet, and other databases, the goal is to extract useable patterns in it. The techniques include the automatic grouping of documents or files, categorizing them into directories, and analyzing patterns and interrelationships within them. A number of online search engines, such as Google, use such software to analyze information across billions of links connecting webpages in order to determine which pages are the most popular or what relevance they have to various fields, interests, domains, etc. This information is then used to rank search results. Given the widespread use of data mining by marketers, government agencies, and others, some social critics have charged that it is leading to an information society in which personal data can be used in many ways—to monitor habits and routines, from shopping practices to workplace productivity. In a sense, this whole situation has created an unconscious HMC modality, given that we are constantly reading and using the information processed by machine intelligences that literally inhabit cyberspace.

Of special relevance to the possibility for HMC are those robots that can interact pragmatically with humans, called *cobots*, which are designed to operate with limited guidance, and based on a high degree of AI that gives them the ability to respond to situations through learning algorithms that are stored in their memory systems and which can construct responsive patterns that are interpreted by humans as relevant. Now, the question becomes: human communication involves nonverbal modalities, so can these be incorporated in HRC in such a way that the communicative event is truly simulative of human-to-human communication?

This question was addressed directly in the 1980s. An early example of a machine designed to incorporate human NVC was the robot head named Kismet, created in the 1990s at MIT, programmed to produce a broad range of facial expressions (Breazeal 2002) (Figure 9.2).

Kismet responded to human signals via input devices that processed auditory, visual, and proprioception information. The robot also had the ability to simulate emotions with artificial facial microexpressions, vocalizations, and head-nodding movements. The software system, called a synthetic nervous system, was designed, in effect, to mimic human intelligence as it is encoded in facial expressivity, that is, by transforming the nonverbal cues to which it is exposed into an identification system that it then turns into its own artificial expressions. Kismet can thus identify and construct verbal and nonverbal cues conveying approval, denial, attention, comfort, and neutrality. As Cynthia Breazeal (2002), Kismet's creator asserted, the robot head was meant to be verisimilar in its automated facial

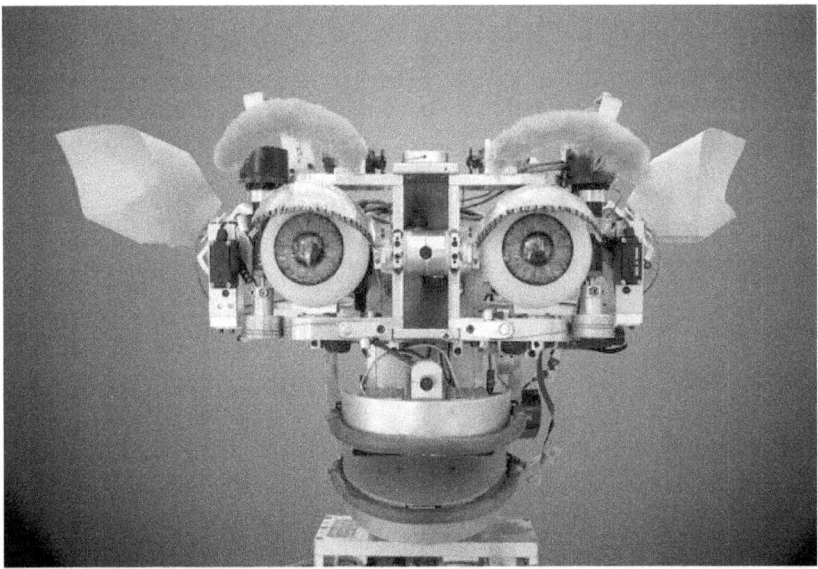

**Figure 9.2** Kismet (Wikimedia Commons).

expressions so that human subjects could be fooled into believing that the device is actually communicating with them. And indeed, experiments showed that this was the case—Kismet had passed the Turing Test. But, Breazeal added a cautionary note: Kisment can express feelings by simulation, but it cannot *feel them*. It needs a biological body to do so. Kismet can also utter words with a variety of phonemes, similar to babbling. As the Kismet system has shown, for robots to eventually be capable of communicating with humans effectively and pragmatically, NVC algorithms will have to evolve more and more. At present, a vast array of robotic systems have been devised to recognize facial expressions and gestures made by humans (Mavridis 2015; Bonarini 2020). Also, robotic faces now allow for a large number of facial expressions to be conveyed because of rubber facial coating, and embedded motors are being produced increasingly. Robotic arms, robotic simulators, and the like are making HMC increasingly viable. But, as Breazeal remarked, it is unlikely that the robots will *feel* or *know* in human terms what they are doing.

It is relevant to revisit John Searle's (1984) response to the Turing Test here to illustrate what Breazeal asserted. Searle argued that a computer does not know what it is doing when it processes symbols, because it lacks intentionality. Just like an English-speaking human being who translates Chinese symbols in the form of little pieces of paper by using a set of rules for matching them with other symbols, or little pieces of paper, knows nothing about the "story" contained in the Chinese pieces of paper, so too a computer does not have access to the "story" inhering in human symbols, implying that HMC may always remain a unidirectional process, with humans the only interlocutor that understands what is going on. The goal of cybernetics is, ultimately, to turn mechanical communication systems, which are allopoietic, into autopoietic ones. Whether or not this goal is realizable, the relevant work will shed light not only on HMC but on communication generally, at least in how it unfolds.

## 9.4 Epilogue

Before the Internet age, Peter Russell popularized the term "global brain" in his 1983 book of the same name, anticipating the effects of the digitized world on human consciousness and the emergence of a form of disembodied communication carried out through virtual media. Global Brain theory claims essentially that our brains are shaped by the environments in which we live and which we ourselves have made. The Internet has provided an environment in which a single information-communication system is constantly emerging which functions as if it were a nervous system connecting the entire planet. Intelligence in this environment is perceived as collective or distributed, not centralized in any particular person, institution, or system. This means that no one individual can control it; the system organizes itself—called emergence—from the networks and processes of interaction between the components. The hyperlinks among webpages resemble synaptic connections, forming a huge associative network along which information is distributed, and thus are illustrative of the Global Brain concept.

It was philosopher Pierre Teilhard de Chardin who saw all this coming in 1945. His term for what is now the Internet was the *noosphere*, a locus which would show the "planetization" of humanity, implying an irreversible and irresistible form of evolution that he called "macrobiological." From this a "global mind" would emerge that no longer would be capable of individuating ideas or assigning importance to authorship. De Chardin's theory is often called *cosmogenesis* or *organicism*—it envisioned individuals and societies as interconnected communicatively for reasons of species survival. The cliché "two heads are better than one" translates in this framework to "all heads are better than one."

De Chardin's term captures perfectly the kind of consciousness we have developed by living in an electronically mediated space where information is available to one and all. Communication over the Internet has led to an impulse to be constantly in contact with others and with machines (given that retrieving information on sites is a form of HMC). It has made communication an obsession.

The foregoing caveat was articulated at the threshold of the Internet in *Technopoly: The Surrender of Culture to Technology* (1992), written by Neil Postman, who defined a society that had become totally reliant on technology and which seeks authorization in it, and even takes its orders from it as a *technopoly*, which he defined as a "totalitarian technocracy" that reduces humans to seeking information constantly for its own sake. Postman's reaction to technology was a reaction to the philosophy known as *cosmism*, or the view that humans and machines are amalgamating to enhance human survival. The basic tenets of cosmism are described by Goertzel (2010) as follows:

- The merging of humans with their own increasingly sophisticated technologies constitutes a new evolutionary phase of the species.

- The dichotomy between natural and artificial intelligence is becoming irrelevant as human-robot interactions become increasingly sophisticated, leading to augmented intelligence.
- AI will become sentient and self-aware, and may parallel and even surpass biological intelligence.
- Science will eventually eliminate the faults in biology, such as mortality and aging.

Early on in the growth of AI, Terry Winograd (1991: 220), a leading researcher, spotted a weakness in the cosmic argument, suggesting that we can only understand what we have ourselves made:

> Are *we* machines of the kind that researchers are building as "thinking machines"? In asking this kind of question, we engage in a kind of projection—understanding humanity by projecting an image of ourselves onto the machine and the image of the machine back onto ourselves. In the tradition of artificial intelligence, we project an image of our language activity onto the symbolic manipulations of the machine, then project that back onto the full human mind.

As American philosopher William Barrett (1986: 160) pointed out in a similar vein, at the start of the AI revolution, if a machine is ever to be built with the features of the human mind it would have "a curiously disembodied kind of consciousness, for it would be without the sensitivity, intuitions, and pathos of our human flesh and blood. And without those qualities we are less than wise, certainly less than human."

## 9.5 Final Remarks

The goal of this textbook has been to describe nonverbal communication in its various manifestations as key to understanding human communication generally both in evolutionary and cultural terms—that is, as something we have inherited from our evolution and which we have transformed creatively to interact meaningfully with each other in specific ways. Eye contact, facial expression, tactile communication, gesture, and proxemic behavior are thus not only part of our survival mechanisms, but also modes of understanding ourselves—a fact that is evidenced by how these are extended beyond the body with artifacts such as clothing and architecture and how they are represented in art and language as intrinsic to human nature.

The three main objectives of this book have been: (a) to describe the traditional study of F2F communication; (b) to examine its extensions into material culture, including clothing and architecture; and (c) to extend it into the domain of HMC. Its overarching theme has been that human beings communicate their ideas and feelings, not only through verbal language, but through the body, not only to reinforce speech but to complete it. Across the world, nonverbal forms of communication are perceived as meaningful, not just decorative accompanying features of spoken or written language. The powerful role of nonverbal communication in human interaction cannot be overemphasized. The eye-contact patterns that we deploy when speaking, the kinds of touching routines utilized during discourse, the gestures and postures that accompany speech are all part of the script of life (so to speak). NVC makes it obvious that humans require their bodies to make sense of the world, and that the body is the source of how we sense things. It is the initial phase in a semiotic interconnection between the body, the mind, and culture, which can be shown graphically as in Figure 9.3.

As Charles Peirce (1931–58, volume I: 538) cogently argued, "Every thought is a sign." But, as he also wrote, "Not only is thought in the organic world, but it develops there" (1931–58, volume V: 551). The relatively simple, nonverbal models that animals produce allow them to cope sufficiently to secure the survival of a species in its ecological niche. In human beings, however, the making of such models transcends mere survival functions. And it is so pervasive and powerful that it diffuses itself throughout human life, manifesting itself in art, symbolism, rituals, etc.

Interpretation is the key to understanding how we turn information into meaning, as discussed throughout. The instant children start to interpret the

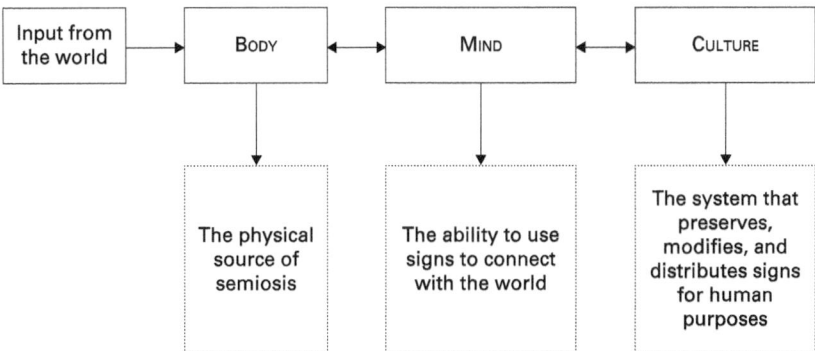

**Figure 9.3** Connection between the body, mind, and culture.

world with signs, they make a vital psychosocial connection between their developing bodies and conscious thoughts to that world. To put it figuratively, signs constitute the "conceptual glue" that interconnects their body, their mind, and the world around them in a holistic fashion. Once children discover that signs are effective tools for thinking, planning, and negotiating meaning with others in certain situations, they gain access to the knowledge domain of their culture. At first, children will compare their own instinctive attempts at communication, such as gesture forms, against the modes to which they exposed in specific contexts. But through protracted usage, the communicative sign systems acquired in such contexts will become cognitively dominant in children, and eventually mediate and regulate their thoughts, actions, and behaviors. Most of the raw, unorganized sensory information that comes from seeing, hearing, and the other senses is organized into meaningful wholes by signs. Our understanding of the world is thus not a direct sensory one. It is mediated by signs and, thus, by the images that they elicit within our mind-space.

Hopefully this trek through the science studying how we make nonverbal messages and meanings will have been a useful one. Many other kinds of paths could have been undertaken, given the interdisciplinary nature of the field. And, indeed, the reader is encouraged to seek these through the reference works provided at the back. The theme I have attempted to expound is that, in effect, the study of NVC in tandem with verbal communication is a critical one in understanding who we are. Indirectly, it is a study in a basic question of existence: Why do we communicate beyond emitting survival cues? We can gain insights into the meaning of this question by describing the activities that communication and its extension into symbolism and representational activities animates. These reflect the human need for *meaning*, of the "metaphysical story" behind human signs.

# Glossary

**addressee** receiver of a message; the individual(s) to whom a message is directed

**addresser** the sender of a message; the creator of a message

**aesthesia** the experience of sensation; in art appreciation, it refers to the fact that our senses and feelings are stimulated holistically by art works

**allokine** a variant of a bodily unit of communication, such as a gesture or facial expression

**alphabet** the graphic code whereby individual characters stand for individual sounds (or sound combinations)

**archetype** an original model or type after which other similar things are patterned

**artifact** an object produced or shaped by human craft, especially a tool, a weapon, or an ornament of archaeological or historical interest; by extension, any media form (a TV program, a recording, etc.)

**artifactual medium** any human artifact (a book, a painting, etc.) that extends the natural modes of message creation and delivery

**artificial intelligence** the branch of computer science concerned with the development of machines having the ability to carry out human mental functions

**asynchronous** communication that takes place over time (not simultaneously)

**augmented reality** interactive experience of a real-world environment enhanced by computer-generated images

**autopoiesis** view that organisms participate in their own evolution

**bimodality** view that verbal and nonverbal communication are integrated systems, mirroring each other structurally and semiotically

**biometrics** applying statistical analysis to biological data

**biosemiotics** the study of signs and sign systems in all species

**bipedalism** capacity to walk upright on two feet

**channel** the physical means by which a signal or message is transmitted

**chronemics** study of the role of time in communication

**CMC** computer-mediated communication, communication that occurs through computers

**co-speech** any aspect of nonverbal communication that accompanies speech

**code** the system in which signs are organized and which determines how they relate to each other and can thus be used for representation and communication

**communication** social interaction through messages; the production and exchange of messages and meanings; the use of specific modes and media to transmit messages

**conative** the effect of a message on the addressee

**conceptual metaphor** a generalized metaphorical formula that defines a specific abstraction (*love = sweet*)

**conceptual metonym** a generalized metonymical formula that defines a specific abstraction (*the face = the person*)

**connotation** the extended or secondary meaning of a sign; the symbolic or mythic meaning of a certain signifier (word, image, etc.)

**contact** the physical channel employed in communication and the psychological connections between addresser and addressee

**context** the situation—physical, psychological, and/or social—in which a sign or text is used or occurs, or to which it refers

**conventional sign** a sign that has no apparent connection to any perceivable feature of its referent; a sign created by human beings in specific social contexts

**cultural modeling** the association of various concrete ideas with an abstract one, producing an overall, or culture-specific model, of the abstract idea

**cybernetics** study of communication and control in humans, animals, and machines

**dactylonomy** counting using one's fingers

**decoding** the process of deciphering a text on the basis of the code or codes and the media used

**denotation** the primary, intentional meaning of a sign, text, etc.

**digital media** computer-based systems of transmission

**discourse** written or spoken communication or debate using keywords, codes, and the like to make the message meaningful to a specific group

**displacement** the ability of the human mind to conjure up the things to which signs refer even though these might not be physically present for the senses to perceive

**double bind** idea that communication often involves mixed messages that need to be connected logically, otherwise a breakdown occurs

**electronic media** devices such as records and radios that allow for the sending and reception of electromagnetic signals

**emoji** picture words selected from a keyboard or app to construct messages

**emotive** the addresser's emotional intent in communicating something

**encoding** the use of a code or codes to select or create a sign or text according to a medium through which the sign will be transmitted

**ethology** science of animal behavior

**extension** idea that human communication can be extended via technology

**eye avoidance** avoiding the gaze of another during interaction for strategic reasons

**eye contact** communicating via the eyes

**feedback** reaction to transmitted messages that informs the sender as to the nature of its reception

**gaze** look steadily during interaction

**gesticulant** gestural movement accompanying speech

**gesture** use of the hands and arms to communicate

**ground** the part of a metaphor that generates meaning

**Gutenberg Galaxy** term coined by Marshall McLuhan to characterize the radical new social order ushered in by the invention of the printing press

**haptics** use of the hands to communicate

**icon** sign made to resemble its referent

**iconicity** the process of representing referents with iconic signs

**image schema** mental impression of locations, movements, shapes, etc.

**index** a sign that has an existential connection to a referent (indicating that something or someone is located somewhere)

**indexicality** the process of representing referents with indexical signs

**information** measure of data that can be stored and retrieved by humans or machines

**interactive** medium where audiences can participate in the medium directly, not passively

**interpretant** the process of adapting a sign's meaning to personal and social experience

**interpretation** the process of figuring out what some sign (word, text, program, etc.) means

**intertextuality** the allusion within a text to some other text

**kine** basic unit of bodily movement

**kinegraph** symbol to annotate specific bodily movements

**kineme** basic unit of bodily-based communication

**kinesic code** social system based on bodily communication

**kinesics** study of bodily communication

**lexigram** symbol representing a word

**mass communication** communication via technology that reaches mass audiences

**meaning** the concept that anything in existence has a design or purpose beyond its mere occurrence

**mechanical medium** any device or technological system that extends both natural and artifactual media (a telephone, a radio, etc.)

**media convergence** convergence of all media into digital formats and, thus, their integration into a single transmission system

**media ecology** view that media extend faculties and thus are part of how humans interact ecologically

**mediascape** the virtual or imaginary landscape of the mind created by the media

**mediation** intercession of a medium between a referent and its representation, and thus between what people perceive and the reality behind the perception

**medium** the physical means or process required to encode a certain type of message and deliver it through some channel to a specific type of receiver

**metacommunication** co-occurrence of various modes of communication that form an overall system

**metalingual** the communicative function by which the code being used is identified

**metaphor** the signifying process by which two signifying domains are connected, explicitly or implicitly

**metonymy** the signifying process by which an entity is used to refer to another that is related to it

**microexpression** unit of facial expression

**multimedia** combined use of several media, such as movies, music, print, etc. producing a type of representation on a computer system that integrates printed text, graphics, video, and sound

**multimodal** use of several communicative or representation modes

**natural medium** any biologically-inherited ability or capacity for encoding and decoding a message, including the voice (speech), the face (expressions), and the body (gesture, posture, etc.)

**natural sign** a sign that is produced by Nature (such as a symptom)

**noise** some interfering element (physical or psychological) in the channel that distorts or partially effaces a message

**object** a synonym for referent or signified; what a sign refers to

**oculesics** study of eye contact

**opposition** the process by which signs are differentiated through a minimal change in their forms (signifiers)

**orality** the use of spoken language to transmit knowledge

**paralanguage** tone, rhythm, and other non-lexical aspects of speech

**persona** the Self that one presents in specific social situations

**phatic** a communicative function by which contact between addresser and addressee is established

**poetic** a communicative function based on poetic language

**pose** particular way of standing or orienting the body

**posture** particular way of standing or sitting

**pragmatics** study of language as used in social contexts

**prosody** patterns of accent and intonation in a language

**prosopagnosia** inability to recognize faces

**receiver** individual or group to whom a message is intended

**redundancy** repetition of parts of a message built into codes for counteracting noise

**referent** what is referred to by a sign (any object, being, idea, or event in the world)

**referential** the communicative function by which a straightforward transmission is intended

**representamen** Peirce's term for the physical part of a sign

**representation** the process of giving a form to some referent with signs

**semantics** the study of meaning in language

**semiology** Ferdinand de Saussure's term for the study of signs, now restricted, by and large, to the study of verbal signs

**semiosis** the comprehension and production of signs

**semiosphere** the universe of signs complementing the biosphere, the universe of organisms

**semiotics** the science or doctrine that studies signs and their uses in representation

**sender** the transmitter of a message

**sensory ratio** the level at which one of the senses is activated during the encoding and decoding of forms

**servomechanism** device that regulates feedback mechanisms

**setting** the place and conditions where a narrative takes place

**sign** something that stands for something (someone) else in some capacity

**signal** any transmission, natural or mechanical

**signification** the relation that holds between a sign and its referent

**significs** study of the relation of signs to bodily processes

**signified** that part of a sign that is referred to (the referent); also called image, object, or concept

**signifier** that part of a sign that does the referring/the physical part of a sign

**simulacrum** inability to distinguish between simulated and real environments

**source domain** the set of vehicles (concrete forms) that is used to deliver the meaning of an abstract concept

**structure** any repeatable or predictable aspect of signs, codes, and texts

**symbol** a sign that has an arbitrary (conventional) connection with a referent

**symbolism** symbolic meaning in general

**symptom** a bodily sign that stands for some ailment, physical condition, disease, etc.

**synchronous** communication that occurs in real time

**synecdoche** the signifying process by which a part stands for the whole

**synesthesia** the evocation of one sense modality (e.g. vision) by means of some other (e.g. hearing); the juxtaposition of sense modalities (e.g. *loud colors*)

**tactility** use of the hands to communicate

**target domain** what a conceptual metaphor is about (the abstract concept that is metaphorized)

**technology** the system of objects made by humans

**technopoly** view that technology can become itself despotic if people rely on it completely

**territoriality** sense of territory for survival purposes

**tetrad** operation of the four laws of communication, according to Marshall McLuhan

**text** a complex sign put together in a specific way

**textuality** the complex of meanings generated by texts

**topic** the subject of a metaphor

**transmission** the sending and reception of messages

**trope** a figure of speech; figurative language generally

**Turing Test** test use to determine if a machine is intelligent

**vehicle** the part of a metaphor that makes a concrete statement about the tenor

**virtual reality (VR)** computer simulation of a real or imaginary system that enables a user to perform operations on the simulated system, which shows the effects in real time

**Yerkish** artificial language developed for communication with non-human primates

**zone** space maintained between people during interactions

# References

Adolphs, Ralph. (2002). "Neural Systems for Recognizing Emotion." *Current Opinion in Neurobiology* 12: 169–77.
Allen, Gary L., Mary A. Peterson and Gillian Rhodes. (2006) "Review: Seeking a Common Gestalt Approach to the Perception of Faces, Objects, and Scenes." *American Journal of Psychology* 119: 311–19.
Allport, Gordon W., and Phillip E. Vernon. (1933) *Studies in Expressive Movement*. New York: Macmillan.
Anacleto, Junia, and Sidney Fels. (2015) "Towards a Model of Virtual Proxemics for Wearables." In: J. Abascal et al. (eds.), Human-Computer Interaction—Lecture Notes in Computer Science, volume 9299. Cham: Springer.
Andersen, Peter A. (1996) *Nonverbal Communication: Forms and Functions*. Mountain View: Mayfield.
Apicella, Coren L., Anthony C Little, and Frank W. Marlowe. (2007) "Facial Averageness and Attractiveness in an Isolated Population of Hunter-Gatherers." *Perception* 36: 1813–20.
Ardrey, Robert (1966). *The Territorial Imperative*. New York: Atheneum.
Argyle, Michael (1975). *Bodily Communication*. New York: Methuen.
Argyle, Michael, and Mark Cook. (1976) *Gaze and Mutual Gaze*. Cambridge: Cambridge University Press.
Argyle, Michael, and Janet Dean. (1965) "Eye Contact, Distance, and Affiliation." *Sociometry* 28: 289–304.
Aristotle. (1895) *Nicomachean Ethics*, ed. by R. W. Browne. London: George Bell.
Aristotle. (1952) *Poetics*, in *The Works of Aristotle*, vol. 11, ed. by W. D. Ross. Oxford: Clarendon Press.
Armstrong, David F., William C. Stokoe, and Sherman E. Wilcox. (1995) *Gesture and the Nature of Language*. Cambridge: Cambridge University Press.
Arnheim, Rudolph. (1969) *Visual Thinking*. Berkeley: University of California Press.
Arnold, Magda. (1960) *Emotion and Personality*. New York: Columbia University Press.
Ascher, Marcia. (1991) *Ethnomathematics: A Multicultural View of Mathematical Ideas*. Pacific Grove: Brooks.
Axtell, Roger. (1991) *Gestures*. New York: John Wiley.

Bailenson, Jeremy N., Jim Blascovich, Andrew C. Beall, and Jack M. Loomis. (2001) "Equilibrium Theory Revisited: Mutual Gaze and Personal Space in Virtual Environments." *Presence: Teleoperators & Virtual Environments* 10: 583–98.

Bänziger, Tanja, Didier Grandjean, Didier, and Klaus R. Scherer. (2009) "Emotion Recognition from Expressions in Face, Voice, and Body: The Multimodal Emotion Recognition Test (MERT)." *Emotion* 9: 691–704.

Barrett, William (1986). *The Death of the Soul: From Descartes to the Computer.* New York: Anchor

Barthes, Roland (1967). *Système de la mode.* Paris: Seuil.

Bateson, Gregory (1936). *Naven.* Stanford: Stanford University Press.

Bateson, Gregory (1942). *Balinese Character: A Photographic Analysis.* New York: New York Academy of Science.

Bateson, Gregory (1951). *Communication: The Social Matrix of Psychiatry.* New York: Norton.

Bateson, Gregory (1956). "A Theory of Play and Fantasy." *Psychiatric Research Reports. American Psychiatric Association* 2: 39–51.

Bateson, Gregory (1972). *Steps to an Ecology of Mind: Collected Essays un Anthropology, Psychiatry, Evolution, and Epistemology.* Chicago: University of Chicago Press.

Bateson, Gregory (1979). *Mind and Nature: A Necessary Unity.* New York: Hampton Press.

Bateson, Gregory, and Margaret Mead. (1942) *Balinese Character: A Photographic Analysis.* New York: New York Academy of Science.

Bateson, Gregory, Don D. Jackson, Jay Haley, and John Weakland. (1956) "Towards a Theory of Schizophrenia." *Behavioral Science* 1: 251–4.

Baudrillard, Jean (1983). *Simulations.* New York: Semiotexte, 1983)

Bavelas, Janet Beavin, Linda Coates, and Trudy Johnson. (2002) "Listener Responses as a Collaborative Process: The Role of Gaze." *Journal of Communication* 52: 566–80.

Beaken, Mike (1996). *The Making of Language.* Edinburgh: Edinburgh University Press.

Beattie, Geoffrey (1978). "Sequential Temporal Patterns of Speech and Gaze in Dialogue." *Semiotica* 23: 29–52.

Berger, John (1972). *Ways of Seeing.* Harmondsworth: Penguin.

Bergin, Thomas G. and Max Fisch. (1984) *The New Science of Giambattista Vico.* Ithaca: Cornell University Press.

Bettoni, Marco (2007). "The Yerkish Language. From Operational Methodology to Chimpanzee Communication." *Constructivist Foundations* 2: 32–4.

Binetti Nicola, Charlotte Harrison, Antoine Coutrot, Alan Johnston, and Isabelle Mareschal. (2016) "Pupil Dilation As an Index of Preferred mutual gaze duration." *Royal Society Open Science* 3. http://doi.org/10.1098/rsos.160086.

Birdwhistell, Ray L. (1952). *Introduction to Kinesics*. Ann Arbor: University of Ann Arbor.
Birdwhistell, Ray L. (1955). "Background to Kinesics." *ETC* 13: 10–18.
Birdwhistell, Ray L. (1960). "Kinesics and Communication." In: E. Carpenter and M. McLuhan, (eds.), *Explorations in Communication*, 54–64. New York: Beacon.
Birdwhistell, Ray L. (1961). "Paralanguage 25 Years after Sapir." In: J. Laver and S. Hutcheson, S. (eds.), *Communication in Face to Face Interaction*, 82–100. Harmondsworth: Penguin.
Birdwhistell, Ray L. (1963). "The Kinesic Level in the Investigation of the Emotions." In: P. Knapp (ed.), *Symposium on Expressions of the emotions in Man*, 123–39. New York: International University Press.
Birdwhistell, Ray L. (1970). *Kinesics and Context: Essays on Body Motion Communication*. Harmondsworth: Penguin.
Birdwhistell, Ray L. (1974). "The Language of the Body." In: A. Silverstein (ed.), *Human Communication*, 203–11. Hillsdale, NJ: Erlbaum.
Birdwhistell, Ray L. (1979). "Kinesics." In *International Encyclopedia of the Social Sciences*, Vol. 8, 379–85. New York: Macmillan.
Black, Max (1962). *Models and Metaphors*. Ithaca: Cornell University Press.
Blackledge, Catherine (2003). *The Story of V*. London: Phoenix.
Bonarini, Andrea (2020). "Communication in Human-Robot Interaction." *Current Robotics Reports*. https://doi.org/10.1007/s43154-020-00026-1
Bottomore, Tom (1984). *The Frankfurt School*. London: Routledge.
Bower, Gordon H. (1980). *Theories of Learning*. 5th ed. Boston: Pearson.
Breazeal, Cynthia (2002). *Designing Sociable Robots*. Cambridge: MIT Press.
Briñol, Pablo, Richard E. Petty, and Benjamin Wagner. (2009) "Body Posture Effects on Self-Evaluation: A Self-Validation Approach." *European Journal of Social Psychology* 39: 1053–64.
Broca, Pierre Paul (1861). "Remarques sur le siège de la faculté du langage articulé suivies d'une observation d'aphémie." *Bulletin de la Société d'Anatomie* 36: 320–57.
Brooks, Rechelle and Andrew N. Meltzoff. (2002) "The Importance of Eyes: How Infants Interpret Adult Looking Behavior." *Developmental Psychology* 38: 958–66.
Bühler, Karl (1934). *Sprachtheorie: Die Darstellungsfunktion der Sprache*. Jena: Fischer.
Bulwer, John (1644). *Chirologia: or the Naturall Language of the Hand*. London: Thomas Harper.
Burgoon, Judee K., Laura, K. Guerrero, and Kory Floyd. (2016) *Nonverbal Communication*. New York: Routledge.
Candland, Douglas K. (1993). *Feral Children and Clever Animals*. Oxford: Oxford University Press.

Caradec, François, and Philippe Cousin. (2018) *Dictionary of Gestures: Expressive Comportments and Movements in Use Around the World.* Cambridge: MIT Press.

Cartmill, Matt, David Pilbeam, and Glynn Isaac. (1986) "One Hundred Years of Paleoanthropology." *American Scientist* 74: 410–20.

Chadwick, John, and William N. Mann. (1950) *The Medical Works of Hippocrates.* Oxford: Blackwell.

Chapple, Eliot D. (1939) "Quantitative Analysis of the Interaction of Individuals." *Proceedings of the National Academy of Science* 25: 295–307.

Chapple, Eliot D. (1940) "Measuring Human Relations." *Genetic Psychology Monographs* 22: 3–147.

Charcot, Jean Martin. (1886) *Oeuvres complètes.* Bureaux du progrès medical.

Chardin, Teilhard de. (1945) *The Phenomenon of Man.* New York: Harper.

Chatterjee, A., A. Thomas, S. E. Smith, and G. K. Aguirre. (2009) "The Neural Response to Facial Attractiveness." *Neuropsychology* 23: 135–43.

Classen, Constance. (1991) "The Sensory Order of Wild Children." In: D. Howes (ed.), *The Varieties of Sensory Experience*, 47–60. Toronto: University of Toronto Press.

Cohen, Doron, Geoffrey Beattie, and Heather Shovelton. (2010) "Nonverbal Indicators of Deception: How Iconic Gestures Reveal Thoughts That Cannot Be Suppressed." *Semiotica* 182: 133–74.

Cole, Fay-Cooper. (1956) *The Bukidnon of Mindanao.* Natural History Museum, Publication No. 792. Chicago: The Museum.

Cooperrider, Kensy, Natasha Abner, and Susan Goldin-Meadow. (2018) "The Palm-Up Puzzle: Meanings and Origins of a Widespread Form in Gesture and Sign." *Frontiers in Communication* 3(23). doi: 10.3389/fcomm.2018.00023.

Corballis, Michael. (2010) "The Gestural Origins of Language." *WIREs Cognitive Science* 1: 2–7.

Craik, Jennifer. (1993) *The Face of Fashion: Cultural Studies in Fashion.* London: Routledge.

Danesi, Marcel. (1993) *Vico, Metaphor, and the Origin of Language.* Bloomington: Indiana University Press.

Danesi, Marcel. (2001) "Layering Processes in Metaphorization." *International Journal of Computing Anticipatory Systems*, 8: 157–73.

Danesi, Marcel. (2004) *Poetic Logic: The Role of Metaphor in Thought, Language, and Culture.* Madison: Atwood Publishing.

Danesi, Marcel. (2009) *X-Rated! The Power of Mythic Symbolism in Popular Culture.* New York: Palgrave.

Danesi, Marcel. (2013a) *Signs of Crime: Introduction to Forensic Semiotics.* Berlin: Mouton de Gruyter.

Danesi, Marcel. (2013b) *The History of the Kiss: The Birth of Popular Culture.* New York: Palgrave.

Danesi, Marcel. (2016) *The Semiotics of Emoji*. London: Bloomsbury.
Danesi, Marcel. (2019). *Understanding Media Semiotics*. London: Bloomsbury.
Danesi, Marcel. (2020) *The Quest for Meaning: A Guide to Semiotic Theory and Practice*. Toronto: University of Toronto Press.
Darwin, Charles. (1871) *The Descent of Man*. New York: Modern Library.
Darwin, Charles. (1872) *The Expression of the Emotions in Man and Animals*. London: John Murray.
Davis, Fred. (1992) *Fashion, Culture, and Identity*. Chicago: University of Chicago Press.
de Jorio, Andrea. (1832) *Gesture in Naples and Gesture in Classical Antiquity*. Bloomington: Indiana University Press.
de Lacy, Phillip. (2010) "Galen (*c.* 139–199)." In: T. A. Sebeok and M. Danesi (eds.), *Encyclopedic Dictionary of Semiotics*, Volume 2, 288. Berlin: Mouton de Gruyter.
de Paulo, Bella M., Deborah A. Kashy, Susan E. Kirkendol, Melissa M. Wyer, and Jennifer A. Epstein. (1996) "Lying in Everyday Life." *Journal of Personality and Social Psychology* 70: 979–95.
de Ruiter, Jan. (2006) "Can Gesticulation Help Aphasic People Speak, or Rather, Communicate?" *Advances in Speech Language Pathology* 8: 124–27.
Derrida, Jacques, and David Wills. (2002) "The Animal that Therefore I Am (More to Come)." *Critical Inquiry* 28: 369–418.
Dessoir, Max. (1892) *Über den Hautsinn*. Universität von Berlin: Archiv für Anatomie und Physiologie.
Dubin, Lois Sherr. (1987) *The History of Beads*. New York: Abrams.
Duchenne, Guillaume. (1862) *Mécanisme de la physionomie humaine*. Paris: Archives Générales de Médecine, P. Asselin.
Duncan, Starkey, and Donald W. Fiske. (1977) *Face-to-Face Interaction*. Hillsdale, NJ: Erlbaum.
Dundes, Alan. (1992) *The Evil Eye: A Casebook*. Madison: The University of Wisconsin Press.
Eco, Umberto. (1968) *Einführung in die Semiotik*. München: Fink.
Eco, Umberto. (1976) *A Theory of Semiotics*. Bloomington: Indiana University Press.
Efron, David. (1941) *Gesture, Race, and Culture*. The Hague: Mouton.
Ekman, P. (1976) "Movements with Precise Meanings." *Journal of Communication* 26: 14–26.
Ekman, P. (1980) "The Classes of Nonverbal Behavior." In: W. Raffler-Engel (ed.), *Aspects of Nonverbal Communication*, 89–102. Lisse: Swets and Zeitlinger.
Ekman, P. (1982) "Methods for Measuring Facial Action." In: K. R. Scherer and P. Ekman (eds.), *Handbook of Methods in Nonverbal Behavior*, 45–90. Cambridge: Cambridge University Press.

Ekman, Paul. (1985) *Telling Lies.* New York: Norton.
Ekman, Paul. (1989) "The Argument and Evidence about Universals in Facial Expressions of Emotion." In: H. Wagner and A. Manstead (eds.), *Handbook of Social Psychophysiology,* 143–64. Chichester: Wiley.
Ekman, Paul. (1999) "Basic Emotions." In: T. Dalgleish and T. Power, (eds.). *The Handbook of Cognition and Emotion*, 45–60. New York: John Wiley & Sons.
Ekman, Paul. (2003) *Emotions Revealed.* New York: Holt.
Ekman, Paul, ed. (2006) *Darwin and Facial Expression: A Century of Research in Review.* Cambridge: Malor Books.
Ekman, Paul. (2009) "Darwin's Contributions to Our Understanding of Emotional Expressions." *Philosophical Transactions of the Royal Society of London, B Biological Sciences* 364: 3449–551.
Ekman, Paul, Richard J. Davidson, and Wallace V. Friesen. (1990) "The Duchenne Smile: Emotional Expression and Brain Physiology II." *Journal of Personality and Social Psychology* 58: 342–53.
Ekman Paul, and Wallace V. Friesen. (1969a) "The Repertoire of Nonverbal Behavior: Categories, Origins, Usage, and Coding." *Semiotica* 1: 49–98.
Ekman Paul, and Wallace V. Friesen. (1969b) "Nonverbal Leakage and Clues to Deception." *Psychiatry* 32: 88–106.
Ekman, Paul, and Wallace V. Friesen. (1971) "Constants across Cultures in the Face and Emotion." *Journal of Personality and Social Psychology* 17: 124–9.
Ekman, Paul, and Wallace V. Friesen. (1975) *Unmasking the Face.* Englewood Cliffs: Prentice-Hall.
Ekman, Paul and Wallace V. Friesen. (1978) *Facial Action Coding System: A Technique for the Measurement of Facial Movement.* Palo Alto: Consulting Psychologists Press.
Ekman, Paul, Wallace V. Friesen, and Phoebe Ellsworth. (1972) *Emotion in the Human Face: Guidelines for Research and a Review of Findings.* New York: Permagon.
Ellsberg, Michael. (2010) *The Power of Eye Contact.* New York: Harper.
Emerson, Ralph Waldo. (1903) *The Complete Works of Ralph Waldo Emerson: Letters and Social Aims*, vol. 8. Boston: Houghton, Mifflin, and Company.
Enninger, Werner. (1992) "Clothing." In: R. Bauman (ed.), *Folklore, Cultural Performances, and Popular Entertainments*, 123–45. Oxford: Oxford University Press.
Epes-Brown, Joseph (1992) "Becoming Part of It." In: D. M. Dooling and P. Jordan-Smith (eds.), *I Become Part of It: Sacred Dimensions in Native American Life*, 1–15. New York: Harper Collins.
Epstein, R., R. P. Lanza, and B. F. Skinner. (1980) "Symbolic Communication Between Two Pigeons." *Science* 207: 543–5.

Exline, R. (1972) Visual Interaction: The Glances of Power and Preference. In: J. Cole (ed.), *Nebraska Symposium on Motivation 1971,* 163–206. Lincoln: University of Nebraska Press.
Farroni Teresa, Mark H. Johnson, and Gergely Csibra. (2004) "Mechanisms of Eye Gaze Perception during Infancy." *Journal of Cognitive Neuroscience* 16: 1320–6.
Fernández-Dols, José-Miguel, and James A. Russell, eds. (2017) *The Science of Facial Expression.* Oxford: Oxford University Press.
Fisher, Helen E. (1992) *Anatomy of Love.* New York: Norton.
Flegg, Graham. (1989) *Numbers Through the Ages.* London: Macmillan.
Foucault, Michel. (1963) *The Birth of the Clinic.* London: Routledge.
Foucault, Michel. (1975) *Discipline and Punish: The Birth of the Prison.* New York: Vintage.
Foucault, Michel. (1976) *The History of Sexuality.* London: Allen Lane.
Fouts, Roger, and Stephen Tukel Mills. (1998) *Next of Kin: My Conversations with Chimpanzees.* New York: William Morrow.
Frazer, James. (1890) *The Golden Bough.* London: Macmillan.
Freud, Sigmund. (1931) *Civilization and its Discontents.* London: Hogarth.
Fridlund, Alan J. (1994) *Human Facial Expression.* San Diego: Academic Press.
Frutiger, Adrian. (1989) *Signs and Symbols.* New York: Van Nostrand.
Galanti, Geri-Ann. (2004) *Caring for Patients from Different Cultures.* Philadelphia: University of Pennsylvania Press.
Gardner, Beatrix T., and R. Allen Gardner. (1975) "Evidence for Sentence Constituents in the Early Utterances of Child and Chimpanzee." *Journal of Experimental Psychology* 104: 244–62.
Gardner, R. Allen, and Beatrix T. Gardner. (1967) Teaching Sign Language to a Chimpanzee. *Science, New Series* 165 (3894): 664–72.
Gardner, Maitland. (2017) *Posture and Gesture in Ancient Maya Art and Culture.* Doctoral thesis, University College London.
Gauthier, Isabel, Pawel Skudlarski, John C. Gore, and Adam W. Anderson. (2000) "Expertise for Cars and Birds Recruits Brain Areas Involved in Face Recognition." *Nature Neuroscience* 3: 191–7.
Gauthier Isabel, Michael J Tarr., Adam W. Anderson, Pawel Skudlarski, and John C. Gore. (1999) "Activation of the Middle Fusiform 'Face Area' Increases with Expertise in Recognizing Novel Objects." *Nature Neuroscience* 2: 568–73.
Gerbner, George, and Larry Gross. (1976) "Living with Television: The Violence Profile." *Journal of Communication* 26: 172–99.
Gibson, James J. (1966) *The Senses Considered as Perceptual Systems.* Boston: Houghton Mifflin.
Gillespie, Maureen, Ariel N. James, Kara D. Federmeier, and Duane G. Watson. (2014) "Verbal Working Memory Predicts Co-Speech Gesture: Evidence from Individual Differences." *Cognition* 132: 174–80.

Gladstone, Gemma L. (2002) "When You're Smiling, Does the Whole World Smile for You?" *Australasian Psychiatry* 10: 144–46.

Glasersfeld, Ernst von. (1974) "The Yerkish Language for Non-Human Primates." *American Journal of Computational Linguistics*. https://www.aclweb.org/anthology/J74-3007.pdf

Glass, Lillian (2013) *The Body Language of Liars*. Pompton Plains: The Career Press.

Goertzel, Ben (2010) *A Cosmist Manifesto: Practical Philosophy for the Posthuman Age*. Humanity+ Press.

Goffman, Erving. (1959) *The Presentation of Self in Everyday Life*. New York: Anchor.

Goffman, Erving. (1963) *Behavior in Public Places*. New York: Free Press.

Goldin-Meadow, Susan. (2003) *Hearing Gesture: How Our Hands Help Us Think*. Cambridge, Mass.: Belknap Press.

Good, Irving J. (1965) "Speculations Concerning the First Ultraintelligent Machine." *Advances in Computers* 6: 31–83.

Gramsci, Antonio. (1947) *Lettere dal carcere*. Torino: Einaudi.

Greenfield, Susan. (2015) *Mind Change*. New York: Random House.

Guddemi, Phillip. (2020) *Gregory Bateson on Relational Communication: From Octopuses to Nations*. Cham: Springer.

Guterstam, Arvid, Andrew I. Wilterson, Davis Wachtell, and Michael S. A. Graziano. (2020) *PNAS* 117: 13162–7.

Foley, Gretchen N., and Julie P. Gentile. (2010) "Nonverbal Communication in Psychotherapy." *Psychiatry (Edgmont)* 7: 38–44.

Frank, L. K. (1957) "Tactile Communication." *Genetic Psychology Monographs* 56: 209–55.

Griffin, Donald R. (1992) *Animal Minds*. Chicago: University of Chicago Press.

Güttgemanns, Erhardt. (2010) "Liturgy." In: T. A. Sebeok and M. Danesi (eds.), *Encyclopedic Dictionary of Semiotics*, Volume 3, 89–96. Berlin: Mouton de Gruyter.

Haakana, Markuu. (2010) "Laughter and Smiling: Notes on Co-occurrences." *Journal of Pragmatics* 42: 1499–1512.

Hakanen, Ernest A. (2007) *Branding the Teleself: Media Effects Discourse and the Changing Self*. Lanham: Rowman & Littlefield.

Haase, Richard F., and Donald T. Tepper. (1972) Nonverbal Components of Empathic Communication. *Journal of Counseling Psychology* 19: 417–24.

Hadjikhani, Nouchine, and Beatrice de Gelder. (2003) "Seeing Fearful Body Expressions Activates the Fusiform Cortex and Amygdala." *Current Biology* 13: 2201–05.

Haggard, Ernest A., and Kenneth S. Isaacs. (1966) "Micro-Momentary Facial Expressions as Indicators of Ego Mechanisms in Psychotherapy." In: L. A.

Gottschalk and A. H. Auerbach (eds.), *Methods of Research in Psychotherapy*, 154–65. New York: Appleton-Century-Crofts.

Hailman, Jack P. (2010) "Optic Signs." In: T. A. Sebeok and M. Danesi (eds.), *Encyclopedic Dictionary of Semiotics*, Volume 4, 88–90. Berlin: Mouton de Gruyter.

Hains, S. M. J., and D. W. Muir. (1996) "Infant Sensitivity to Adult Eye Direction." *Child Development* 67: 1940–51.

Hall, Edward T. (1959) *The Silent Language*. New York: Anchor.

Hall, Edward T. (1963) "System for the Notation of Proxemic Behavior." *American Anthropologist* 65: 1003–26.

Hall, Edward T. (1964) "Silent Assumptions in Social Communication." *Disorders of Communication* 42: 41–55.

Hall, Edward T. (1966) *The Hidden Dimension*. Garden City: Anchor Books.

Hall, Edward T. (1968) "Proxemics." *Current Anthropology* 9: 83–108.

Hall, Edward T. (1974) *Handbook for Proxemic Research*. Washington, D.C.: Society for the Anthropology of Visual Communication.

Hall, Edward T. (1976) *Beyond Culture*. Garden City: Anchor Books.

Hall, Edward T. (1983) *The Dance of Life*. Garden City: Anchor Books.

Hall, Edward T., and Mildred Reed Hall. (1975) *The Fourth Dimension in Architecture: The Impact of Building on Behavior*. Santa Fe: Sunstone Press.

Hall, Stuart. (1973) *Encoding and Decoding in Television Discourse*. University of Birmingham, Centre for Contemporary Cultural Studies.

Hamilton, Antonia. (2016) "Gazing at Me: The Importance of Social Meaning in Understanding Direct-Gaze Cues." *Philosophical Transactions of the Royal Society* B 371: 20150080. http://dx.doi.org/10.1098/rstb.2015.0080.

Hamilton, W. D. (1971). "Geometry for the Selfish Herd." *Journal of Theoretical Biology* 31: 295–311.

Hanna, Judith Lunne. (2010). "Dance." In: T. A. Sebeok and M. Danesi (eds.), *Encyclopedic Dictionary of Semiotics*, Volume 1, 92–5. Berlin: Mouton de Gruyter.

Harwood, William. (2011) *Dictionary of Contemporary Mythology*. Oklahoma City: World Audience.

Heidegger, Martin. (1962) *Being and Time*. New York: Harper & Row.

Henley, Nancy. (1977) *Body Politics: Power, Sex and Nonverbal Communication*. Englewood Cliffs: Prentice-Hall.

Herodotus. (440 BCE) *The Histories*. Library of Alexandria 2014.

Hertenstein Matthew J., Dacher Keltner, Betsy App, Brittany A. Bulleit, and Ariane R. Jaskolka. (2006) "Touch Communicates Distinct Emotions." *Emotion* 6: 528–33.

Heussen, Yana, Ferdinand Binkofski, and Jacob Jolij. (2011) "The Semantics of the Lying Face." *International Journal of Psychophysiology* 77: 206–07.

Hewes, Gordon W. (1955) "World Distribution of Certain Postural Habits." *American Anthropology* 57: 231–44.

Hewes, Gordon W. (1973) "Primate Communication and the Gestural Origin of Language." *Current Anthropology* 14: 5–24.

Hewes, Gordon W. (1976) "The Current Status of the Gestural Theory of Language Origin." In: S. R. Harnad, H. D. Steklis, and J. Lancaster (eds.), *Origins and Evolution of Language and Speech*, 482–504. New York: New York Academy of Sciences.

Hickock, Gregory, Ursual Bellugi, and Edward S. Klima. (2001) "Sign Language in the Brain." *Scientific American* 284 (6): 58–65.

Hietanen, Jari (2018) "Affective Eye Contact: An Integrative Review." *Frontiers in Psychology*. 28 August 2018 | https://doi.org/10.3389/fpsyg.2018.01587.

Hofstadter, Douglas. (1979) *Gödel, Escher, Bach: An Eternal Golden Braid*. New York: Basic.

Hollander, Anne. (1988) *Seeing Through Clothes*. Harmondsworth: Penguin.

Hollander, Anne. (1994) *Sex and Suits: The Evolution of Modern Dress*. New York: Knopf.

Honeck, Richard P., and Robert R. Hoffman, eds. (1980) *Cognition and Figurative Language*. Hillsdale: Lawrence Erlbaum Associates.

Hjortsjö, Carl-Herman. (1970) *Man's face and Mimic Language*. Lund: Studentlitteratur.

Ifrah, Georges. (2000), *The Universal History of Numbers: From Prehistory to the Invention of the Computer*. New York: John Wiley and Sons

Insolla, Timothy. (2012) The New Hakodate Jomon Culture Center, Minamikayabe, Japan. *Material Religion* 8: 262–4.

Irons, David. (1894) "Prof. James' Theory of Emotion." *Mind* 3: 77–97.

Izard, Carroll E. (1971) *The Face of Emotion*. New York: Appleton-Century-Crofts.

Jack, Rachael E., Oliver G. B. Garrod, Hui Yu, Roberto Caldara, and Philippe G. Schyns. (2012) "Facial Expressions of Emotion Are Not Culturally Universal." *Proceedings of the National Academy of Sciences* 109 (19): 7241–4.

Jackson, Danielle. (2017) "Persona of Anime: A Depth Psychological Approach to the Persona and Individuation." *ProQuest* 1964903170.

Jakobson, Roman. (1960) "Linguistics and Poetics." In: T. A. Sebeok (ed.), *Style and Language*. Cambridge, MA: MIT Press.

James, William. (1884) "What Is an Emotion?" *Mind* 9: 188–205.

Jensvold, Mary L., and R. Allen Gardner. (2000) "Interactive Use of Sign Language by Cross-Fostered Chimpanzees (*Pan troglodytes*)." *Journal of Comparative Psychology* 114: 335–6.

Jespersen, Otto. (1922) *Language: Its Nature, Development and Origin*. London: Allen and Unwin.

Johnson, Mark. (1987) *The Body in the Mind: The Bodily Basis of Meaning, Imagination and Reason.* Chicago: University of Chicago Press.

Jokinen, Kristiina. (2009) "Nonverbal Feedback in Interactions." In: J. Tao and T. Tan (eds.), *Affective Information Processing,* 227–40. London: Springer.

Jolly, Stephen. (2000) "Understanding Body Language: Birdwhistell's Theory of Kinesics." *Corporate Communications: An International Journal* 5: 133–9.

Jones, Stanley E., and A. Elaine Yarbrough. (2009) "A Naturalistic Study of the Meanings of Touch." *Communication Monographs* 52: 19–56.

Joos, Martin. (1967) *The Five Clocks: A Linguistic Excursion Into the Five Styles of English Usage.* New York: Harcourt, Brace and World.

Jordania, Joseph. (2009) "Times to Fight and Times to Relax: Singing and Humming at the Beginnings of Human Evolutionary History." *Kadmos* 1: 272–7.

Jordania, Joseph. (2011) *Why do People Sing? Music in Human Evolution.* Tbilisi: Logos, International Research Center for Traditional Polyphony.

Jourard, S. M. (1966) "An Exploratory Study of Body Accessibility." *British Journal of Social and Clinical Psychology* 5: 221–31.

Jung, Carl Gustav. (1956) *Symbols of Transformation.* Princeton: Princeton University Press.

Jung, Carl Gustav. (1959) *The Archetypes and the Collective Unconscious.* New York: Pantheon Books.

Jung, Carl Gustav. (1971) *Collected Works of C. G. Jung,* volume 6. Princeton: Princeton University Press.

Jung, Carl Gustav. (1973) *Letters,* Vol. 1: 1906–1950. Princeton: Princeton University Press.

Katz, Elihu. (2002) *Canonic Texts in Media Research: Are There Any? Should There Be? How About These?* New York: Polity Press.

Kaufman, Lynne. (1971) "Tacesics, The Study of Touch: A Model for Proxemic Analysis." *Semiotica* 4: 149–61.

Keltner, Dacher. (2009) "Darwin's Touch: Survival of the Kindest." *Greater Good Magazine.* https://greatergood.berkeley.edu/article/item/darwins_touch_survival_of_the_kindest.

Kendon, Adam. (1967) "Some Functions of Gaze-Direction in Interactions." *Acta Psychologica* 26: 22–63.

Kendon, Adam. (1972) "Some Relationships Between Body Motion and Apeech: An Analysis of an Example." In:. R. Seigman and B. Pope. Elmsford (eds.), *Studies in Dyadic Communication.* New York: Pergamon Press.

Kendon, Adam. (1977) *Studies in the Behavior of Social Interaction.* Lisse: Peter De Ridder Press.

Kendon, Adam. (1979) "Some Methodological and Theoretical Aspects of the Use of Film in the Study of Social Interaction." In: G. P. Ginsburg (ed.), *Emerging Strategies in Social Psychological Research.* New York: Wiley.

Kendon, Adam. (1980) "Gesture and Speech: Two Aspects of the Process of Utterance." In: M. R. Key (ed.), *Nonverbal Communication and Language*, Mary R. Key, 207–27. The Hague: Mouton.

Kendon, Adam. (1982) "The Study of Gesture: Some Observations on Its History." *Recherches Sémiotiques/Semiotic Inquiry* 2: 45–62.

Kendon, Adam. (2004) *Gesture: Visible Action as Utterance*. Cambridge: Cambridge University Press.

Kendon, Adam. (2010) "Nonverbal Communication." In: T. A. Sebeok and M. Danesi (eds.), *Encyclopedic Dictionary of Semiotics*, Volume 2, 45–57. Berlin: Mouton de Gruyter.

Kendon, Adam. (2017) "Reflections on the 'Gesture-First' Hypothesis of Language Origins." *Psychonomic Bulletin & Review* 24: 163–70.

Kendon, Adam, Richard M. Harris, and Mary R. Key. (1975) *Organization of Behavior in Face-to-Face Interaction*. The Hague, Netherlands: Mouton.

Kennedy Daniel P., Jan Phillip Gläscher, Julian Michael Tyszka, and Ralph Adolphs. (2009) "Personal Space Regulation by the Human Amygdala." *Nature Neuroscience* 12: 1226–7.

Knapp, Mark L. (1978) *Nonverbal Communication in Human Interaction*. New York: Holt.

Knapp, Mark L., and Judith Hall. (2010) *Nonverbal Communication in Human Interaction*. Boston: Wadsworth.

Kobayashi, Hiromi, and Shiro Kohshima. (2001) "Unique Morphology of the Human Eye and Its Adaptive Meaning: Comparative Studies on External Morphology of the Primate Eye." *Journal of Human Evolution* 40: 419–35.

Kowalski, Gary. (1991) *The Souls of Animals*. Walpole: Stillpoint Publishing.

Krampen, Martin. (2010) "Code." In: T. A. Sebeok and M. Danesi (eds.), *Encyclopedic Dictionary of Semiotics*, Volume 1, 39–45. Berlin: Mouton de Gruyter.

Krys, Kuba, C. Melanie Vauclair, Colin A. Capaldi, Vivian Miu-Chi, Michael H. Bond, Alejandra Domínguez-Espinosa, Claudio Torres, Ottmar V. Lipp, and Sam S. Manickam. (2016) "Be Careful Where You Smile: Culture Shapes Judgments of Intelligence and Honesty of Smiling Individuals." *Journal of Nonverbal Behavior* 40: 101–16.

Laban, Rudolf. (1950) *The Mastery of Movement*. London: MacDonald & Evans.

Lacan, Jacques. (1977) *Écrits: A Selection*. New York: W. W. Norton.

Lakoff, George. (1987) *Women, Fire, and Dangerous Things: What Categories Reveal about the Mind*. Chicago: University of Chicago Press.

Lakoff, George. (2012) "The Contemporary Theory of Metaphor." In: M. Danesi and S. Maida-Nicol (eds.), *Foundational Texts in Linguistic Anthropology*, 128–71. Toronto: Canadian Scholars' Press.

Lakoff, George, and Mark Johnson. (1980) *Metaphors. We Live By*. Chicago: University of Chicago Press.

Lakoff, George, and Mark Johnson. (1999) *Philosophy in the Flesh: The Embodied Mind and Its Challenge to Western Thought.* New York: Basic.

Lamarck, Jean-Baptiste. (1809) *Philosophie zoologique.* Paris: Librairie F. Savy.

Lance, Brent, and Stacy C. Marsella. (2007) "Emotionally Expressive Head and Body Movement During Gaze Shifts." In: C. Pelachaud, J. C. Martin, E. André, G. Chollet, K. Karpouzis, and D. Pelé (eds.), *Intelligent Virtual Agents. Lecture Notes in Computer Science,* Vol 4722. Berlin: Springer.

Langer, Susanne K. (1948). *Philosophy in a New Key.* Cambridge, MA: Harvard University Press.

Langer, Susanne K. (1957). *Problems of Art.* New York: Scribner's.

Lasswell, Harold D. (1927). *Propaganda Techniques in World War I.* Cambridge: MIT Press.

Law, Franzo (2017). "Vocabulary Size and Auditory Word Recognition in Preschool Children." *Applied Psycholinguistics* 38: 89–125.

Lazarsfeld, Paul F., and Elihu Katz. (1955) *Personal Influence: The Part Played by People in the Flow of Mass Communications.* Glencoe: Free Press.

Leary, Mark R. (1996) *Self-Presentation: Impression Management and Interpersonal Behavior.* Boulder: Westview Press.

Leary, Mark R. (2011) "Personality and Persona: Personality Processes in Self Presentation." *Journal of Personality* 79: 1191–1218.

Leonard, Crystal. (2017) "The Sense of Touch and How It Affects Development." serendip.brynmawr.edu/exchange/crystal-leonard/sense-touch-and-how-it-affects-development. Accessed April 11, 2017.

Leube, Dirk T., Michael Erb, Wolfgang Grodd, Mathias Bartels, and Tilo T. J. Kircher. (2003). "Successful Episodic Memory Retrieval of Newly Learned Faces Activates a Left Fronto-Parietal Network." *Cognitive Brain Research* 18: 97–101.

Lévi-Strauss, Claude. (1952) "Language and the Analysis of Social Class." *American Anthropologist* 53: 155–63.

Lewis, Richard D. (1996) *When Cultures Collide: Leading Across Cultures.* Boston: Nicholas Brealey Publishing.

Li, Stan Z., and Anil K. Jain, eds. (2011) *Handbook of Face Recognition.* New York: Springer.

Lieberman, Phillip. (1972). *The Speech of Primates.* The Hague: Mouton.

Lieberman, Phillip. (1975). *On the Origins of Language.* New York: MacMillan.

Lieberman, Phillip. (1984). *The Biology and Evolution of Language.* Cambridge, Mass.: Harvard University Press.

Lieberman, Phillip. (1991). *Uniquely Human: The Evolution of Speech, Thought, and Selfless Behavior.* Cambridge, MA: Harvard University Press.

Lin, Dennis, Jilin Tu, Shyamsundar Rajaram, Zhenqui Zhang, and Thomas Huang. (2006) "Da Vinci's Mona Lisa: A Modern Look at a Timeless Classic." In: S. Renals, S. Bengio, and J. G. Fiscus (eds.), Machine Learning for

Multimodal Interaction MLMI 2006, Lecture Notes in Computer Science, volume 4299 (Berlin: Springer, 2006).

Lin, Xu. (2007) "Cultural Dimensions and Conversational Strategies—Conversational Strategies Adopted in Different Cultures and the Way to Bridge the Gap." *US-China Foreign Language* 5: 71–6.

Link, Frederick C., and D. Glenn Foster. (1984) *The Kinesic Interview Technique*. Atlanta: Interrotec Associates.

Lippmann, Walter. (1922) *Public Opinion*. New York: Macmillan.

Loof, Denis de. (1976) "Some American and German Customs Compared." *Le Langage et l'Homme* 30: 37–46.

Lorenz, Konrad. (1952) *King Solomon's Ring*. New York: Crowell.

Lotman, Jurij. (1991) *Universe of the Mind: A semiotic Theory of Culture*. Bloomington: Indiana University Press.

Malinowski, B. (1922) *Argonauts of the Western Pacific*. New York: Dutton.

Malinowski, Bronislaw. (1923) !The Problem of Meaning in Primitive Languages." In: C. K. Ogden and I. A. Richards (eds.), *The Meaning of Meaning*, 296–336. New York: Harcourt, Brace and World.

Mallery, Garrick. (1972) *Sign Language among North American Indians Compared with That among Other Peoples and Deaf-Mutes*. The Hague: Mouton.

Marey, E. J. (1879) *Animal Mechanism*. New York: D. Appleton and Co.

Marr, David. (1982) *Vision: A Computational Investigation into the Human Representation and Processing of Visual Information*. New York: W. H. Freeman.

Marsh, Peter. (1991) *Eye to Eye: How People Interact.* Salem House (Internet Archive)

Matsumoto, David. (1992) More Evidence for the Universality of a Contempt Expression. *Motivation and Emotion* 16: 363–8.

Matsumoto, David. (2001) "Culture and Emotion." In: D. Matsumoto (ed.), *The Handbook of Culture and Psychology*, 171–94. New York: Oxford University Press.

Matsumoto, David, and Bob Willingham. (2009) "Spontaneous Facial Expressions of Emotion of Congenitally and Non-congenitally Blind Individuals." *Journal of Personality and Social Psychology* 96: 1–10.

Maturana, Humberto, and Francisco Varela. (1973) *Autopoiesis and Cognition* Dordrecht: Reidel.

Mavridis, Nikolaos. (2015) A Review of Verbal and Non-Verbal Human–Robot Interactive Communication. *Robotics and Autonomous Systems* 63: 22–35.

McCracken, Grant. (1995) *Big Hair: A Journey into the Transformation of Self.* Toronto: Penguin.

McGann, Jerome. (2000) "Marking Texts of Many Dimensions." In: S. Schreibman, R. G. Siemens, and J. M. Unsworth (eds.), *A Companion to Digital Humanities*, 358–76. Hoboken: Wiley & Sons.

McHugh, Joanna Edel, Rachel McDonnell, Carol O'Sullivan, and Fiona N. Newell. (2009) "Perceiving Emotion in Crowds: the Role of Dynamic Body Postures on the Perception of Emotion in Crowded Scenes." *Experimental Brain Research* 204: 361–72.

McLuhan, Marshall. (1951) *The Mechanical Bride: The Extensions of Man*. London: Routledge and Kegan Paul.

McLuhan, Marshall (1962) *The Gutenberg Galaxy: The Making of Typographic Man*. Toronto: University of Toronto Press.

McLuhan, Marshall. (1964) *Understanding Media: The Extensions of Man*. Cambridge: MIT Press.

McLuhan, Marshall. (1968) *Through the Vanishing Point*. New York: Harper & Row.

McLuhan, Marshall. (1970) *Culture is Our Business*. New York: Wipf & Stock.

McLuhan, Marshall. (1972) *Take Today: The Executive as Dropout*. New York: Harcourt, Brace, & Jovanovich.

McLuhan, Marshall. (1998) *The Agenbite of Outwit*, published posthumously in *McLuhan Studies*, Volume 1, Issue 2 (January 1998)

McLuhan, Marshall, and Quentin Fiore. (1967) *The Medium is the Massage: An Inventory of Effects*. New York: Random House.

McLuhan, Marshall, and Eric McLuhan. (1988) *The Laws of Media*. Toronto: University of Toronto Press.

McNeill, David. (1992) *Hand and Mind: What Gestures Reveal about Thought*. Chicago: University of Chicago Press.

McNeill, David. (2005) *Gesture & Thought*. Chicago: University of Chicago Press.

McNeill, David, Susan D. Duncan, Jonathan Cole, Shaun Gallagher, and Bennett Bertenthal. (2008) "Growth Points from the Very Beginning." *Interaction Studies: Social Behaviour and Communication in Biological and Artificial Systems* 9: 117–32.

McQuail, Denis. (2000) *Mass Communication Theory: An Introduction*. London: Sage.

Mead, Margaret. (1964) *Continuities in Cultural Evolution*. New Haven: Yale University Press.

Mead, Margaret, and Frances C. MacGreggor. (1951) *Growth and Culture: A Photographic Study of Balinese Childhood*. New York: Putnam.

Mehrabian, Albert. (1968) "Inference of Attitude from the Posture, Orientation, and Distance of a Communicator." *Journal of Consulting and Clinical Psychology* 32: 296–308.

Mehrabian, Albert. (1972) *Silent Messages: Implicit Communication of Emotions and Attitudes*. Belmont: Wadsworth.

Meltzoff, Andrew N., and M. Keith Moore. (1977) "Imitation of Facial and Manual Gestures by Human Neonates." *Science* 198 (4312): 74–8.

Merleau-Ponty, Maurice. (1993) *The Merleau-Ponty Aesthetics Reader*. Evanston: Northwestern University Press.

Messinger, Daniel S., Alan Fogel, and K. Laurie Dickson. (2001) "All Smiles Are Positive, but Some Smiles Are More Positive Than Others." *Developmental Psychology* 37: 642–53.

Meyer, Pamela. (2010) *Liespotting: Proven Techniques to Detect Deception*. New York: St. Martin's.

Mondada, Lorenza. (2018) "Multiple Temporalities of Language and Body in Interaction: Challenges for Transcribing Multimodality." *Research on Language and Social Interaction* 51: 85–106.

Money, John. (1986) *Lovemaps: Clinical Concepts of Sexual/Erotic Health and Pathology, Paraphilia, and Gender Identity from Conception to Maturity* Baltimore: Johns Hopkins University Press.

Montagu, Ashley. (1983) "Toolmaking, Hunting, and the Origin of Language." In: B. Bain (ed.), *The Sociogenesis of Language and Human Conduct*, 3–14. New York: Plenum.

Montagu, Ashley. (1986) *Touching: The Human Significance of the Skin*. New York: Harper and Row.

Moore, Jerry D. (1996) The Archaeology of Plazas and the Proxemics of Ritual: Three Andean Traditions. *American Anthropologist* 98: 789–802.

Morris, Desmond. (2019) *Postures; Body Language in Art*. London: Thames & Hudson.

Morris, Desmond, Peter Collett, Peter Marsh, and Marie O'Shaughnessy. (1979) *Gestures: Their Origins and Distributions.* London: Cape.

Morsella, Ezequiel, and Robert M. Krauss. (2004) "The Role of Gestures in Spatial Working Memory and Speech." *The American Journal of Psychology* 117: 411–24.

Müller-Lyer, Franz Carl. (1889) "Optische Urteilstäuschunge." *Archiv für Physiologie Suppl.*: 263–70.

Mulvey, Laura. (1975) "Visual Pleasure and Narrative Cinema." *Screen* 16: 6–18.

Murphy, Nora A., Jonathan M. Lehrfeld, and Derek M. Isaacowitz. (2010) "Recognition of Posed and Spontaneous Dynamic Smiles in Young and Older Adults." *Psychology and Aging* 25: 811–21.

Nakashima, Satoshi F., Stephen R. H. Langton, and Sakiko Yoshikawa. (2012) "The Effect of Facial Expression and Gaze Direction on Memory for Unfamiliar Faces." *Cognition and Emotion* 26: 1316–25.

Navarro, Joe. (2010) "Body Language of the Hands." *Psychology Today*. https://www.psychologytoday.com/ca/blog/spycatcher/201001/body-language-the-hands.

Nelson, Nicole L., and James A. Russell. (2013) "Universality Revisited." *Emotion Review* 5 (1): 8–15.

Nielsen, Gerhard. (1964) *Studies in Self-Confrontation*. Copenhagen: Munksgaard.

Neugebauer, Otto. (1952) *The Exact Sciences in Antiquity*. Princeton: Princeton University Press.
Noble, William, and Ian Davidson. (1996) *Human Evolution, Language and Mind*. Cambridge: Cambridge University Press.
Ogden, Charles K. (1932) *Opposition: A Linguistic and Psychological Analysis*. London: Paul, Trench, and Trubner.
Ogden, Charles K., and I. A. Richards. (1923) *The Meaning of Meaning*. London: Routledge and Kegan Paul.
O'Leary, Michael Boyer, Jeanne M. Wilson, Anca Metiu, and Quintus R. Jett. (2008) "Perceived Proximity in Virtual Work: Explaining the Paradox of Far-but-Close." *Organization Studies* 29: 979–1002.
Olson, Gary M., and Judith S. Olson. (2000) "Distance Matters." *Human-Computer Interaction* 15: 139–78.
Olson, Matthew H., and B. R. Hergenhahn. (2009) *An Introduction to Theories of Learning*, 8th ed. Upper Saddle River: Pearson.
Ortony, Andrew, ed. (1979) *Metaphor and Thought*. Cambridge: Cambridge University Press.
Pacioli, Luca. (1509) *De divina proportione*. Venice: Paganini.
Paget, Richard. (1930) *Human Speech*. London: Kegan Paul.
Patterson, Francine. (1978) "The Gesture of a Gorilla: Language Acquisition in Another Pongid." *Brain and Language* 5: 72–9.
Patterson, Francine, and Eugene Linden. (1981) *The Education of Koko*. New York: Holt, Rinehart and Winston.
Peck, Stephen R. (1987) *Atlas of Facial Expression*. Oxford: Oxford University Press.
Peirce, Charles S. (1931–58) *Collected Papers of Charles Sanders Peirce*, Vols. 1–8, C. Hartshorne and P. Weiss (eds.). Cambridge, MA.: Harvard University Press.
Pelc, Jerzy. (1992) "The Methodological Status of Semiotics: Signs, Semiosis, Interpretation and the Limits of Semiotics." In: M. Balat and J. Deledalle-Rhodes (eds.), *Signs of Humanity*, 247–59. Berlin: Mouton de Gruyter.
Pereira-Kohatsu, Juan Carlos, Lara Quijano-Sánchez, Federico Liberatore, and Miguel Camacho-Collados. (2019). "Detecting and Monitoring Hate Speech in Twitter." *Sensors* 19, 4654.
Phillips, Stephen. (1980) *Extrasensory Perception of Quarks*. Wheaton: Theosophical Publishing House
Piaget, Jean. (1969) *The Child's Conception of the World*. Totowa: Littlefield, Adams and Company.
Piaget, Jean. (1971) *Genetic Epistemology*. New York: W. W. Norton.
Picard, Rosalind. (1997) *Affective Computing*. Cambridge: MIT Press.
Pinker, Steven. (1994) *The Language Instinct: How the Mind Creates Language*. New York: William Morrow.

Pinxten, Rik, Ingrid Van Dooren, and Frank Harvey. (1983) *Anthropology of Space*. Philadelphia: University of Pennsylvania Press.
Plato. (1992) *The Republic*. Grube: Hackett Publishing Company.
Plato. (2020) *The Sophist*. Project Gutenberg: http://www.gutenberg.org/ebooks/1735.
Plutarch. (2015) *Moralia*. Cambridge: Harvard University Press.
Plutchik, Robert. (1991) *The Emotions*. Lanham, MD: University Press of America.
Pliny the Elder. (1857) *Natural History*. London: Bohn.
Pollio, Howard R., Jack M. Barlow, Harold J. Fine, and Marylin R. Pollio. (1977) *Psychology and the Poetics of Growth: Figurative Language in Psychology, Psychotherapy, and Education*. Hillsdale: Lawrence Erlbaum Associates.
Popper, Karl. (1976) *The Unending Quest*. Glasgow: Collins.
Popper, Karl, and John Eccles. (1977) *The Self and the Brain*. Berlin: Springer.
Porter, Stephen, Leanne ten Brinke, and Brendan Wallace. (2012) "Secrets and Lies: Involuntary Leakage in Deceptive Facial Expressions as a Function of Emotional Intensity." *Journal of Nonverbal Behavior* 36 (1): 23–37.
Postman, Neil. (1992) *Technopoly: The Surrender of Culture to Technology*. New York: Alfred A. Knopf.
Postman, Neil. (2006) "Media Ecology Education." *Explorations in Media Ecology* 5: 5–14.
Premack, Ann. (1976) *Why Chimps Can Read*. New York: Harper and Row.
Premack, David. (1976) "Language in Chimpanzee?" *Science* 172: 808–22.
Premack, David, and Ann Premack. (1981) *The Mind of an Ape*. New York: Norton.
Preziosi, Donald. (2010) "Architecture." In: T. A. Sebeok and M. Danesi (eds.), *Encyclopedic Dictionary of Semiotics*, Volume 1, 59–65. Berlin: Mouton de Gruyter.
Radcliffe-Brown, Alfred (1922) *The Andaman Islanders*. Cambridge: Cambridge University Press.
Ramachandran, Vilayanur S. (2011) *The Tell-Tale Brain: A Neuroscientist's Quest for What Makes Us Human*. New York: Viking.
Reid, John E. (1991) *Interviewing and Interrogation: The Reid Technique*. Minneapolis: John E. Reid and Associates.
Reid, Vincent M., and Tricia Striano. (2005) "Adult Gaze Influences Infant Attention and Object Processing: Implications for Cognitive Neuroscience." *European Journal of Neuroscience* 21: 1763–66.
Richards, I. A. (1936) *The Philosophy of Rhetoric*. Oxford: Oxford University Press.
Richmond, Virginia. (2008) *Nonverbal Behavior in Interpersonal Relations*. Boston: Pearson.

Riggio, Ronald E. and Riggio, H. R. (2012) "Face and Body in Motion." In: T. Cash (ed.), *Encyclopedia of Body Image and Human Appearance*. London: Elsevier.

Rinn, William E. (1984) "The Neuropsychology of Facial Expression: A Review of the Neurological and Psychological Mechanisms for Producing Facial Expressions." *Psychological Bulletin* 95: 52–77.

Rios-Martinez, Jorge, Anne Spalanzani, and Christian Laugier. (2015) "From Proxemics Theory to Socially-Aware Navigation: A Survey." *International Journal of Social Robotics* 7: 137–53.

Rogers, Everett M. (2000) "The Extensions of Men: The Correspondence of Marshall McLuhan and Edward T. Hall." *Mass Communications and Society* 3: 117–35.

Rosch, Eleanor, Evan Thomson, and Francisco J. Varela. (1991) *The Embodied Mind: Cognitive Science and Human Experience*. Cambridge, MA: MIT Press.

Rossano, Federico. (2012) *Gaze Behavior in Face-to-Face Interaction*. Nijmegen: Radboud University.

Rousseau, Jean-Jacques. (1966) *Essay on the Origin of Language*. Chicago: University of Chicago Press.

Rubinstein, Ruth P. (1995) *Dress Codes: Meanings and Messages in American Culture*. Boulder: Westview.

Ruesch, Jurgen, and Gregory Bateson. (1951) *Communication: The Social Matrix of Psychiatry*. New York: Norton.

Ruesch, Jurgen, and Weldon Kees. (1956) *Nonverbal Communication; Notes on the Visual Perception of Human Relations*. Berkeley: University of California Press.

Rumbaugh, Duane M., ed. (1977) *Language Learning by a Chimpanzee: The Lana Project*. New York: Academic.

Russell, Peter. (1983) *The Global Brain*. New York: Tarcher.

Russell, James. (1994) "Is There Universal Recognition of Emotion From Facial Expression? A Review of the Cross-Cultural Studies." *Psychological Bulletin* 115: 102–41.

Russell, James, and José Fernandez Dols, eds. (1997) *The Psychology of Facial Expression*. Cambridge: Cambridge University Press.

Russell, Stuart J., and Peter Norvig. (2003) *Artificial Intelligence: A Modern Approach*. Englewood Cliffs, NJ: Prentice Hall.

Sacks, Oliver. (1985) *The Man Who Mistook His Wife for a Hat*. London: Macat Library.

Samuel, Arthur L. (1959) "Some Studies in Machine Learning Using the Game of Checkers." *IBM Journal of Research and Development* 3: 210–29.

Samuels, Curtis A. (1985) "Attention to Eye Contact Opportunity and Facial Motion by Three-Month-Old Infants." *Journal of Experimental Child Psychology* 40: 105–14.

Sapir, Edward. (1949) "The Unconscious Patterning of Behavior in Society." In: D. Mandelbaum (ed.), *Selected Writing of Edward Sapir in Language, Culture and Personality*, 544–59. Berkeley: University of California Press.
Sartre, Jean-Paul. (1943) *Being and Nothingness*. London: Routledge.
Saussure, Ferdinand de. (1916) *Cours de linguistique générale*. Paris: Payot.
Savage-Rumbaugh, E. Sue. (1986) *Ape Language: From Conditioned Response to Symbol*. New York: Columbia University Press.
Savage-Rumbaugh, E. Sue, Mary A. Romski, Rose Sevcik, and James L. Pate, James L. (1983) "Assessing Symbol Usage Versus Symbol Competency." *Journal of Experimental Psychology: General* 112: 508–12.
Savage-Rumbaugh, E. Sue, Duane M. Rumbaugh, and Sally L. Boysen. (1978) "Symbolic Communication between Two Chimpanzees." *Science* 201: 641–44.
Schachter, Stanley, and Jerome Singer. (1962) "Cognitive, Social, and Physiological Determinants of Emotional State." *Psychological Review* 69 (5): 379–99.
Schafer, Edward H. (1951) "Ritual Exposure in Ancient China." *Harvard Journal of Asiatic Studies* 14: 130–84.
Scheflen, Albert E. (1964) "The Significance of Posture in Communication Systems." *Psychiatry* 27: 316–31.
Scheflen, Albert E. (1966) "Natural History Method in Psychotherapy: Communicational Research." In: L. A. Gottschalk and A. H. Auerbach (eds.), *Methods of Research in Psychotherapy*. New York: Appleton-Century-Crofts.
Scheflen, Albert E. (1973) *Communicational Structure: Analysis of a Psychotherapy Transaction*. Bloomington: Indiana University Press.
Schmandt-Besserat, Denise. (1992) *Before Writing*, 2 vols. Austin: University of Texas Press.
Schmandt-Besserat, Denise. (1999) *The History of Counting*. New York: Harper-Collins.
Schramm, Wilbur. (1963) *The Science of Human Communication*. New York: Basic Books.
Schrier, Karen, and David Schaenfield. (2016) "Collaboration and Emotion in Way." In: S. H. Tettegah and W. D. Huang (eds.), *Emotions, Technology, and Digital Games*. Amsterdam: Elsevier.
Schroeter, Melani, and Charlotte Taylor, eds. (2018) *Exploring Silence and Absence in Discourse: Empirical Approaches*. New York: Palgrave.
Searle, John R. (1984) *Minds, Brain, and Science*. Cambridge, MA: Harvard University Press.
Sebeok, Thomas A. (1990) *Zoosemiotics*. Toronto: Toronto Semiotic Circle.
Sebeok, Thomas A., and Marcel Danesi. (2000) *The Forms of Meaning: Modeling Systems Theory and Semiotics*. Berlin: Mouton de Gruyter.
Segaud, Marion. (1973) Anthropologie de l'espace. *Espaces et Sociétés* 9: 29–38.

Senju, Atsushi, and Mark H. Johnson. (2009) "The Eye Contact Effect: Mechanisms and Development." *Trends in Cognitive Sciences* 13: 127–34.

Shannon, Claude E. (1948) "A Mathematical Theory of Communication." *Bell Systems Technical Journal* 27: 379–423.

Shannon, Claude E., and Warren Weaver. (1949) *The Mathematical Theory of Communication*. Urbana: The University of Illinois Press.

Simmel, Georg. (1921) "The Sociology of the Senses." In: R. E. Park and E. W. Burgess (eds.), *Introduction to the Science of Sociology*. Chicago: University of Chicago Press.

Simon, Mark. (2005) *Facial Expression*. New York: Watson-Guptill.

Sirius, R. U., and Jay Cornell. (2015) *Transcendence: The Disinformation Encyclopedia of Transhumanism and the Singularity*. San Francisco: Disinformation Books.

Sorokowska, Agnieszka, Piotr Sorokowska, and Peter Hilpert. (2017) "Preferred Interpersonal Distances: A Global Comparison." *Journal of Cross-Cultural Psychology* 48: 577–92.

Stross, Brian. (1976) *The Origin and Evolution of Language*. Dubuque, IA: W.C. Brown.

Sturken, Marita, and Lisa Cartwright. (2009) *Practices of Looking: An Introduction to Visual Culture*. Oxford: Oxford University Press.

Sweetser, Eve. (1990) *From Etymology to Pragmatics: The Mind-as-Body Metaphor in Semantic Structure and Semantic Change*. Cambridge: Cambridge University Press.

Tanner, Dennis C., and Matthew E. Tanner. (2004) *Forensic Aspects of Speech Patterns: Voice Prints, Speaker Profiling, Lie and Intoxication Detection*. Tucson: Lawyers & Judges Publication Company.

Terrace, Herbert S. (1979) *Nim*. New York: Knopf.

Terrace, Herbert S. (1983) "Apes Who Talk: Language or Projection of Language by Their Teachers?" In: J. de Luce and H. T. Wilder (eds.), *Language in Primates: Perspectives and Implications*. 22–39. New York: Springer-Verlag.

Terrace, Herbert S., Laura-Ann Petitto, Richard J. Sanders, and Thomas G. Bever. (1979) "Can an Ape Create a Sentence?" *Science* 206: 891–902.

Thom, René. (1975) *Structural Stability and Morphogenesis: An Outline of a General Theory of Models*. Reading: Benjamin

Tomasello, Michael, Brian Hare, Hagen Lehmann, and Josep Call. (2007) "Reliance on Head Versus Eyes in the Gaze Following of Great Apes and Human Infants: The Cooperative Eye Hypothesis." *Journal of Human Evolution* 52: 314–20.

Tomkins, Silvan. (1962) *Affect, Imagery, and Consciousness*. New York: Springer.

Tomkins, Silvan, and R. McCarter. (1964) "What and Where Are the Primary Affects? Some Evidence for a Theory." *Perceptual and Motor Skills* 18: 119–58.
Tomkins, Silvan, and Carroll E. Izard. (1965) *Affect, Cognition, and Personality: Empirical Studies*. New York: Springer.
Tracy, Jessica L., and Alec T. Beall. (2011) "Happy Guys Finish Last: The Impact of Emotion Expressions on Sexual Attraction." *Emotion* 11: 1379–87.
Trumble, Angus. (2004) *A Brief History of the Smile*. New York: Basic.
Tulving, Endel. (1972) "Episodic and Semantic Memory." In: E. Tulving and W. Donaldson (eds.), *Organization of Memory*, 23–46. New York: Academic.
Turing, Alan. (1936) "On Computable Numbers with an Application to the Entscheidungs Problem." *Proceedings of the London Mathematical Society* 41: 230–65.
Turing, Alan. (1950) "Computing Machinery and Intelligence." In: E. A. Feigenbaum and J. Feldman (eds.), *Computers and Thought*, 123–34. New York: McGraw-Hill.
Uexküll, Jakob von. (1909) *Umwelt und Innenwelt der Tierre*. Berlin: Springer.
Ulam, Stanislaw. (1958) "Tribute to John von Neumann." *Bulletin of the American Mathematical Society* 64: 5.
Uono, Shota, and Jari K. Hietanen. (2015) "Eye Contact Perception in the West and East: A Cross-Cultural Study." *PLOS One,* February 25, 2015. https://doi.org/10.1371/journal.pone.0118094.
Urban, Greg. (2002) "Metasignaling and Language Origins." *American Anthropologist* 104: 233–46.
Vick, Sarah-Jane, Bridget M. Waller, Lisa A. Parr, Marcia C. Smith Pasqualini, and Kim A. Bard. (2007) "A Cross-Species Comparison of Facial Morphology and Movement in Humans and Chimpanzees Using the Facial Action Coding System (FACS)." *Journal of Nonverbal Behavior* 31 (1): 1–20.
Vygotsky, Lev S. (1962) *Thought and Language*. Cambridge, MA: MIT Press.
Walcot, Peter. (1978) *Envy and the Greeks*. Liverpool: Liverpool University Press.
Ward, Ben. (1999) "Koko: Fact or Fiction?" *American Language Review* 3: 12–15.
Watson, O. Michael (1970) *Proxemic Behavior*. The Hague: Mouton.
Watson, O. Michael (1974) "Proxemics." In: T. A. Sebeok (ed.), *Current Trends in Linguistics* 12: 311–44. The Hague: Mouton.
Watson, O. Michael, and Myrdene Anderson. (1987) "The Quest for Coordinates in Space and Time." *Reviews in Anthropology* 14: 78–89.
Weissman, Benjamin, and Dean Tanner. (2018) "A Strong Wink Between Verbal and Emoji-Based Irony: How the Brain Processes Ironic Emojis During Language Comprehension." *Plos One* (https://doi.org/10.1371/journal.pone.0201727).

Weizenbaum, Joseph. (1966) "ELIZA—A Computer Program for the Study of Natural Language Communication Between Man and Machine." *Communications of the ACM* 9: 36–45.

West, Martin L. (1994) *Ancient Greek Music.* Oxford: Oxford University Press.

Wiener, Norbert. (1948) *Cybernetics, or Control and Communication in the Animal and the Machine.* Cambridge, MA: MIT Press.

Wiener, Norbert. (1950) *The Human Use of Human Beings: Cybernetics and Society.* Boston: Houghton, Mifflin.

Willems, Roel M., and Peter Hagoort. (2007) "Neural Evidence for the Interplay between Language, Gesture, and Action: A Review." *Brain and Language* 101: 278–89.

Wilson, Frank R. (1998) *The Hand: How Its Use Shapes the Brain, Language, and Human Culture.* New York: Pantheon.

Winograd, Terry. (1991) "Thinking Machines: Can There be? Are We?" In: J. J. Sheehan and M. Sosna (eds.), *The Boundaries of Humanity*, 198–223. Berkeley: University of California Press.

Ye, Zhengdao. (2004) "Chinese Categorization of Interpersonal Relationships and the Cultural Logic of Chinese Social Interaction: An Indigenous Perspective." *Intercultural Pragmatics* 1-2: 211–30.

Yee, Nick, Jeremy N. Bailenson, Mark Urbanek, Francis Change, and Dan Merget. (2007) "Unbearable Likeness of Being Digital: The Persistence of Nonverbal Social Norms in Online Virtual Environments." *CyberPsychology & Behavior* 10: 115–21.

Yerkes, Robert M. (1943) *Chimpanzees: A Laboratory Colony.* New Haven: Yale University Press.

Zaremba Filipczak, Z. (1977) "New Light on Mona Lisa: Leonardo's Optical Knowledge and His Choice of Lighting." *The Art Bulletin* 59: 518–23.

# Index

action unit (AU) 80, 86
adaptor 32
addressee 6, 177, 203, 204, 207
addresser 5, 6, 177, 203, 204, 205, 207
affect display 32
Affective Computing (AC) 47, 88, 188
allokine 30, 36, 203
allophone 30
allopoietic 194, 195, 198
American Sign Language (ASL) 124, 125, 136, 137, 138, 139, 140, 141
animal mechanism 142
archetype 60, 62, 64, 73, 92, 103, 203
architecture 25, 50, 148, 164, 168, 170, 171, 200, 201
Arcimboldo, Giuseppe 94, 95
Argyle, Michael 14, 38, 57
Aristotle 88, 116, 211
art 11, 22, 40, 41, 49, 50, 64, 66, 68, 69, 71, 85, 86, 89, 90, 97, 115, 116, 117, 146, 170, 171, 200, 201, 203
artifactual media 8, 161, 203
Artificial General Intelligence (AGI) 194
Artificial Intelligence (AI) 24, 47, 88, 188, 193, 194, 195, 196, 200
asynchronous 11, 12, 203
audition 7
autopoiesis 13, 184, 194, 195, 198, 203

Bateson, Gregory 14, 24, 29, 30, 41, 42, 43, 91, 93, 94, 95, 188
Baudrillard, Jean 11
bimodality 1, 20, 21, 22, 25, 29, 30, 35, 54, 56, 111, 155, 203
biometrics 88, 203
bipedalism 23, 97, 98, 99, 101, 203

Birdwhistell, Ray 14, 27, 29, 30, 31, 35, 36, 37, 51, 75
Blake, William 71, 72
brain 20, 22, 23, 24, 45, 54, 61, 64, 66, 77, 79, 87, 88, 99, 100, 111, 114, 119, 135, 154, 166, 167, 180, 189, 194, 198, 199
Broca, Pierre Paul 114
bull's-eye model 5
Bulwer, John 126, 127

Chapple, Eliot 43
Chardin, Pierre Teilhard de 199
chimpanzees 1, 23, 99, 114, 122, 136, 137, 138, 139, 140
chronemic 36, 203
clothing 19, 25, 27, 35, 51, 90, 164, 167, 171, 172, 173, 174, 200, 201
co-speech 13, 14, 15, 32, 43, 44, 57, 76, 129, 130, 131
cobot 196
code (definition) 6, 7
Cole, Fay-Cooper 112
collocation 193
communication (definition) 2, 3, 4, 5
computer-mediated communication (CMC) 11, 12, 14, 159, 175, 204
conative 6, 204
conceptual metaphor theory 58
connotation 19, 28, 33, 35, 53, 58, 59, 104, 160, 170, 172, 173, 174, 175, 177, 178, 204
connotatum 19
contact 6
context analysis 24, 30
context (definition) 6
cooperative eye hypothesis 55, 56

corporeality 8
cosmism 199
counting 101
cybernetics 5, 158, 159, 187, 188, 189, 190, 191, 198, 204
cyberspace 2, 25, 119, 167, 196

dactylonomy 101
dance 7, 9, 15, 36, 51, 55, 101, 121, 141, 142, 143, 144, 170, 196, 205
Darwin, Charles 12, 24, 34, 44, 49, 53, 76, 77, 78, 92, 95, 106, 117, 119, 123, 142, 173
decoder 5
denotation 19, 20, 28, 172, 175
denotatum 19
Derrida, Jacques 56
destination
digital 11, 16, 88, 101, 104, 166, 204
displacement 7, 204
divine eye 60
divine proportion 88
double bind 42, 93, 204
dress code 20, 174
Duchenne, Guillaume 77, 78
Dürer, Albrecht 117, 118
dyadic 13

Efron, David 29, 32, 129, 132
Ekman, Paul 44, 46, 51, 53, 75, 76, 77, 78, 79, 80, 123, 129, 132
electronic 9, 10, 11, 166, 190, 191, 199, 205
emblem 31, 133
emergence 199
emoji 7, 11, 16, 159, 175, 176, 177, 178, 183, 184
emotional leakage 44, 46
emotive 6, 7, 32, 35, 37, 38, 42, 54, 81, 87, 108, 109, 122, 138, 143, 154, 177
encoder 5
Escher, Maurits C. 115, 116
evil eye 60, 61, 62, 104, 126, 128, 129
evolution 2, 3, 8, 12, 13, 20, 22, 23, 25, 33, 53, 58, 60, 61, 65, 76, 79, 93, 95, 97, 98, 99, 105, 112, 122, 130, 134, 135, 136, 143, 144, 146, 151, 154, 160, 161, 164, 166, 171, 181, 185, 199, 200
extended nonverbal communication (ENVC) 164, 171, 175, 178
extension theory 163, 164, 165, 172, 185
eye avoidance 55
eye contact 2, 12, 14, 15, 24, 25, 27, 28, 29, 32, 34, 35, 39, 42, 44, 49, 50, 51, 52, 53, 54, 55, 56, 58, 59, 69, 71, 83, 90, 150, 154, 156
Eye of Providence 60, 51

face recognition 54, 75, 76, 86, 87
face-to-face (F2F) 11, 32, 34, 37, 147, 148, 159, 163, 170, 175, 177, 178
Facial Action Coding System (FACS) 80
facial expression 7, 12, 13, 16, 21, 47, 54, 75, 76, 79, 80, 81, 82, 87, 93, 95, 104, 175
feedback 5, 154, 179, 189, 190, 196
feral children 13, 138
Fisher, Helen 78, 91, 172
forced smile 81
forensics 27, 44, 45
Foucault, Michel 28, 56, 175
frame analysis 90
Frazer, James 92
Freud, Sigmund 62, 92

Galen of Pergamon 49
Gardner, Allen 136, 137, 138, 140, 141
Gardner, Beatrix 136, 137, 138, 140, 141
gaze 43, 53, 55, 56, 57, 58, 61, 65, 66, 67, 68, 69, 71, 81, 87, 130, 159, 191
Gerbner, George 10
gesticulant 34, 121, 130, 131, 132, 178, 190
gesticulation 20, 47, 121, 131, 132, 133, 144
gestural theory 133
gesture 1, 3, 6, 7, 8, 12, 13, 15, 16, 19, 20, 21, 22, 23, 24, 27, 28, 29, 31, 32, 34, 36, 37, 40, 41, 44, 47, 53, 54, 64, 82, 88, 104,

108, 111, 112, 118, 121, 122, 123, 124, 127, 128, 129, 130, 140, 188, 198, 200
global brain 198, 199
global village 11, 104
Goffman, Erving 90, 91, 148, 173, 177
gorilla 1, 99, 136, 138
Gross, Larry 10
gustation 8

hair 82, 83, 84, 91, 167, 171, 172, 173
hairstyle 27, 35, 83, 84, 85, 90
Hall, Edward T. 41, 51, 108, 147, 148, 149, 150, 151, 152, 153, 154, 155, 157, 158, 161, 163, 164, 168, 170, 179, 185
Hall, Stuart 10
handedness 97, 100, 111, 112, 113, 114, 119
handshake 8, 97, 106, 107, 108, 113, 158, 161, 178
haptics 8, 34, 97, 98, 101, 103, 105, 110, 111, 120, 121, 130, 150, 161, 177
head 28, 29, 30, 32, 36, 37, 38, 39, 55, 56, 57, 58, 64, 71, 75, 82, 83, 102, 108, 124, 130, 131, 141, 179, 197
headgear 174
Herodotus 91
Hippocrates 43
hologram 120
holophrase 137
homeostasis 95
homo sapiens 22
honey bees 7
Horus 63
human-computer interaction (HCI) 160
hyperreal 11, 12
Hypodermic Needle Theory (HNT) 9

iconic 122, 123, 124, 131, 146, 160, 175, 176, 177, 195
illustrator 32, 132
image schema 59, 73, 91, 110
indexical 30, 122, 124, 178
interdisciplinary 16, 24
Internet 119, 167, 180, 181, 196, 198, 199
interpretant 17

Jakobson, Roman 5, 6, 54, 55
Joos, Martin 155, 156
Jorio, Andrea de 126, 128
Jung, Carl 62, 90, 92, 172

Katz, Elihu, 9, 10
Kendon, Adam 13, 14, 30, 43, 53, 57, 122, 126, 129, 130, 131, 132, 133, 135, 148, 154
kine 30
kinegraph 31, 36
kineme 29, 30, 31, 32, 35, 37, 53, 120, 137
kinesics 14, 15, 27, 28, 29, 30, 31, 32, 33, 34, 35, 37, 38, 39, 41, 42, 43, 44, 45, 46, 47, 51, 58, 75, 88, 98, 123, 150
Klimt, Gustav 70

Lakoff, George 58, 59, 60
Lamarck, Jean-Baptiste 114
Langer, Susanne 69
larynx 23, 45, 99
Lasswell, Harold 9
laws of media 179, 180
Lazarsfeld, Paul 9, 10
lexical 129, 130, 132, 137, 139, 141, 193
lexigram 136
Lichtenstein, Roy 69, 70
Lippmann, Walter 9, 10
Lorenz, Konrad 151
lovemap 91

Machine Intelligence (MI) 187, 191, 192, 195
Machine Learning (ML) 193
McLuhan, Marshall 3, 10, 11, 13, 120, 163, 164, 165, 166, 167, 168, 179, 180, 181, 182, 183, 184, 185, 186, 188
McNeill, David, 130, 131, 132
macrospace 149
Malinowski, Bronislaw 141
mass communications 1, 9, 10, 11, 168
mass media 9, 10, 168
Maturana, Humberto 13, 184, 194
Maya art 40, 41, 90, 101

Mead, Margaret 29, 30, 77, 125, 144
mechanical media 8
medium (definition) 7, 8, 9
mesospace 149
message (definition) 8, 9, 10
metacommunication 41, 188
metalingual 6
metaphor 58, 59, 60, 62, 73, 124, 134, 178
Michelangelo 68, 97, 112, 113
microexpression 80, 82, 88, 175, 197
microspace 148, 149, 151
morphogenesis 93, 105
Mudra 126
Müller-Lyer Illusion 50, 51
multimedial 7, 8
multimodal 7, 8
mutual gazing 51, 52, 53, 54, 56, 57, 159

Namaste 108, 118
Natural Language Programming (NLP) 194
natural media 8
neoteny 24
Netscher, Caspar 39, 40
noise 4, 33, 98, 154
nonverbal communication (definition) 12, 13, 14
noosphere 199

oculesics 51
Ogden, Charles 113, 114
olfaction 8
one-step flow 10
opposition 105, 113, 114, 174
optical illusion 95
osmosis 79, 135

Pacioli, Luca 88, 89
Paget, Richard 134, 135
paradigmatic 19
paralinguistic 34, 35, 45
Patterson, Francine 138, 139
Peirce, Charles S. 17, 18, 32, 124
perceived proximity 147, 158, 159

persona 89, 90, 91, 92, 171
phatic 6, 7, 55, 106, 108, 123, 130, 156, 157, 177
pheromone 8, 9
phoneme 4, 20, 29, 30, 35, 105, 167, 183, 198
Piaget, Jean 21
Picasso, Pablo 70
pivot grammar 137
Plato 11, 60, 68, 188
Pliny the Elder 61
Plotinus 71
Plutarch 60
poetic 6
Popper, Karl 21, 22
portraiture 69, 76, 85, 89, 90
pose 8, 27, 34, 35, 37, 38, 39, 41, 68, 82, 83, 90
Postman, Neil 181, 182, 199
posture 1, 2, 8, 12, 15, 23, 24, 27, 28, 29, 32, 33, 34, 35, 36, 37, 38, 40, 41, 44, 46, 47, 64, 88, 99, 104, 149, 150, 154, 156, 188
pragmatic 129, 132, 135, 196, 198
prehensile 23, 99, 109
Premack, Ann 139
Premack, David 139
print age 10, 166, 183
printing press 166
probability 4, 5
prosody 7
prosopagnosia 86
proxeme 150
proxemics 8, 12, 15, 34, 35, 106, 147, 148, 149, 150, 151, 153, 155, 156, 157, 158, 159, 160, 161, 163, 164, 165, 168, 169, 170, 171, 179, 200
proxetic 150
psychotherapy 41, 42, 80

Quintilian 104

Radcliffe-Brown, Alfred 18
receiver 4, 5, 6

redundancy 4
referential 6, 13, 20, 124
register 25, 155, 156, 157, 158
regulator 32, 122, 190
representamen 17
rites 91, 92, 141, 142
rituals 28, 34, 55, 56, 92, 106, 108, 112, 142, 158
robot 47, 119, 160, 187, 195, 196, 197, 200
robotics 119, 179
Rousseau, Jean-Jacques 134
Rumbaugh, Duane 138, 139, 140
Russell, Peter 198

Sacks, Oliver 86
Sartre, Jean-Paul 68
Saussure, Ferdinand de 16, 17
Savage-Rumbaugh, Sue 138
Scheflen, Albert 14, 30, 36, 38, 41
Schramm, Wilbur 5
semaphore 3
semiosis 17, 19, 21, 44, 47, 105
semiotics (definition) 16, 17, 19
sender 4, 5
sensorium 183, 184
servomechanism 189, 190, 196
Shannon, Claude E. 4, 5, 191
sign (definition) 17, 18
signal (definition) 2
signified 16, 17
signifier 16, 17, 20
silence 33, 34, 122
simulacrum 11, 12, 178
simulated nonverbal communication 163, 175
snapping 101
spatial code 163, 168, 169
spatiality 8
steepling 37
symbolism 49, 60, 62, 63, 64, 68, 73, 76, 83, 110, 112, 113, 126

sympathetic magic 61, 119
synchronous 11, 12, 46
syntagmatic 19

tactile communication 3, 7, 8, 31, 34, 51, 58, 59, 97, 98, 106, 108, 109, 110, 111, 119, 121, 149, 150, 151, 158, 177, 179, 183
tactility 3, 8, 106, 109, 110, 119, 120, 150, 159, 164
technopoly 199
Terrace, Herbert S. 138
territoriality 147, 149, 151, 160, 161
tetrad 163, 179, 180, 181, 182, 183, 184
third eye 64, 71, 73
Tomkins, Silvan 78
transmitter 4
Turing, Alan 191
Turing Test 192, 198
turn-taking 43, 57, 129, 130
Twitter 12, 167
two-step flow 10

universality hypothesis 77, 78

Varela, Francisco 13, 184, 194
Vermeer, Johannes 67, 68, 69
vervet monkeys 18
Vico, Giambattista 111
Vinci, Leonardo da 65, 66, 67, 68, 117
virtual reality (VR) 178, 179
visuality 7, 164, 184, 191
vocalism 7, 135
voiceprinting 45
Vygotsky, Lev S. 21

Waterhouse, John William 66
Weizenbaum, Joseph 194
Wiener, Norbert 188, 289, 190
writing 8, 45, 61, 71, 115, 146

Yerkish 136, 139

www.ingramcontent.com/pod-product-compliance
Lightning Source LLC
Chambersburg PA
CBHW050326020526
44117CB00031B/1805